Current Perspectives in Psychology

Improving Literacy in America

Guidelines from Research

Frederick J. Morrison,
Heather J. Bachman,
and Carol McDonald Connor

YALE UNIVERSITY PRESS   NEW HAVEN AND LONDON

Designed by Sonia Shannon.
Set in Garamond and Gill Sans types by The Composing Room of Michigan, Inc.
Printed in the United States of America

Library of Congress Cataloging-in-Publication Data
Morrison, Frederick J.
    Improving literacy in America : guidelines from research / Frederick J. Morrison,
Heather J. Bachman, Carol McDonald Connor.
        p.   cm. — (Current perspectives in psychology)
    Includes bibliographical references and index.
    ISBN 0-300-10645-9 (cloth : alk. paper)
        1. Literacy—United States—Psychological aspects.   2. Literacy—Social as-
pects—United States.   3. Language arts (Primary)—United States.   4. Readiness
for school—United States.   I. Bachman, Heather J.   II. Connor, Carol McDonald.   III. Title.   IV. Series.

LC151.M69 2005
372.6'0973—dc22

                                                                        2004043130

A catalogue record for this book is available from the British Library.

The paper in this book meets the guidelines for permanence and durability of
the Committee on Production Guidelines for Book Longevity of the
Council on Library Resources.
10 9 8 7 6 5 4 3 2 1

*To Marshall and Jerry, the yin and yang of
my intellectual journey—FJM
To Fred—CMC
To Fred and Lindsay, with gratitude—HJB*

Contents

V—GUIDELINES FOR IMPROVEMENT

Series Foreword

Current Perspectives in Psychology presents the latest discoveries and developments across the spectrum of the psychological and behavioral sciences. The series explores such important topics as learning, intelligence, trauma, stress, brain development and behavior, anxiety, interpersonal relationships, education, child rearing, divorce and marital discord, and child, adolescent, and adult development. Each book focuses on critical advances in research, theory, methods, and applications and is designed to be accessible and informative to nonspecialists and specialists alike.

This book focuses on the challenges of improving literacy in America. The ongoing failure of educational reform and social policy to have significant and enduring impact on literacy makes this topic current. Policy makers, educators, and social scientists often move from one program to the next to improve literacy among our nation's youth. Each program is funded and tested, but produces little or mixed effects. This book explains why there has been little impact on literacy and what can be done to rectify the situation. It draws on advances in theory and research on the underpinnings of illiteracy and influences that can be mobilized to effect change.

The authors address literacy by focusing on multiple levels of analysis. Critical topics include parenting, ethnic and cultural differences, teacher selection and training, daycare, and early schooling. The authors describe the influences affecting literacy, and, more important, the pathways and mechanisms through which these influences operate. Among the many findings are those that establish differences in literacy in the earliest school contact with the child. Moreover, these early differences predict later literacy. Much of the effect of illiteracy is evident and established before school begins. Parenting is accorded a pivotal role in literacy. Child language skills (sounds, words, grammar), based on how parents speak to and reason with their children, prepare children for school and account significantly for the prediction of early school skills and later literacy. The work that is cited does not gainsay the importance of educational reform and changes in the schools but rather conveys that much can be and ought to be done outside of the educational system.

Drs. Morrison, Bachman, and Connor have drawn from theory and research in diverse areas of development, education, and social policy. They provide a fresh perspective on the foundations of literacy and how these can be translated to have impact on children at the levels of both the family and social policy. The book is thorough, authoritative, and engaging.

Alan E. Kazdin
Series Editor

Acknowledgments

This work was a true collaboration; each of us contributed substantially to all of the chapters in the book, although each of us took responsibility for drafting specific chapters: Fred Morrison for chapters 1, 8, and 9; Heather Bachman for chapters 2, 4, and 5; and Carol Connor for chapters 3, 6, and 7. Nascent ideas for this book were explored in an advanced seminar at the University of Michigan in Winter 2002. We would like to thank Valerie Cumming, Tina Danek, Bryce Hella, Mary Leone, and Regan Preston for their ideas and enthusiasm. We thank the families, teachers, school administrators, and others who have participated in our research over the past decade. We thank also the colleagues, research assistants, associates, and students who supported the research efforts with their hard work and good ideas. Lisa Slominski helped us with the final formatting of the book. Jay Connor offered excellent advice regarding the content and presentation. Alan Kazdin's intellectual guidance and professional support were invaluable. Robin DuBlanc, along with Yale University Press staff Erin Carter, Nancy Moore, Keith Condon, and the designers, lent critical advice and expertise.

I

Introduction

1

The Scope of the Problem

A doctor for schools calls Philadelphia's very sick.
New York Times
Education chief takes steps to close ailing school system.
New York Times
Drastic action urged for 15 city schools.
Chicago Tribune

These headlines and others in newspapers and magazines throughout the country in recent years have trumpeted the continuing problems the United States is experiencing in educating all of its children. A steady drumbeat of evidence in scientific journals and the popular media continues to declare that significant numbers of American children are not developing the skills they need to be successful in school and in the workplace. Despite growing national awareness and the efforts of three separate administrations to address the problem, little progress seems to have been made in improving the levels of literacy of American children from elementary through high school in the last ten to fifteen years (National Center for Educational Statistics 2003b).

In our view, part of the problem rests with the manner in which we have tackled this problem. First, most discussions have focused on single issues with an either-or quality to them. For example, recent discussions have concentrated on whether we should allow vouchers or not, or whether we should decrease class size or not. These issues are all presented and debated in isolation as holding the key to understanding the literacy problems of American children. Little effort has been made to integrate these issues into a more systematic and coherent attack on the problem. Second, most of these single-issue solutions have a silver bullet quality to them. That is, the solutions are offered as the one way to solve all of our nation's problems. If only we could pour more money into the public school system, one argument goes, our problems would evaporate. Another quick-fix solution is seen in reducing class sizes.

The failure of many of these proposals to quickly and dramatically turn around our children's educational outcomes is seen by critics as demonstrable proof that the solution was misguided. Seldom do we see discussions of these individual solutions as part of a more comprehensive strategy that must be implemented across a variety of contexts and over a significant period of time. Finally, and most crucial, the dominant analyses of the causes and cures of America's literacy problems have tended to focus primarily on the schooling years. Here, too, while scientists and analysts have identified a number of very important issues pertaining to schools, the exclusive focus of concern on the schooling years has blinded us to a much larger picture about the nature and origins of problems children can experience as they develop.

A Comprehensive Perspective

In contrast to this single-issue, silver bullet mentality, research accumulating quietly over the past ten to twenty years paints a decidedly more complex picture of the extent, nature, and sources of problems facing American children, families, and society as we strive to improve education in this country. Theoretical and empirical advances have documented clearly that many factors operating over long periods of time in the child's life combine cumulatively to produce greater or lesser academic and literacy skills. Single-factor solutions focus on only one facet of the problem, when in reality it is embedded in a complex network of factors operating at different levels. In some instances, as we hope to demonstrate, concentrating on a single factor (like class size) may merely be treating the symptoms of the disorder, distracting attention from more genuinely causal influences. As is the case in medicine, treating symptoms produces some degree of short-term gain but does not eliminate the problem by tackling the underlying cause. Silver bullet proposals, while they attract attention and headlines, likewise distract us from appreciating the systemic nature of the forces operating across broad segments of society and over long periods of time in the child's life to shape each child's pattern of strengths and weaknesses.

Critically, as we will document, psychologically and educationally meaningful individual differences among children emerge and begin to stabilize well before school begins. These differences among children cut across a range of important language, cognitive, literacy, and even social skills that shape and support academic growth as children transition to and progress through school. Any lasting solution to America's literacy problems must recognize and confront the importance of these early differences.

The Preschool Years

Growth of these early foundational skills is significantly related to many complex factors operating in the life of the preschool child. Most notable, we will argue, is parenting. As we shall see, parenting for successful academic performance is a complicated, multifaceted task, bringing together many different dimensions operating simultaneously in a child's life. Effective parents teach, mentor, and provide love and support, yet at the same time they establish rules, standards, and limits, all in the service of nurturing and facilitating their child's growth. While parenting is emerging as the most potent environmental force in young children's lives, it is becoming equally clear that preschool experiences can and do have discernible effects on children (albeit in complex ways) and that certain preschool interventions, appropriately focused and implemented, can yield important gains for our most at-risk children and families. We will attempt to identify which are the most productive features of those preschool environments and interventions.

Likewise, we will examine the role of socioeconomic and racial/ethnic factors. Parental income and education levels are often credited with producing wide variability in children's development, especially when we are trying to understand the nature and sources of minority gaps in academic achievement. Here we will present the results of some surprising and counterintuitive findings: (1) that racial differences in academic achievement are not limited to lower socioeconomic families; and (2) high levels of school success have been achieved by minority children in low-income families. For example, some children from poor immigrant groups (such as Indo-Chinese refugees) have tended to perform well in U.S. schools, while other immigrant children from low-income families have shown more academic problems (for example, Mexicans). In addition, recent evidence has revealed that discrepancies in White and African American children's academic performance (the so-called "Black-White test score gap") are evident in middle- and upper-income communities and emerge well before the children ever get to school. Yet these findings do not lead inexorably to a focus on genetic differences between Blacks and Whites. As we will attempt to illustrate throughout the book, multiple cultural, linguistic, and psychological influences come together in complex ways to shape the growth of academic skills starting early and continuing throughout childhood.

Yet these forces—parenting, preschool, sociocultural—themselves do not operate monolithically. The child brings to the task of development a profile of unique skills and characteristics that parents and teachers are, in part, responding to. Hence the impact of particular parental practices will vary depending on the child. Some children require more discipline than others, some more cognitive stimulation. In proffering suggestions for optimizing literacy in America, we will need to include the child's qualities in our discussion and tailor our recommendations accordingly.

The School Years

As complex and intricate as this picture is of the young child's development, this is only part of the story. The process of schooling now comes into play, but as we can now appreciate, schooling operates on a backdrop of substantial variation in children's skills and the environments that have been operating for five years or more and continue to exert their influence. Hence understanding the role and importance of schooling, as well as making recommendations for improving it, will benefit, we will show, from inclusion of individual child factors in the description. Specifically, instructional strategies designed to promote growth in reading have been shown to differ distinctly depending on the entering skill level of the child in vocabulary, phonological skills, and reading.

Fresh data and new insights about the nature of learning in children emerging from current research point to a distinct conclusion that children learn important literacy skills like vocabulary and letter and word naming in a reasonably specific fashion as a function of the amount and type of instruction they receive. In other words, growth in the foundational skills necessary for successful literacy does not proceed in a broad, universal fashion where progress in one skill is necessarily generalized to all related skills in a more global developmental progression. Rather, specific skills are nurtured by specific instructional or other environmental practices (Wachs 1984). Consequently, we must pay closer attention to the specific factors in the environment that nurture or impede the learning of specific skills. On an optimistic note, the conclusions emerging from recent research point to a program of instruction in the early grades that could, in principle, optimize each individual child's progress in reading.

The goal—or perhaps dream—of individualized instruction has seemingly eluded scientists and practitioners in contemporary educational discussions. As we will argue, progress toward that lofty goal is currently impeded by a number of entrenched problems in the field of education. The first impediment, variability in the qualifications of people entering the teaching field, is yielding variable levels of quality in teaching and hence in student outcomes. Second, unevenness in teacher training and knowledge compounds the problem of qualifications and further erodes the level of instruction children are receiving. Third, constant political and philosophical wars being waged in educational circles divert attention from the systematic pursuit of research that can serve to improve education for all children. Finally, the ongoing separation of research and practice in the field of education has stifled progress and innovation in understanding and improving education for our children.

The Historical Roots of the Problem

We will round out our treatment of the scope of America's literacy problems with some thoughts about how we got ourselves into this predicament. Diverse sources of evidence point to historical changes in two broad domains of societal functioning in America—parenting and schooling—as crucial to how we got here and where we need to focus our efforts to move ahead. As a working metaphor for these large-scale long-term trends, we have adopted the phrase "the perfect educational storm" to describe the coming together in the 1980s and 1990s of two broadly historical forces that independently appeared quite manageable but whose combined force has produced calamitous results for some children. We will try to be careful not to blame parents and teachers, for some of these historical changes have reaped enormous benefits for our society. Yet we must acknowledge the possibility at least that one of the unintended consequences of these trends has been the erosion of the academic progress of some of our children. Finally, we will offer a series of specific recommendations for improving literacy in America, based on our interpretation of the implications of the scientific research accumulating over the past thirty years.

Plan of the Book

There are four major sections that follow in the book. Part 2 focuses on the preschool years, reviewing and analyzing major factors hypothesized to influence literacy development during early childhood. Included is a discussion of the impact of socioeconomic status and race/ethnicity (chapter 2), preschool experience and intervention (chapter 3), parenting (chapter 4), and child factors (chapter 5). Part 3 focuses squarely on the school years, including discussion of the nature of learning and interactions between child characteristics and instructional practices (chapter 6), followed by examination of factors implicated in fuller implementation of our best instructional practices (chapter 7). The next section, part 4, takes a broader historical perspective on our current situation, examining the role played by significant shifts in parenting and schooling over the past half century (chapter 8). The final section, part 5, makes specific suggestions about ways to improve literacy in America that are based on our reading of the best scientific evidence currently available.

What Is Literacy?

At the outset we would like to define what we mean by *literacy* and how we are using the term in the present volume. According to the standard dictionary definition, literacy is "the state of being literate." Looking further for the definition of *literate,* one traditionally, until recently, has found the simple definition "able to read and write" or sometimes more generally "educated, cultured." Recently, however, the term has come to have a broader meaning that is slowly being included in standard definitions. Recent dictionary editions include the entry "having knowledge or competence." This sense of *literate* recognizes that the term is being used to encompass a broader range of skills and areas of functioning. Hence it has become commonplace to speak of computer literacy or geographical literacy or historical literacy. In this sense literacy includes knowledge and skills needed for functioning in particular segments of society. We will be using *literacy* in this broader sense to include developing knowledge and skills that facilitate learning.

One other aspect of the focus we have adopted merits explication. In our discussion of schooling we will be focusing heavily on the early school years, from kindergarten through third grade, and our discussion will lean heavily on research and development of reading skills during those years. We chose this focus for two reasons. First, the majority of solid empirical work in the past two decades has emphasized early reading skills acquired during the first three to four years of school. In addition, the evidence is pretty clear that a child's performance during early years strongly predicts later performance in elementary and high school. Nevertheless, it is important to recognize that important topics and areas of literacy will not receive the full treatment they deserve. Hence our discussions of mathematical and scientific literacy will not be as detailed as our discussions of literacy in reading. In addition, broader theoretical topics and controversies surrounding notions of intelligence and its role in academic development will not be emphasized (Ferrari and Sternberg 1998; Gardner 1983; Sternberg 1988).

The Nature of the Problem

As we mentioned, at its simplest level, too many American children are not reaching adequate levels of language, cognitive, literacy, and social skills. Obviously there have always been children in our society who have had problems in school (and there will likely be children who will continue to struggle). But there are several things that make our current situation particularly puzzling and worrisome. First, modern problems have seemed to be curiously intransigent, despite increasing public concern and steadily increasing public expenditures. By some accounts the amount of money devoted to education has more than doubled in the last twenty years. Second, the literacy demands being placed on American workers have escalated dramatically over the same period. Without a corresponding improvement in functional literacy levels among prospective employees, productivity, competitiveness, and personal as well as national levels of economic well-being are bound to suffer. Third, it is troubling and unacceptable in a free, democratic society that large gaps in educational opportunities between rich and poor or across racial or ethnic lines should be allowed to persist. Finally, there is evidence that the problem may have been getting worse in the recent past. Although the bulk of the evidence from the National Assessment of Educational Progress (NAEP) studies over the last few decades has shown little change in the levels of literacy evidenced overall by American children (Campbell, Hombo, and Mazzeo 1999), these general trends may not present the whole story. In recent analyses examining the progression of reading scores from the 1990s, NAEP data revealed that differences in reading scores between the highest- and lowest-performing students have increased over approximately the last ten years (National Center for Educational Statistics 2003b). In other words, although the general trend in literacy has not worsened over time, that may be because some of our children are doing better, but others are not. This implies that forces operating during the 1980s and 1990s (and maybe before) may have conspired to exacerbate the achievement gap among American children.

Two Literacy Cultures, Two Literacy Problems?

While the focus of this book is on children who are struggling to acquire adequate language, literacy, and related skills, it would be incomplete if we did not at least mention another emerging concern at the other end of the literacy spectrum—the superachievers. In parallel with trends that have served to erode basic literacy in a sizable percentage of American children, a contrasting culture has arisen that seems absolutely obsessed with academic success and prestige. Starting with competitive preschool entrance exams and culminating in anxiety-ridden, pressure-cooker high schools, for a significant and influential minority of affluent, upwardly mobile parents and professionals, the academic stakes have risen steadily higher. Piling ever more hours of homework on increasingly tough academic courses, coupled with stressful extracurricular schedules, more and more sleep-deprived adolescents are arriving at our most elite universities burned out and exhausted. Full discussion of this other literacy culture and its implications for our children's development is beyond the scope of this volume. But one consequence may be that the achievement gap may be widening systematically, ironically creating problems at both ends of the scale.

The Concept of Variability

Throughout the book in our discussions of literacy problems we will continually be referring to "individual differences" or, more generally, to the notion of "variability." This is an important concept for several reasons, and it contrasts with the general tendency to describe America's literacy problems in more universal terms. Hence in contrast to statements like "American children have poor literacy skills," which one often sees, we prefer to describe the situation with sentences like "There is great variability in American children's literacy skills." This is not just a semantic distinction. It will greatly help clarify our understanding of the state of literacy in our children and what we need to do to improve it. For the truth is that significant numbers of American children, perhaps the majority, are doing fine in reading and writing, math, and science. Claims about literacy problems in American children in general mischaracterize the problem and hence misdirect our attention to its causes and ultimate solution. Likewise, in describing parenting and teaching and their role in contributing to literacy problems, it is more accurate and useful to describe variability across parents and teachers rather than to make general statements about parenting or teaching, which tend to indict the whole group.

Picturing the Complexity of Development

As we will reiterate throughout this volume, the development of literacy skills is influenced by a complex set of factors in the child, family,

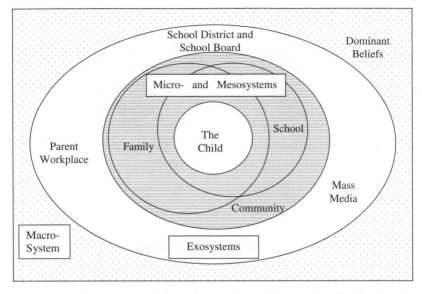

Figure 1.1. Bronfenbrenner's ecological approach (1986).

school, and larger sociocultural context. Psychologists and other social scientists have grappled with ways to capture this complexity. A particularly influential conceptualization is the ecological approach of Uri Bronfenbrenner (1986). In his view, depicted pictorially in figure 1.1, each child is embedded or encircled in an ever-widening and broader set of environmental influences that interact with one another. The most immediate or proximal sources of influence (the micro- and mesosystems) include the child's own characteristics and the settings he or she encounters on a daily basis—for example, home, school, peers. Outside these influences are more remote or distal sources (exo- and macrosystems), which include the parents' workplace, local government, religious institutions, and broader cultural and social beliefs and values.

For purposes of the present book, there are two important ideas that emerge from this conceptualization. The first is that factors at different levels in this ecological system interact to shape children's development. Consequently, it is important to distinguish the role of distal factors (like cultural beliefs or socioeconomic status) from proximal factors (like parenting practices or instructional influences) in shaping a child's literacy growth. Second, it is helpful to view the influence of distal factors as operating through the more proximal factors. For example, if administrators of a school district hold the belief that the whole language approach to teaching reading is the best method (a distal macrolevel factor), they will encourage teachers to use it in instructing their children (a proximal microlevel factor). In this sense, the distal factor (beliefs) exerts its influence via the proximal factor (instructional practices). Put another way, the proximal factor mediates the relation between the distal factor and the outcome.

While these concepts of ecological systems, distal and proximal factors, and mediation may seem abstract and academic, they will help us to understand how the various forces (culture, socioeconomic status, parenting, teaching) relate to one another in shaping literacy acquisition.

Our Starting Point: Individual Differences

The foundation of our discussion is accumulating evidence over the past twenty years or more that there are large individual differences in the language, reading, and math skills of American children. National assessments of reading, mathematics, and science achievement have documented that sizable percentages of children and adolescents (20 percent or more) are not acquiring literacy skills necessary for academic and vocational success (Applebee, Langer, and Mullis 1989). For over thirty years, the NAEP has regularly tested America's nine-, thirteen-, and seventeen-year-olds on a range of skills including reading, mathematics, and science (as well as other subjects, though less systematically). In general, the findings across time and academic areas paint a disturbing picture. For most students, not much improvement occurred in the latter third of the twentieth century. A distinct upturn in scores for African American students was noted during the 1970s, but that trend stalled in the 1980s and may even be reversing itself in the 1990s and 2000s.

More distressing is the level of proficiency exhibited by students. The NAEP divided children's reading skills into five functional levels. At the most basic level, children could follow brief written directions and identify facts from simple paragraphs. At the next, intermediate-level readers could search for, locate, and organize information in relatively lengthy passages. At the higher levels, readers could understand complicated literary and informational passages, and could analyze and integrate less familiar material about topics they studied at school. At the highest level, they could expand and restructure the ideas presented in specialized and complex texts. NAEP found that most American children possess basic or rudimentary reading and math skills, and that seventeen-year-olds have some mastery of intermediate-level skills, but less than half of the seventeen-year-olds reached the higher levels, and only 4.8 percent were classified as advanced readers. Overall, despite clear national recognition of this poor performance over the last fifteen years, the most recent assessments still showed little change in the final decade of the twentieth century (National Center for Educational Statistics 2003b).

Perhaps more striking, evidence has revealed substantial variability in the literacy skills of American children at surprisingly early ages (Alexander and Entwisle 1988; Stevenson et al. 1976). In a seminal study, albeit with a small sample (forty-two families), Hart and Risley (1995) conducted in-depth observations of conversations between mothers and children from professional, working-class, and welfare families from the time the children began to utter their first words, sometime around ten to twelve months of age. Every month for an hour, the researchers taped the conversations and noted the amount and complexity of talk occurring between parent and child. They then followed the children into school.

Of particular significance was how each child's vocabulary was developing. Vocabulary is an essential feature of a child's language skill; it indirectly indexes the growth in a child's knowledge about the world and predicts later reading and academic achievement. Hart and Risley's findings were eye-opening. By three years of age, dramatic differences had emerged in the children's vocabularies. Children from professional families were estimated to know approximately 1,100 different words, those from working-class families 750 words, and welfare children 500 words. Equally startling, the differences among the groups of children could be clearly seen as early as eighteen months of age. Subsequent research with larger, more representative samples has confirmed Hart and Risley's basic results (Kessenich, Raviv, and Morrison 2000; Stipek and Ryan 1997). One analysis on a national sample of two- and three-year-olds from the NICHD Early Child Care Research Network (1999) found that on measures of language and cognitive skills, some American children were functioning at the level of a one-year-old, while others were performing like five-year-olds. Stipek and Ryan (1997) uncovered large socioeconomic status (SES) differences in both cognitive and early literacy skills among a sample of preschoolers and kindergartners. In addition, on several of the cognitive measures, such as word knowledge, number memory, conceptual grouping, and letter reading, the disadvantaged kindergartners scored lower than the advantaged preschoolers at the beginning of the year.

Even more disconcerting is the stability of the individual differences over time. Children's scores on early literacy tasks at kindergarten entry consistently predicted academic performance throughout the first three years of formal schooling experience (Stevenson et al. 1976). Additional literature has pointed to an unbroken line of predictability from first grade reading ability to eleventh grade reading experience and ability, even after accounting for children's cognitive abilities (Cunningham and Stanovich 1997; Cunningham, Stanovich, and West 1994). Taken together, a growing body of evidence testifies to the very early emergence and stability of meaningful differences among children in important literacy and related skills. Clearly, then, one key to improving literacy is to understand the factors responsible for creating these differences so early in a child's life. The next section turns to a discussion of the dominant explanation for the early emergence of this wide variability.

II

Before Children Enter School

2

Sociocultural Factors

In 1998 [one of our most economically prosperous years as a nation] child poverty was over 10 percent in every state. In three states, over a quarter of all children under age 18 were poor: Louisiana (25.7 percent), New Mexico (27.1 percent), and the District of Columbia (30.5 percent).

Census Bureau

As a black parent, I acknowledge there might be differences in what we do with our preschool children that would put them on a more equal footing with whites on the first day of kindergarten.

Dr. Ronald Ferguson

Whether politicians, researchers, teachers, or parents, most people, when asked to speculate about the source(s) of the literacy problems facing American children, nominate as likely culprits disparities stemming from poverty, unemployment, and low levels of parental education. Even achievement discrepancies among children of different racial groups are more commonly attributed to the economic hardship endured by minority group members than any meaningful cultural distinctions. As a result, tremendous social and scientific efforts have been expended to track the academic and vocational successes of the haves and the have-nots. Moreover, many Americans have used the size of the achievement gaps among children from advantaged and disadvantaged classes as a touchstone to gauge the equity and efficacy of our educational system.

Despite a number of political attempts in recent decades to empower schools to act as great equalizing forces for societal ills, such as the implementation of desegregation policies, teacher certification mandates, and school accountability standards, it has become painfully obvious that our current educational system is not the potent agent of social change that many may have hoped. The difficulties school administrators and educators have encountered in reducing achievement discrepancies across racial and socioeconomic lines do not bode well for future instructional efforts with an increasingly diverse student population. For example, the number of minority children attending public elementary and secondary schools is steadily rising (National Center for Educational Statistics 2001a), and Hispanic youth are projected to compose 25 percent of the population in grades K–12 by 2030 (National Center for Educational Statistics 1995a). Furthermore, the United States still reports one of the highest child poverty rates of any industrialized nation (Smeeding and Rainwater 1995).

In this chapter, we will endeavor to tease apart the unique and combined influences of sociocultural factors, including socioeconomic, racial, and ethnic minority status, in shaping children's early literacy development.

Socioeconomic Disadvantage and Academic Achievement

Socioeconomic status (SES) has traditionally been measured by three indicators: parental income, education, and occupational status. National analyses of literacy trends reveal that nine-, thirteen-, and seventeen-year-old children from families with lower levels of parental education (that is, high school graduation or less) consistently score lower on reading, mathematics, and science assessments than do children whose parents completed some education after high school (National Center for Educational Statistics 1999). Most striking is the fact that children from lower SES families begin kindergarten and first grade behind their more affluent peers and make less progress throughout their early elementary school years (Alexander and Entwisle 1988; Stipek and Ryan 1997). In other words, SES-related achievement disparities, which are apparent at the beginning of school, are not significantly diminished by traditional instructional practices; instead, these differences are sustained, or even exacerbated, over time. Furthermore, long durations of poverty in the first few years of life can lead to very deleterious effects on general cognitive and verbal skills, as well as on achievement throughout early childhood (Smith, Brooks-Gunn, and Klebanov 1997).

Not only are substantial achievement gaps between children from low and high SES homes detectable from kindergarten through twelfth grade, equally apparent are disparities in language and emergent literacy skills (for example, knowledge of colors, shapes, sizes, letters, and numbers) throughout the prekindergarten years. For example, within a national sample of approximately 1,000 three-year-olds, children's vocabulary comprehension and production skills ranged from approximately two years below age level to two years above (Kessenich, Raviv, and Morrison 2000). Moreover, children living in low SES families during the first two years of life displayed significant lags in developing emergent literacy and language skills by thirty-six months of age compared to children whose parents had higher levels of income or education (Bachman and Morrison 2002). Psychologists studying parent-child conversations found that children whose families were on welfare spoke with smaller vocabularies and showed slower rates of growth in vocabulary acquisition than did their same-aged peers from working-class and professional families (Hart and Risley 1995).

Parental Education and Income

There is little argument that children exposed to economic deprivation during early childhood are more likely to experience a number of adverse outcomes, such as impeded language and literacy acquisition. However, just because SES indicators, like family income or maternal education, consistently discriminate between low- and high-achieving students does not necessarily mean that the silver bullet has been located and the source of literacy problems in America has been identified. What does a two-year-old understand about the dollars and cents in his mother's wallet? And why is a preschooler more likely to know the letters of the alphabet if her parent has a Ph.D. rather than a GED?

We in no way want to minimize the negative impact of socioeconomic disadvantage on children's early development. Yet our goals would not be achieved if our investigative pursuits ended here. Simply categorizing children according to SES indices is ultimately unsatisfying and incomplete because the processes by which factors like paren-

tal education and income influence literacy development remain un-
defined. Remembering our discussion in chapter 1 regarding distal and
proximal sources of influence, we must consider SES a distal factor. A
major movement under way in psychological research right now involves trying to determine how distal factors, like socioeconomic status, wield their influence. Do these SES discrepancies arise because
fewer resources (educational, psychological, physical, community, and
neighborhood) are available to poorer children? Perhaps parents with
less education or income interact differently with their children than
parents from more affluent backgrounds?

The Context of Poverty

Accumulating evidence illustrates that both direct and mediated pathways of influence are operating in low SES families, which act to depress children's academic performance. Nevertheless, the vast majority
of the research has concentrated on describing the context of poverty
and identifying environmental risk factors associated with economic
deprivation. For instance, children living in poverty are much more
likely to experience negative perinatal outcomes, like prematurity (Saigal et al. 1991) and low birth weight (2,500g or less), as well as less adequate nutrition and health care in early childhood (Korenman and
Miller 1997). Their mothers are less likely to receive timely prenatal
care during the first trimester (McCormick et al. 1992). These children
are more frequently raised in single-parent households (McLanahan
and Sandefur 1994) and exposed to neighborhoods with fewer community resources and higher rates of unemployment, violence, and
delinquency (Brooks-Gunn, Duncan, and Aber 1997). The lack of material and economic resources leads to a host of adverse outcomes, such
as weaker cognitive skills, a high rate of classroom behavior problems,
greater academic failure, and higher school dropout rates (Duncan,
Brooks-Gunn, and Klebanov 1994; Duncan et al. 1998; Hansen, McLanahan, and Thompson 1997).

Poverty and Family Relations

Although the deleterious effects of low-income status pervade many
aspects of children's family environment and physical surroundings,

research has also demonstrated that lower SES parents' interactions with their children appear qualitatively different from those of higher SES households. Parents living in poverty tended to talk less to their children and often communicated with a more limited vocabulary than did parents with more education or financial security. Instead, the language directed to young children in lower SES households was generally more repetitive, with less varied words in mothers' speech. Moreover, parents offered fewer questions or descriptive statements, which can elicit greater understanding and more advanced vocabulary acquisition (Hart and Risley 1995; Hoff-Ginsberg 1991). Hart and Risley provided the following vignettes of the parent-child interaction styles in professional and welfare families:

> In the professional families the extraordinary amount of talk, the many different words, and the greater richness of nouns, modifiers, and past-tense verbs in parent utterances suggested a culture concerned with names, relationships, and recall . . . parents spent time and effort developing their children's potential, asking questions and using affirmatives to encourage their children to listen, to notice how words refer and relate, and to practice the distinctions among them. In the welfare families, the lesser amount of talk with its more frequent parent-initiated topics, imperatives, and prohibitions suggested a culture concerned with established customs. To teach socially acceptable behavior, language rich in nouns and modifiers was not called for; obedience, politeness, and conformity were more likely to be the keys to survival. (133–134)

After children begin school, those with less-educated parents also lose ground academically over the summer months compared to children with higher levels of parental educational attainment. These "summer effects" (Entwisle and Alexander 1993) again indicate that parents with fewer economic or educational resources generally are less likely to provide cognitively stimulating or enriching home environments compared to higher SES parents. Recent work has further substantiated that parental education and income indicators, measured when children were babies, are substantially less predictive of children's language skills at three years of age after accounting for the influence of parenting practices and children's cognitive abilities (Raviv, Kessenich, and Morrison in press).

It is difficult to imagine how parents' income or educational attainment might directly shape their child's language and literacy development. In fact, increasing parental income or educational attainment has resulted in relatively modest gains in children's academic achievement (Magnuson and McGroder 2002; Mayer 1997). Instead, a robust literature, spanning several decades, has demonstrated that powerful proximal variables, such as the characteristics of childcare, the parent, and the child, transmit the influence of SES onto children's well-being. The exclusive focus on distal influences provides an incomplete picture of the variability in American children's early literacy development.

Race, Ethnicity, and Academic Achievement

Similar problems and confusion arise when examining the nature and sources of racial and ethnic differences in the academic achievement of American students. Cultural comparisons garnering the most attention include: (1) African Americans and European Americans (commonly referred to as the "Black-White test score gap"); (2) Asians, Asian Americans, and European Americans; and (3) Hispanic immigrants, Hispanic Americans, and European Americans.

The Black-White Test Score Gap

Perhaps the most salient ethnic group comparison has focused on the persistent discrepancies in academic performance between Black and White American children. In general, African American children do not perform as well as their White peers on a variety of academic assessments. Even in recent decades, during periods of national economic prosperity, this gap in Black and White children's academic achievement has endured. According to the National Assessment of Educational Progress, discrepancies in reading, mathematics, science, and writing scores decreased significantly from 1980 to 1988, with Black students' scores improving over time and White students' scores remaining stable. However, this rate of progress did not continue, and after the late 1980s, the trends reversed, eliminating much of the earlier growth (Ferguson 2002; Thernstrom and Thernstrom 1998). A recent report that tracked four cohorts of children in the early 1990s revealed that while the Black-White gap in reading and mathematics achievement fluctuated somewhat across grades, with a reduction noted during elementary school, significant differences were still evident from elementary to high school (National Center for Educational Statistics 2001b). Not only did average levels of performance differ, significant gaps emerged for Black and White students who had previously shown quite similar levels of performance just one or two years earlier.

Why Make Ethnic and Racial Comparisons?

Before plunging in to explore the sources of these racial gaps, we might worry that simply making comparisons of Black and White children's scores is invidious and inappropriate. There is a long history in the social sciences, particularly in the early to mid-1900s, of promoting cultural inferiority as a viable explanation for the lower academic performance and socioeconomic disadvantage experienced by Black Americans. Over the last few decades, minority researchers have rightly criticized these "deficit models" of development because they minimize the impact of over two hundred years of discriminatory policies, which limited social advancement and educational attainment, and failed to recognize the positive characteristics and contributions of ethnic minorities (Garcia-Coll et al. 1996; McLoyd 1990; Slaughter-Defoe et al. 1990).

So, in the twenty-first century, what is the utility of even making these comparisons? What do we hope to accomplish by pointing out the early emergence, size, and persistence of the Black-White gaps in language and literacy acquisition? In our efforts to uncover the nature and sources of individual differences in literacy development, we are following the lead of prominent sociologists, economists, and historians who have demonstrated that the Black-White test score gap has significant, far-reaching implications for educational and vocational success and economic security. In the recent collaboration commissioned by the National Academy of Sciences, *America Becoming: Racial Trends and Their Consequences* (Smelsen, Wilson, and Mitchell

2001), Harvard University researcher Ronald Ferguson maintained: "If test scores were equal, on average, among the races, there would be little need for current debates about affirmative action in college admissions. Certification testing for new teachers would not so dramatically affect the racial composition of the nation's teacher work-force. The hourly earnings gap among racial groups would be only a fraction of what it is currently. Whether we like it or not, test scores, and the skills they measure, matter" (348).

In like manner, in *The Black-White Test Score Gap,* sociologists Christopher Jencks and Meredith Phillips claimed: "In a country as racially polarized as the United States, no single change in isolation could possibly eliminate the entire legacy of slavery and Jim Crow or usher in an era of full racial equality. But if racial equality is America's goal, reducing the Black-White test score gap would probably do more to promote this goal than any other strategy that commands broad political support. Reducing the test score gap is probably both necessary and sufficient for reducing racial inequality in educational attainment and earnings. Changes in education and earnings would in turn help reduce racial differences in crime, health, and family structure, although we do not know how large these effects would be" (1998a, 3–4). Clearly, the racial gap in achievement is important and we ignore it at our own peril. Therefore, we proceed with the following review not simply as an intellectual exercise but to provide a scholarly analysis of the nature and sources of racial achievement discrepancies based on recent multidisciplinary research. In this way, we hope ultimately to elucidate ways to improve literacy in America for all children.

Common Explanations

Sociocultural explanations are frequently offered as reasons for the achievement gap. One interpretation (Ogbu 1988, 1991) posits that despite Black parents' encouragement of their children's educational pursuits, their castelike status undermines their efforts. Consequently, Black children's educational aspirations diminish as they observe their parents' encounters with job ceilings and high levels of unemployment in their communities. Moreover, their concomitant economic hardship is associated with higher parental stress, fewer material resources, and more adverse child outcomes (McLoyd 1998; Wilson 1987). Other work has demonstrated that among high school and college students, the anxiety evoked during test taking, when confronted with the threat of fulfilling a negative stereotype about one's group, can also depress academic performance (Steele 1998; Steele and Aronson 1995). Consequently, as a self-protective mechanism, minority students may identify less with the high-achieving student role.

Other scientists have looked to the schooling environment as a source of bias against Black students and families. For example, it has been found that by the end of first grade, White children outperform Black children, even though the two groups had performed similarly earlier in the school year (Alexander and Entwisle 1988). One hypothesis is that African American children may experience greater difficulties during the transition to a formal schooling environment (Entwisle and Alexander 1988). Additionally, parents in disenfranchised groups, such as African Americans, may have less educational experience and "cultural capital." This may limit their opportunity to effectively negotiate with teachers and school officials to support their children's educational progress (Bourdieu 1985; Lareau and Horvat 1999).

Additional explanations have been offered by biogenetic researchers who attempt to distinguish genetic from environmental sources of influence in the Black-White test score gap (for example, Rowe, Vazsonyi, and Flannery 1994, 1995). However, the work has not provided conclusive evidence, particularly given the malleability of heritable traits to environmental forces (Collins et al. 2000). Therefore, the present review focuses on interpretations that represent more robust research.

How Cultural and Schooling Factors Affect Young Children

The research on achievement disparities between Black and White children parallels the literature on SES and school performance by offering a detailed analysis of the environmental context children experienced yet places less emphasis on the mediating processes by which familial stress, economic insecurity, and discrimination influence early academic achievement. Some argue that the protective behaviors Black children adopt emerge after prolonged experience with the school system during which they develop an awareness of stereotypes. However, applying these explanations to young children in the prekindergarten and elementary school years is strained. Findings from other research clearly reveal that African American elementary school children report liking and doing well in school, despite the gap in test scores (Stevenson, Chen, and Uttal 1990); at least at this point in their schooling, they are not actively expressing disengagement or disidentification with their roles as high-achieving students.

Two Important Caveats for the Cultural and Schooling Perspectives

Overall, cultural, economic, and schooling approaches have not yielded completely satisfactory explanations, especially as compelling evidence builds in two important areas. First, meaningful racial/ethnic gaps in literacy and language development emerge at very young ages. Research with national data sets has revealed that eliminating the Black-White gap in literacy skills in first grade could reduce the test score gap in twelfth grade by half (Phillips, Crouse, and Ralph 1998). By three years of age, substantial variation has been detected for Black and White children on cognitive test scores (Johnson et al. 1993). By kindergarten entry (Bachman 1999) and in first grade (Entwisle and Alexander 1988; Phillips et al. 1998; Stevenson, Chen, and Uttal 1990), there are substantial gaps observed on assessments of reading, mathematics, and vocabulary.

Second, it has become increasingly clear that racial/ethnic differences develop at least somewhat independently of SES. In other words, traditional socioeconomic indices such as income, education, and occupational status do not fully explain these early academic disparities. Sizable differences in literacy and language skills at the beginning of kindergarten were not significantly diminished when Black and White children of highly educated parents were compared (Bachman and Morrison 2002). In national surveys, Black children scored about seventeen points lower than did White children on a standardized vocabulary comprehension measure in first grade (Phillips et al. 1998). This vocabulary gap did not consistently narrow when Black and White children with similar socioeconomic backgrounds were contrasted.

The presence of significant Black-White achievement discrepancies among students in higher SES families with more educated parents has drawn growing attention from the media as well. In 1999, the *New York Times* featured the lag in middle SES Black students' performance with an illustration from a high school in Evanston, Illinois, a racially diverse, middle to upper SES suburb of Chicago. The Evanston school district reported that in the 1997–98 academic year, "nearly 25 percent of black students had failed at least one class, compared with 4 percent of white students. Seven percent of black students' grades were A's, compared with 25 percent for whites. In 1996, on a state reading test, 49 percent of African Americans at the school were reading below grade level, compared with 9 percent of whites. And while the college attendance rate of both blacks and whites here is above the national average, 66 percent of blacks go to college, compared with 95 percent of whites" (Belluck 1999). An African American woman who managed a high school program to assist minority students described her frequent encounters with middle SES Black students from stable, well-educated families who had fallen behind academically. She commented: "The first thing that came to my head is 'Oh, they're poor' or 'Oh, they're in a single-parent home. . . .' To my surprise, the students were living in the better part of Evanston. Students were living with two-parent families who have college degrees. They have computers. They have personal tutors. And they're getting C's and D's, and why?" (Belluck 1999).

Researchers and educators have recently combined efforts to better understand why the test score gap may exist even in higher SES communities and schools. In 1999, the Minority Student Achievement Network (MSAN) was created to address the racial achievement gaps in primary and secondary schools in fifteen middle- and upper-middle-income school districts from California, Illinois, Massachusetts, Michigan, New Jersey, New York, North Carolina, Ohio, Virginia, and Wisconsin (Ferguson 2002). From a sample of over 30,000 seventh and eleventh graders, half of White students reported A or A– grade averages compared to only 15 percent of Black students. Likewise, 44 percent of Black students and 14 percent of White students reported C+ averages or below. Socioeconomic differences between the Black and White families, like parental education, home resources (for example, books and computers), family size, and marital status, predicted some of the GPA discrepancy but did not completely explain the gap.

Predictably, single demographic factors predicted GPA differences even less well for Black and White students in higher SES families. The test score gap was actually *larger* among higher SES students. Another way to characterize this pattern is that there were smaller SES differences in GPA among Black students than among White students. Overall, the financial and educational gains experienced by Black families in these school districts have not yet produced the corresponding gains in student achievement that many parents, educators, and researchers expected.

Completing the Ecological Perspective: Investigating Proximal Sources of Influence

It is discouraging to acknowledge that several decades of social reform have not ameliorated centuries of systematic discrimination, but that is exactly what current research suggests. While economic and educational reforms may have been critical agents of change for many aspects of Black families' lives, such as their neighborhood quality, their physical and psychological health, and their greater career mobility and economic security, gains have been less dramatic for Black children's early literacy development or later academic performance.

So, if increases in income or educational attainment do not fully reduce the achievement gap, where do we look next? This dilemma has proven to be a major sticking point in psychological and educational research—until now, most investigations have essentially stopped here, with a few notable exceptions. Researchers have been exceedingly reluctant to delve much further into characteristics of the home environments or parent-child dynamics in Black families for fear of appearing to place blame on parents who have already endured tremendous hardships and have overcome innumerable obstacles in order to reach a position of higher socioeconomic status. However, the pursuit of substantive solutions for these persistent racial gaps should not be considered a cause for concern or offense, especially when the ramifications of these achievement disparities are so far-reaching and important to our society as a whole.

An alternative, and less implemented, strategy for addressing this perplexing disparity in achievement is to consider the influence of minority status on more proximal factors that shape children's early development. For example, infant mortality rates are disproportionately higher in Black families than in White families (Centers for Disease Control and Prevention 2000), and this rate of incidence occurs independently of SES (Schoendorf et al. 1992). The higher infant mortality experienced by Black, college-educated parents is caused in part by higher rates of low birth weight; the mortality rates are much more similar among Black and White infants with normal birth weights (Schoendorf et al. 1992). Further, neither education nor genetics offers an adequate explanation. As reported recently in the *New York Times,* "It now seems that education cannot explain much about the racial gap in the outcome of pregnancies. The infant mortality rate experienced by Black women who are college graduates is higher than that for White women who are high school dropouts. This is not because of racially linked genetic differences—the babies of Black women born in the United States die at a higher rate than those of Black immigrant women in similar economic circumstances" (Rothstein 2002). A number of factors may contribute to these racial differences in pregnancy outcomes, including poorer maternal health before conception, insufficient access to care during pregnancy, and greater psychosocial risks and stressors among Black parents (Schoendorf et al. 1992). As more connections are found between mothers' psychological well-being and children's prenatal development (DiPietro et al. 2002), it is possible that the stress middle-class Black mothers experience, among other factors, may be more severe and pervasive than previously considered.

Another proximal source that must be considered is parenting. The Black-White vocabulary gap was reduced by about 25 percent after accounting for racial differences in the type and quantity of learning activities and educational experiences parents provided their children (Phillips et al. 1998). Corroborating evidence has revealed that measures of Black parents' literacy promotion and cognitive stimulation is less predictive of their young children's academic achievement than is found for White parents (Bachman 1999; Berlin and Brooks-Gunn 1995; Johnson et al. 1993; Sugland et al. 1995). Even among more educated parents, significant racial differences are evident in the amount

of shared book reading, print exposure, and hours spent viewing television in Black and White households (Bachman 1999). In general, some
African American parents are less likely to read with their children than
are White parents, there are fewer books in their homes, and their children spend more hours watching television. One explanation may be
that, although parents may have achieved higher levels of income or
education than were previously attained in their families, due to social
and political constraints, "changes in families' class position [could]
take more than one generation to alter parenting practices" (Phillips et
al. 1998, 126). Notably, not only have parents' education levels predicted racial gaps in children's vocabulary skills in national data sets,
but grandparents' educational attainment uniquely contributed as
well. This suggests that generational effects of historically lower socioeconomic status may be shaping current parenting practices (Phillips
et al. 1998).

Other research has sought to determine how some Black children
have achieved academic success, despite being raised in poor families.
Case studies of high- and low-achieving Black adolescents from poor,
one- and two-parent homes revealed that parents of high achievers
were more involved with their children's education, promoted strong
educational values, and expressed personal responsibility for their children's performance compared with parents of low-achieving students
(Clark 1983). When these high-achieving adolescents were in preschool
and elementary school, "parents attempted to prepare children for
school tasks during home conversations, study encounters, and other
activities that called upon the child to speak, read, spell, and solve challenging problems. . . . Parents usually monitor[ed] homework closely,
including work with flash cards, art projects, research projects, reading, and writing assignments, in the child's first school years, while
slowly urging self-regulation in these activities" (136–37). In contrast,
parents of low achievers were less involved with their children's education and held their children responsible for academic failure: "There
are no consistent, regularly performed learning rituals in these homes.
Reading of school materials, writing, and homework are seldom, if
ever, done in the home. Although parents sometimes 'remind' the students of homework obligations, there are no parental attempts to su-
pervise or check student's progress. . . . These parents may have some
vague idea of the student's school performance; they may know that

their child is being only minimally productive, but they feel powerless to help the student improve or to control his or her behavior" (195). As we will discuss further in chapters 3 and 4, parenting practices consistently emerge as one of the most potent influences on early child development for all children.

A third possible proximal source of Black-White literacy gaps may be differences in the frequency and type of childcare used during the preschool years. For example, employed mothers often rely on relatives to provide childcare. However, White children are somewhat more likely to receive care from fathers (34 percent) than from grandmothers (28 percent), whereas Black preschoolers are more likely to be cared for by a grandmother (32 percent) than their father (17 percent) (Smith 2002). This care-giving difference may explain, at least partly, why grandparents' educational attainment significantly predicts the test score gap over and above the contribution of parents' education (Phillips et al. 1998). In addition, more Black children attend center-based care (30 percent) than do White children (24 percent) (Ehrle, Adams, and Tout 2001; Liang, Fuller, and Singer 2000). Because Black mothers of preschoolers are more likely to work full-time than are White mothers (Folk and Beller 1993), national data also indicate that over half of Black infants and toddlers of employed mothers are in full-time childcare (58 percent) compared to about a third of White children (Ehrle, Adams, and Tout 2001). It is not yet clear whether these different patterns of childcare usage have been instrumental in reducing or perpetuating the test score gap.

In summary, multiple cultural and contextual factors, such as acculturation and adaptation, economic hardship, and generational effects of low parental educational attainment, have been shown to impinge upon Black children's early development (McLoyd 1990, 1998; Phillips et al. 1998). However, we currently understand much less well the proximal mechanisms by which these distal factors exert their influence. A substantial proportion of the Black-White gap can be attributed to forces operating in children and families' lives *before* school entry. As a summary, we echo Jencks and Phillips's recommendation:

> Instead of emphasizing the kinds of racial differences that economists and sociologists usually study (parents' eco-

nomic resources, parents' position in the occupational hier-
archy, parents' exposure to formal education, and parents'
living arrangements), successful theories will take more account of the factors that psychologists have traditionally
emphasized (the way family members interact with one another and with the outside world, for example). A good explanation of why White five-year-olds have bigger vocabularies than Black five-year-olds is likely to focus on how
much the parents talk to their children, how they deal with
their children's questions, and how they react when their
children either learn or fail to learn something, not on how
much money the parents have. (1998b, 26)

National and International Comparisons
of Asian and American Children

Another frequently studied racial disparity involves cross-cultural comparisons of Asian and American students in reading, mathematics, and
science. As early as first and fifth grades, children from China and Ja-
pan have been shown to outscore American students in mathematics,
and Chinese children surpassed American children in reading as well
(Stedman 1997; Stevenson, Chen, and Lee 1993). Achievement was
particularly discrepant in mathematics skills; by eleventh grade, only
14.5 percent of Chinese and 8 percent of Japanese students were scoring
lower than the American students' mean level of performance (Stevenson, Chen, and Lee 1993).

Cultural differences in educational beliefs are often cited to explain these international gaps in academic skills, particularly as more
evidence demonstrates that these academic discrepancies persist for
several generations after Asian families immigrate to the United States
(Fuligni 1997). Both Asian and Asian American students devote more
time to homework and educational activities than nonacademic activities such as part-time employment or household chores (Chen and
Stevenson 1995; Stevenson and Lee 1990). In addition, Chinese and
Japanese students report higher educational aspirations for themselves
than do American students. Asian youth and parents were more likely
to attribute academic successes to effort, unlike the American families,

who place relatively higher weight on innate ability (Stevenson, Chen, and Lee 1993).

The Influence of Teacher and Parent Instruction

However, recent evidence highlights the potency of the instructional and parenting practices Asian children receive for shaping their superior academic achievement. When investigating the more advanced mathematics performance of Chinese kindergarten and first grade children, Geary and colleagues found that the Chinese children implemented a variety of arithmetic strategies to complete mathematics problems and also retrieved answers from long-term memory more frequently and rapidly than did the American elementary school children (Geary 1996; Geary et al. 1996). One possible explanation is greater amount of time spent practicing these skills in school. Naito and Miura (2001) found that, after accounting for language characteristics and age-related factors, significant schooling effects on learning of arithmetic concepts were detected for Japanese children in first grade compared to their same-age counterparts in kindergarten. In other words, the acquisition of sophisticated addition strategies and facility with the Base 10 number system were developed as a result of explicit instruction in first grade.

In addition to the curricular advantages experienced by Asian children, Asian and Asian American parents also provide literacy instruction for their children. Asian parents espouse higher educational values and expectations for their children than do European American parents (Chen and Stevenson 1995), and these cultural beliefs shape their parenting practices in a variety of ways (Chao 2000). In one of the few studies of preschool-aged Asian American children, Asian American parents demonstrated much greater involvement in their children's literacy development than did the Euro-American parents. For example, almost 60 percent had taught their children basic reading, mathematics, and writing skills before kindergarten entry, as opposed to only 16 percent of European American parents (Schneider and Lee 1990). Further, after formal schooling began, Asian American parents continued to provide additional literacy supports for their children, including purchasing books, arranging a study area in the home, and enrolling their children in private tutoring and study sessions, including music and language lessons (Hieshima and Schneider 1994; Schneider and Lee 1990).

How Asian Immigrant Parents Promote Literacy Development

Asian parents' involvement in their children's educational progress is often evident independent of SES. In fact, the manifestation of cultural values in the family organization and parenting strategies of Asian parents is observable even among immigrants who do not speak English and are employed in low-wage jobs. Ethnographic work with Indo-Chinese refugees depicts the collaborative efforts of parents and older siblings to assist the younger children's adaptation to the schooling environment and their English literacy acquisition (Caplan, Choy, and Whitmore 1992).

> Among the refugee families . . . homework clearly dominates household activities during weeknights. Although the parents' lack of education and facility with English often prevents them from engaging in the content of the exercise, they set standards and goals for the evening and facilitate their children's studies by assuming responsibility for chores and other practical considerations. After dinner, the table is cleared and homework begins. The older children, both male and female, help their younger siblings. Indeed, they seem to learn as much from teaching as from being taught. It is reasonable to suppose that a great amount of learning goes on at these times—in terms of skills, habits, attitudes, and expectations as well as the content of a subject. The younger children, in particular, are taught not only subject matter but how to learn. Such sibling involvement demonstrates how a large family can encourage and enhance academic success. (39–40)

In summary, diverse findings across several cultural comparisons converge on a coherent interpretation. Literacy acquisition requires environmental support, both to provide instruction and to arrange the setting and time for practice. Even in the context of poverty, instruction from parents and teachers can play a compensatory role that buffers children from more adverse outcomes and promotes academic success.

The Academic Achievement of Immigrant and Native Hispanic Children

Recent reports from the 2002 Census Population Survey (CPS) revealed that Hispanics have surpassed Blacks as the largest minority group in America (Clemetson 2003; Ramirez and de la Cruz 2003). Much of this increase is the result of rising immigration. Currently, 40 percent of Hispanics are foreign born, and approximately two-thirds of the total Hispanic population is of Mexican descent, followed by Central and South America (14 percent), Puerto Rico (9 percent), and Cuba (4 percent) (Ramirez and de la Cruz 2003). Consequently, Hispanic children represent one of the fastest growing ethnic groups in American public schools (National Center for Educational Statistics 1995b). The diversity in ethnic background and English-language proficiency that some school districts are facing is staggering. In California, for example, 32 percent of residents are Hispanic (U.S. Census 2000). Across California's kindergarten classrooms, students speak at least fifty-six different languages, with over 80 percent of these kindergartners speaking Spanish as their first language (State of California Department of Education 1999). The term *Hispanic* is used by the U.S. Census Bureau for all individuals from Central and South America, Cuba, the Dominican Republic, and Spain, whereas *Latino* generally refers to people from Spanish-speaking countries in the Americas (Mendoza 1994). The terms are often used interchangeably in current research. However, since "Hispanic" is the most general designation (Mendoza 1994), and census respondents overwhelming choose "Hispanic" over "Latino" as panethnic descriptors (Guzman and McConnell 2002), we will primarily use "Hispanic" in the following review.

Data from the NAEP have uncovered sizable Hispanic-White gaps in reading, mathematics, and science at nine years of age that persist through age seventeen (National Center for Educational Statistics 1995b). In addition, Hispanic adolescents' high school dropout rates are significantly higher (30 percent) than they are for non-Hispanic

White (9 percent) or Black (12 percent) youths (Cooper, Denner, and Lopez 1999; National Center for Educational Statistics 1995b). Foreign-born Hispanic adolescents are particularly likely to report more academic problems, including dropping out, than are their peers (Fuligni 1997; Landale, Oropesa, and Llanes 1998).

Based on studies with other ethnic groups, we would expect to find that Hispanic children's academic problems emerge quite early. However, very little research has investigated young Hispanic children's school-readiness skills and literacy development (Flores et al. 2002). The existing literature pertains almost exclusively to children of Mexican or Puerto Rican descent. Gaps in White and Hispanic children's reading and math achievement have been detected in first grade, with Hispanic children performing similarly to their Black peers (Stevenson, Chen, and Uttal 1990). Moreover, low levels of English vocabulary comprehension have been detected among Hispanic children at four to six years of age (Crockett, Eggebeen, and Hawkins 1993). Investigation of California school records revealed that Hispanic kindergartners, especially Spanish-speaking kindergartners, experienced social promotion at higher rates than did Anglo students (Cosden et al. 1995). In other words, kindergarten children identified by teachers as struggling to master the skills being taught were advanced to first grade for "social reasons." They were not retained in kindergarten for an additional year. However, whether they were promoted or retained, by the end of first grade, students were performing more poorly than the majority of their peers, even when standardized tests were administered in Spanish (Cosden et al. 1995).

Taken together, growing evidence demonstrates that academic difficulties are evident early for Hispanic children, and that problems are encountered by both English- and Spanish-speaking Latino children.

Commonly Identified Sources of Variability for Hispanic Children

Since Hispanic families face a number of socioeconomic risks, explanations for their children's academic difficulties tend to rely on traditional SES indices. Hispanic families are disproportionately represented among America's poor (Aponte 1993; Ramirez and de la Cruz 2003). Mexican immigrants, for example, are particularly likely to experience higher rates of poverty. When compared to Puerto Rican and Cuban immigrants, this is related to their low educational attainment and poor English (Leyendecker and Lamb 1999; Ramirez and de la Cruz 2003). Child poverty rates are exacerbated by the low number of Mexican American and Puerto Rican mothers who are employed part- or full-time. Yet even among Latino children with one or two employed parents, poverty rates exceed the prevalence encountered by Black children (Lichter and Landale 1995). Approximately 90 percent of Hispanic American families are concentrated in urban areas, which often contain higher-crime neighborhoods and poorer public schools (Leyendecker and Lamb 1999). In addition, the Hispanic population in the United States is younger than are other ethnic groups, and households generally include more children (Mendoza 1994). Foreign-born children often reside with two married parents, whereas native-born Hispanic children increasingly experience single-parent households with each successive generation (Brandon 2002). It should be noted that many of these socioeconomic disparities vary widely across the different Hispanic groups. For example, the incidence of unemployment and single-parent-headed households occurs more frequently in Puerto Rican than in Mexican American families (Landale and Lichter 1997).

However, as we have repeatedly emphasized, the influence of these socioeconomic discrepancies must be, at least partially, transmitted through more proximal developmental factors. Although the research addressing these more process-oriented questions in Hispanic families is still in early stages of development, the initial evidence points to several possible factors. These include parenting practices, low levels of preschool experience, and children's health and behavior problems.

Proximal Sources of Influence on Hispanic Children's Development

Given the large proportion of Hispanic families who are recent immigrants (that is, within three generations of immigration), much of the burgeoning literature on Hispanic parents has focused on parenting expectations, beliefs, and values as well as on how acculturation may alter these characteristics. For instance, highly acculturated Latino parents tend to view children's development as more complex and dynamic and believe that children can engage in independent activities at younger ages more so than do less acculturated parents (Guttierrez and Sameroff 1990; Savage and Gauvain 1998). Hispanic parents' educational aspirations remain quite high during their children's formal school experience, although their expectations may diminish if their children struggle academically over time (Goldenberg et al. 2001; Stevenson, Chen, and Uttal 1990). Immigrant Latino parents place high instrumental value on educational attainment as a means of obtaining higher education, financial security, and greater vocational opportunities, and notably, these beliefs do not significantly diminish the longer they reside in the United States or when faced with perceived discrimination (Goldenberg et al. 2001). In national survey data, Hispanic parents expressed greater concerns about their children's kindergarten readiness than did White parents (Diamond, Reagan, and Bandyk 2000).

In reality, we still know very little about Hispanic parents' literacy-promoting behaviors, for either English or Spanish proficiency. Randomized interventions have reported modest successes in increasing the frequency and quality of Hispanic parents' book-reading interactions with their infants and preschoolers (Golova et al. 1999; Valdez-Menchaca and Whitehurst 1992). However, few studies have examined naturally occurring literacy practices within Hispanic families.

In addition, immigrant parents rely heavily on their children's assistance with "language brokering," or translating between English and Spanish for parents, siblings, teachers, and community members. Children's translating work may enhance their academic motivation and achievement in the long run as they develop sophisticated communication skills and acquire greater access to resources (Orellana 2001). On the other hand, bilingual fifth grade students reported feeling encumbered and stressed by their translating responsibilities, especially if they perceived themselves as not yet acculturated to American society (Weisskirch and Alva 2002). Hispanic parents also enlist older siblings to provide tutoring for younger siblings, although this educational assistance often wanes as the older students themselves experience academic difficulties in high school (Cooper, Denner, and Lopez 1999).

A second proximal factor is childcare. Hispanic parents use relative care arrangements (grandparents, aunts, and so on) more than formal center care (Smith 2002). Moreover, Latino parents enroll their children in preschool less frequently than do parents of other ethnic backgrounds, and this pattern holds even after taking into account the ethnic group differences in income, employment, education, and parenting practices (Fuller, Eggers-Piérola, and Holloway 1996). Despite Hispanic children's high poverty rates, their enrollment in Head Start is substantially lower (19 percent) than that of poor Black children (39 percent) (Smith 2002). Why would this be so? One Latino mother replaced a Colombian babysitter with a formal childcare center and expressed her frustration that "most center teachers and staff are 'Americans.' When her daughter first came home from the center, [the mother] could not understand her newly acquired English" (Fuller, Eggers-Piérola, and Holloway 1996, 410). Another mother was displeased with her childcare center because only one classroom aide could speak Spanish, and she felt like the White staff treated Hispanic parents as "ignorant." Whatever the causes, Hispanic kindergartners enter public school with significantly less preschool experience than do their peers (National Center for Educational Statistics 1995b), even though preschool can provide important literacy and language benefits (as we discuss in chapter 3), especially for immigrant children. For example, bilingual preschool education has been shown to improve the English proficiency of Mexican children while sustaining their Spanish proficiency (Rodriguez et al. 1995).

A third potential source of influence involves children's health and behavior. A leading group of Latino pediatricians has issued a statement that Latino children experience a disproportionate number of health problems, like asthma, diabetes mellitus, and obesity, and are at high risk for behavioral and developmental disorders (Flores et al. 2002). Unfortunately, in spite of these medical and developmental risks, Hispanic children are more likely to be uninsured, to encounter numerous barriers for accessing health care (for example, language and transportation problems, less preventative screening), and to obtain poorer quality health care than are other ethnic groups (Flores et al.

2002; Mendoza 1994). Hispanic children's higher rates of developmental and behavioral problems have been referred to as the "epidemiological paradox" in the medical community, because Hispanic children actually experience good birth outcomes (low rates of prematurity, neonatal and infant mortality, and higher birth weight) despite their high incidence of poverty (Flores et al. 2002; Mendoza 1994; Padilla et al. 2002). Again, these patterns diverge in meaningful ways among children of different Hispanic groups. Puerto Rican children experience higher rates of poor birth outcomes and later behavioral and developmental disorders than do children of Mexican or Cuban descent.

Clearly, there are many more questions than answers that remain regarding Hispanic children's literacy development. Basic descriptive data about Hispanic children's language and literacy development, in both Spanish and English, during the preschool and elementary school years is urgently needed, as is a richer understanding of the proximal factors that shape Hispanic children's early development. Finally, Hispanic children's developmental trajectories will vary significantly depending on their families' degree of acculturation, English-language proficiency, immigrant status, and country of origin.

All together, in attempting to understand the roots of America's literacy problems, primary emphasis has been placed understandably on sociocultural factors. While the impact of poverty and low education are clearly relevant, we have emphasized that income, education, and race/ethnicity wield their influence on children's literacy acquisition indirectly via more proximal processes, especially the interactions that children experience with their parents and childcare providers during the years before they start school.

3

Early Childcare and Preschool

Study links working mothers to slower learning.
New York Times

Given the strong evidence of its benefits to society, preschool education for the poor—and perhaps for all children—is a must.
Business Week

As we discussed in the last chapter, the effect of distal influences such as
SES and ethnicity on children's literacy operate primarily through
more proximal sources of influence. As a more proximal source, early
childhood care and education programs are seen as potent weapons in
the effort to improve children's literacy. Consequently, policy makers
at the federal level have focused closely on early childhood education
and its promise as a long-term cure for illiteracy, school inequities, and
the achievement gap. The passage of Public Law 99–457 in 1986 supported early intervention for children with special needs and attempted to bring to fruition the results of decades of research that
highlighted the importance of early childhood education. The law un-
derscored the "compelling belief that children who begin life at a disadvantage can be helped; that development is malleable; and that society must assist parents of disabled and developmentally vulnerable
children in helping these children reach their potential as fully as possible" (Meisels, Dichtelmiller, and Liaw 1993, 361).

Notwithstanding these high hopes, the precise effect of such programs can be difficult to determine given the complexity of children's
lives and the many forces that influence their development, particularly family and community. Historically, research on early childcare

programs has found them both effective and ineffective in improving children's social and educational future. For example, some research has suggested that, for infants, long days in childcare may lead to delays in development by three years of age (Brooks-Gunn, Han, and Waldfogel 2002). Yet other studies have demonstrated that preschool interventions for children at risk can have long-term positive effects on children's reading, math, and social skills (Barnett 1995). These equivocal results leave parents, researchers, educators, and policy makers in a quandary. To some extent, the effect of childcare and preschool depend on the target population (children at risk for academic failure, special needs children, or more typical children), the goal of the care (educational, remedial, or supervisory), as well as how early childhood program caregivers and researchers define what child success and childcare quality mean (facility and resources or student academic and social outcomes).

Understanding the effects of early childcare is further confounded by philosophical and ideological disputes within the early childhood profession. These differences are reinforced because factions have different goals for children, resulting in different definitions of what is considered a "high-quality" early childhood care and education program. For example, some programs place greater emphasis on the physical plant and the qualifications of the teachers, while others emphasize stimulation of children's social and emotional development or are designed to educate, and still others emphasize the need to keep children safe while their parents work. As we will discuss, deciding what is "high quality" will differ for each kind of program and we, as a society, will be called upon to clarify these goals as demands for greater student academic achievement reach down to the preschool level. In this chapter, we will examine the evidence on the effect of "high-quality" early childhood programs, what "high quality' means, and the overall effect of these programs on children's literacy development. This research has been instrumental in helping us understand the multifaceted challenges of serving young children at risk for academic failure. As an example, we will explore the history and impact of the Head Start and Even Start programs, as well as the policy issues in which they have been embroiled, to illustrate how the complex and competing goals of the early childhood programs drive their definitions of what "high quality" and "child success" are.

We will then review the evidence on which elements of early childhood programs most positively influence children's academic and social skills and why certain early childhood education programs are effective.

Is Day Care Good or Bad for Children?

More than 60 percent of the almost 20 million children under the age of five years living in the United States will spend time in some form of regular childcare (Smith 2002). Thus, whether day care is good, bad, or indifferent is an important question on many levels. Research conducted during the 1990s tended to indicate that maternal employment, especially in the first year of life, has a negative effect on children's cognitive development (Belsky 2001; Blau and Grossberg 1992; Waldfogel, Han, and Brooks-Gunn 2002). However, it has been argued, these studies did not take into account the quality of the childcare children received. Research suggests that high-quality childcare can promote children's literacy development whereas poor-quality childcare may hinder it (Barnett 1995).

However, deciding whether or not day care is bad for children is overly simplistic. The story is much more complex—especially when multiple child, family, and day-care characteristics are considered (McClelland, Kessenich, and Morrison 2003) along with definitions of "quality." For example, in the NICHD studies of early childcare and youth development (NICHD-ECCRN 1997), children were followed from birth through elementary school. These studies investigated the effect of childcare on a number of outcome measures, including parenting, children's social development and interactions with peers, and their cognitive and literacy growth.

Over and over again, the quality of the childcare predicted children's later success in school, almost regardless of how "high quality" was defined. Children who attended high-quality day-care programs tended to do better in school later on than did children in poor-quality day care. For example, when high quality was defined as the "sensitivity, involvement, and stimulation provided by [day-care] caregivers" (NICHD-ECCRN 2001), higher quality was positively associated with more positive mother-child interactions and increasing maternal sensitivity, which, the authors assumed, should lead to stronger child outcomes. More hours in childcare were related to less positive mother-child interactions over the first three years of children's lives. In other words, mothers were more likely to interact with their babies in caring ways when their child was in a high-quality day-care setting with sensitive and caring day-care providers than were mothers whose children were in poor-quality day-care settings. One important note, however: mothers' educational level was a stronger positive predictor of maternal caring and sensitivity than was childcare quality and the number of hours children spent in childcare. As we will discuss in chapter 4, children are more likely to be successful in school when their mothers are caring and sensitive at home.

The same pattern of results emerged in exploring the effects of childcare on children's social interactions with their peers (NICHD-ECCRN 2001). Better-quality childcare, as defined above, was positively associated with better interactions with peers, but only while children were actually in childcare; the effect did not generalize to other social settings. Thus, children in higher-quality day care were more likely to play well with other children while they were at day care than were children in poor-quality day-care settings. Here again, the effect of mothers' sensitivity was much stronger than that of the childcare setting and positively affected peer interactions across a variety of settings. Mothers who were more sensitive and caring tended to have children who played well with other children both at home and at school compared to detached and less responsive mothers. Importantly, children who interacted with their peers more positively also tended to have stronger language and cognitive skills than did children who interacted negatively with their peers.

Children's developing cognitive skills may also be affected by their day-care experiences (Christian, Morrison, and Bryant 1998). The amount of time children spent in childcare was positively associated with their kindergarten mathematics skills, but only for children from families where the mother had less education and the home literacy environment was weaker. Thus for children living in poverty, more time spent in day care led to stronger cognitive outcomes when they reached kindergarten. In contrast, in some studies, the time spent in childcare had no effect, either positive or negative, for children from more affluent homes. Yet in other studies, children from middle-class families enrolled in childcare from infancy displayed poorer reading skills in kindergarten than did their peers who stayed at home (O'Brian Caughy, DiPietro, and Strobini 1994). It has been argued, especially about earlier studies, that the quality of day care must be taken into account, and that high-quality day care will not have negative effects on children's development.

This may not be universally true. There is preliminary evidence that for infants, long hours in childcare, regardless of quality, may have a long-term negative effect on children' early literacy development (Brooks-Gunn, Han, and Waldfogel 2002). In this study, which also used the NICHD-ECCRN data set, infants who spent long days in childcare (more than thirty hours per week) tended to have weaker early reading skills at age three years than did children who spent less time in childcare. This negative effect appeared to be less for children from ethnic minorities than it was for European American non-Hispanic children and for children over nine months of age. Again, the quality of the childcare made an important difference in school readiness (higher quality led to stronger early literacy skills), as did home environment and maternal sensitivity. But even the highest-quality childcare still had a negative effect on literacy development if babies spent more than thirty hours per week in childcare during the first nine months of their life.

The cumulative amount of time children spend in day care may also be important. ECCRN researchers (NICHD-ECCRN 2003) observed that children who spent more time in day care during the first five years of their lives were deemed less socially competent by both mothers and day-care providers and were judged to be more unruly and disruptive by mothers, day-care providers, and kindergarten teachers. Additionally, day-care providers and kindergarten teachers reported more adult-child conflicts.

There are, however, important caveats to these findings. First, not all children have the same response to day care (Crockenberg 2003; Greenspan 2003). For example, some children (especially boys) with behavior problems may find day care challenging, while others find the experience enriching (Langlois and Liben 2003). Also, day care may not be the root cause of children's unruliness. Instead, mothers might be more likely to send unruly children to day care. As we will emphasize throughout this book, there are multiple pathways and multiple effects on children's developing literacy. Childcare experiences are just one part of children's lives.

As an illustration, many of the preceding studies examined the independent effects of childcare and parenting on children's outcomes. However, parenting and childcare do not operate in isolation. The effect of each may interact with child characteristics and with each other to provide simultaneous effects that influence children's developing literacy. Take, for example, the effect of childcare on mother-child interactions (NICHD-ECCRN 2001, 2002a). This effect is made more complex because parents must be considered active agents in selecting childcare. Mothers with more education were, on average, more sensitive than were mothers with less education. In turn, mothers who were more sensitive and responsive to their children may have insisted on higher-quality childcare, knew how to identify and monitor quality, and could afford to pay for it. When the multiple influences of parenting, sociocultural factors, and childcare quality and amount of time are examined simultaneously (NICHD-ECCRN 2002a), we can see more clearly that there is no simple answer. Children who attend higher-quality day care develop stronger early language and literacy skills, on average, than do children who attend poorer-quality day care. But these children are also more likely to have better-educated, more caring, and more sensitive parents.

Overall, parenting appears to be a more important source of influence on children's development than is childcare. Researchers recently examined the simultaneous effects of child characteristics, parenting, early childcare environment, and schooling experiences on children's literacy skills in first grade (NICHD-ECCRN 2004). Both parenting/home environment and early childcare quality positively affected children's language skills at four and one-half years of age, which, in turn, predicted first grade literacy. However, the contribution of parenting was about three to four times greater than that of early childcare quality and affected children's social skills as well as their language skills.

Overall, participation in childcare appears to have relatively small positive or negative effects on developing literacy. Clearly, high-quality day care is better for children than low-quality. Yet for most children, their day-care experience after nine months of age will have little or no long-term effect on their developing literacy; high-quality childcare will not offset the negative effect of poor parenting, and poor-quality childcare will not prevent success for children with effective parents.

However, for infants under nine months of age, long days (more than thirty hours per week) in childcare programs may lead to poorer school readiness, regardless of the parenting and home environment. The social-policy implications of the latter finding for parental nurturance leave are profound and deserve more discussion than we can provide in this chapter. As a society, we need to review family-leave and workplace policies that make it easier for parents of very young children to combine work and family responsibilities.

Early Intervention Programs for "At-Risk" Children

High-quality preschool interventions can make an important difference to the later school success of children with risk factors: poverty, disabilities, learning English as a second language, among others (Barnett 1995). Thus we distinguish between child- or day-care programs that are designed to take care of children while parents work outside the home and preschool interventions, which are provided specifically for children who are at risk for school failure. Early childcare and education/intervention programs have been shown to significantly enhance children's prospects for academic success and reduce the probability of referral to special education, grade retention, and leaving school before high school graduation (Barnett 1995). They promote stronger language and literacy development (Dickinson and Tabors 2001) and demonstrate significant economic return on investment over children's lifetimes, according to cost-benefit analyses (Reynolds et al. 2003).

There are a number of model early childhood interventions that, based on robust research evidence, strongly support children's later academic success. These include (but are not limited to) the Perry Preschool Project, the Abecedarian Project, the School Development Program (Haynes and Comer 1996), and the Chicago Title 1 Child-Parent Centers (Reynolds et al. 2003; Barnett 1995; Campbell and

Ramey 1995; Haynes and Comer 1996). In virtually every case, when compared to children who did not attend these programs, students receiving intervention demonstrated significantly stronger academic and social skill development. Moreover, many of these effects lasted through high school and young adulthood. Just as we saw with the day-care research reviewed earlier, the quality of the intervention program made a difference in children's outcomes. High-quality programs produced positive effects on children's outcomes, whereas poor-quality programs actually yielded negative effects. This conclusion is, perhaps, most compelling when we examine the research on Head Start.

Head Start

Born in the optimistic 1960s, Head Start has been one of the federal government's most extensive forays into education. To date, over 20,302,000 children have participated in Head Start programs, most of them from low-income homes and about 70 percent from ethnic minority families. Separate philosophically and administratively from the state-mandated and -administered public school districts, Head Start was originally conceived as part of the War on Poverty and as one way to promote civil rights and to begin righting social inequities by providing federal dollars directly to local programs rather than through the states. Its goal was to support children and families through health care and nutrition, and by providing an enriching caring environment in which children could experience success (Zigler and Meunchow 1992).

Head Start began as a summer program in 1965. A popular program and one sponsored by Ladybird Johnson, Head Start expanded to a school-year program in 1966 and by 1972 was primarily a school-year program serving over 370,000 children annually. This strong support and rapid expansion created an enduring program, but one with ongoing concerns about oversight and program quality. Because the program had an explicit goal to employ members of the community, Head Start personnel often had little early childhood experience and few credentials. As a civil rights program, the Community Action Program (CAP) staff responsible for managing the Head Start program often discounted the views of prominent early childhood educators. In fact, when a university department head explained that her proposed high-quality educational program needed the minimum budget she requested, she was told by CAP staff, "This is not supposed to be a high quality preschool program; this is Head Start" (Zigler and Meunchow 1992, 44). This is an astounding statement if the primary goal of Head Start is to improve children's literacy but somewhat understandable if the goal is ensuring civil rights by empowering members of the community. For the latter goal, educating children would be but one small part of the total project.

Because Head Start was originally conceived as a comprehensive program rather than one primarily focused on promoting children's academic skills, the founders included prominent pediatricians and psychologists but few early childhood educators. Julius Richmond, the first director and a pediatrician, was adamant that the program serve two nutritious meals per day, teach children how to brush their teeth, and include immunizations, vision, hearing, and health screenings. Urie Bronfenbrenner, a prominent developmental psychologist, was instrumental in advocating an ecological approach encompassing the family and community as well as the child (we described this approach in chapter 1). Civil rights workers insisted that the program's main goal was to empower parents and the community. Initially, developing children's literacy was not an explicit focus of Head Start. Indeed, for a program designed to support children at risk for academic under-achievement, there were, surprisingly, no specific educational goals. Rather, the guidelines noted "that Head Start should: (1) 'provide a flexible schedule and program oriented to the needs of the individual child;' (2) 'encourage exploration and manipulation of the environment;' (3) 'develop such imaginative techniques as role-playing, doll play, puppetry and dramatic activities;' and (4) 'provide maximum variety of and opportunities for communication with special emphasis on conversation to strengthen verbal skills'" (Zigler and Meunchow 1992, 42). Ironically, early efforts to measure the effects of Head Start focused on assessing whether participation raised children's IQ scores rather than whether children's health improved, their parents were more comfortable within a school environment, or the community prospered. Although early studies found short-term increases in children's IQ scores, soon after, other studies found that children who participated in Head Start did not maintain their IQ gains. Such findings put the program immediately in jeopardy and left its reputation tarnished (Zigler and Meunchow 1992).

Also incriminating were studies that compared Head Start with educationally focused preschool programs such as the Abecedarian and Perry Preschool projects (Barnett 1995). These studies found that, in general, early education programs had positive effects on important indicators such as grade retention and referral to special education, but that "poor-quality" programs could have negative effects. Unfortunately, the "poor-quality" programs tended to be Head Start programs, which had less funding, more high-risk children, higher child/staff ratios, and teachers with fewer years of professional training (Barnett et al. 1987; Barnett 1995). Thus the very children who most needed the benefits offered by high-quality early education programs were least likely to find such benefits in Head Start. Fortunately, in 1998 Congress passed standards for Head Start quality, including teacher training; efforts are now under way to enforce implementation of these standards (www.ed.gov). Most recently, Head Start programs are being held accountable for their students' language and early literacy skill growth through twice-yearly assessment of basic language and early literacy skills (Administration for Children and Families 2003).

Changing Goals of Head Start

As our nation focuses more closely on early literacy, many believe that Head Start should become more focused on education, and oversight should be moved to the U.S. Department of Education. Although this move was desperately opposed during the Carter administration because of civil rights issues, the matter is being more carefully considered today.

In July 2001 a task force convened that included representatives of both the Department of Health and Human Services and the Department of Education. U.S. Secretary of Education Paige observed, "Although we know much about how to prepare our children for success, too many of our preschool programs are not doing a good job of preparing disadvantaged children for school." He added, "We have much work to do to improve the academic quality of Head Start and other preschool services and general awareness of the activities that preschool programs and families alike can use to prepare our children for academic success." U.S. Secretary of Health and Human Services Thompson agreed, "I am proud to join Secretary Paige in a concerted effort to make our federal programs worthy of the children they serve" (www.ed.gov).

However, the National Head Start Association (NHSA), a private nonprofit organization representing Head Start children, parents, and staff, adamantly opposed moving Head Start to the Department of Education. For them, the broader goals of Head Start were important. In their position paper they stated:

> It is Head Start's focus on families and fighting poverty in a comprehensive manner which has led to the program's success in getting children ready for school, improving their literacy and numeracy skills, and giving their parents the skills in becoming the child's first and best teacher . . . [the Department of Health and Human Services] administration ensures greater collaboration and integration of all the components providing the education, health, family, and community supports and services that contribute to children's readiness, especially for low-income children and families. . . . Transferring the program to the oversight of the Department of Education holds no guarantee that key program components, such as comprehensive services, career development of community residents, and meaningful parent involvement, including substantial governance responsibility, will remain the approach. (www.nhsa.org/advocacy/advocacy_position_keephhs.htm)

Escalating rhetoric revealed the strong feelings surrounding this controversy. Chester E. Finn Jr., former U.S. assistant secretary of education, argued: "They're [members of the 'preschool establishment'] content with hugs, snowsuits, blocks, swings, gerbils, carrot sticks, and dental visits. . . . They shun responsibility for advancing a child's cognitive development (Robelen 2001, 24). In contrast, NHSA chairman Ron Herndon stated in his address to the 2002 Annual Head Start

Training Conference, "Title 1 [administered by the U.S. Department of Education], billions of dollars going to the school systems all across this country has done little or nothing to raise the reading and math scores of low-income children across the country. If, in fact, Title 1 works, then why do we still have this disparity in achievement in this country today? Black and Hispanic twelfth graders are reading and doing math at the same level as white eighth graders. . . . This is how the Department of Education runs programs."

These conflicting statements demonstrate the competing goals for Head Start. Is it to be a program serving children and focused on specific educational targets? Or will it be a broader program serving a wider population, including parents and community members, with children's education only one (albeit critical) aspect of the program?

Even Start

Even Start, a fairly new federally supported program designed as a complement to Head Start, serves children before they enter Head Start, from birth through age three years. Initiated in 1989, the program has already been amended several times. The entrance age was lowered in 1991 from one year to birth, and community-based organizations were allowed to receive these Title 1 funds. In 1994 Even Start was reauthorized as Part B of Title I of the Elementary and Secondary Education Act (ESEA) as amended by the Improving America's Schools Act. According to this legislation, the Even Start program is intended to "help break the cycle of poverty and illiteracy by improving the educational opportunities of the Nation's low-income families by integrating early childhood education, adult literacy or adult basic education, and parenting education into a unified family literacy program. . . . The program shall (1) be implemented through cooperative projects that build on existing community resources to create a new range of services; (2) promote achievement of the National Education Goals; and (3) assist children and adults from low-income families to achieve challenging State content standards and challenging State student performance standards" (*Improving America's Schools Act* 1994, section 1201).

As part of this amendment, cooperation between schools and communities was strengthened by requiring stronger collaboration in the application and implementation process. In 1996 Congress sought to further strengthen Even Start by passing an amendment "requiring instructional services to be intensive" (St. Pierre et al. 1998).

In general, Even Start programs are required to provide three core services: (1) adult education and adult literacy; (2) parenting education; and (3) early childhood education. Support services, such as transportation, childcare, nutrition assistance, health care, meals, special care for a disabled family member, and referrals for mental health and counseling, services to battered women, child protective services, employment, and screening or treatment for chemical dependency, may also be provided. Even Start has three primary goals:

- to help parents improve their literacy or basic educational skills;
- to help parents become full partners in educating their children;
- to assist children in reaching their full potential as learners.

Proponents claim that combining adult literacy or adult basic education, parenting education, and early childhood education into a unified family literacy program may help break the intergenerational cycle of poverty and low literacy in the nation. One clear advantage of the Even Start program is that parent participation is mandatory (St. Pierre et al. 1995). Indeed, parents in Even Start do demonstrate gains in reading and math skills. However, it is not clear that these gains are due to Even Start participation, because parents whose children were in other preschool programs showed similar gains (St. Pierre et al. 1995). However, parents participating in Even Start were more likely to achieve their GED (high school diploma equivalent) than were parents not participating in Even Start.

Even Start seems to be positively related to home learning environment. Even Start parents improved in providing learning activities, story reading, books in the home, play materials, talking with their children, and teaching their children. However, parents who did not participate in Even Start made similar gains. Even Start families did provide more different kinds of reading materials in the home (books, magazines, newspapers) than did families not participating in Even Start (St. Pierre et al. 1995). While families involved in Even Start made gains in income and employment, so did families not in Even Start. "Even Start families made few changes on measures of adult self-efficacy, social support, and family resources" (St. Pierre et al. 1995, 1; see also Tao, Gamse, and Tarr 1998, 162–63).

Do the fairly modest gains in education and parenting for families participating in Even Start translate into improved child literacy outcomes? Children participating in Even Start did appear to get an "early boost" in language and early literacy skills compared to children who did not participate in Even Start but were in other programs. However, the latter group of children seemed to "catch up" to children who were in Even Start the next year (St. Pierre et al. 1995, 165–74). In another study, children who were in Even Start for longer periods of time demonstrated faster rates of growth in language skills than did children in Even Start for shorter periods of time (that is, there was a dosage effect) (Tao, Gamse, and Tarr 1998). So, children who attended Even Start appeared to get a "boost" in their language and early literacy development, but it is not clear that this translated into stronger academic achievement in the long run (St. Pierre et al. 1998).

However, when intensity and quality of services are taken into account, Even Start appears to offer substantial and important support to families living in poverty. High-quality Even Start programs that were center based and provided intensive services to both children and parents appeared to be more effective than were programs that, for example, visited parents and children in the home. "Literacy-based" intensive programs appeared to be more effective in supporting families than were more diffuse programs where parent services appeared to be a "catch-all for a variety of parent-focused services including health education, nutrition education, and life skills" (St. Pierre et al. 1998, 5). Unfortunately, too many Even Start programs failed to provide intensive high-quality services, and so the overall efficacy of the Even Start program nationwide appears to be negligible.

Even Start and Head Start Future Directions

So we see that some Head Start and Even Start programs are quite effective in supporting children's early literacy, whereas others are not.

Enforcing consistent standards and incorporating what we have learned from current research about the elements of successful preschool interventions into Even Start and Head Start programs will provide an important strategy for improving literacy in America. There is no reason that Head Start and Even Start, properly funded and administered, with clear goals as to their purpose and reasonable assessment of parent and student outcomes, cannot meet the needs of the children and families they were designed to serve. As we will discuss later, we have learned a lot in the last four decades about how children learn and the skills they need to acquire to prevent reading difficulties and academic failure. Head Start and Even Start programs can incorporate this information whether they are administered through the Department of Education or the Department of Health and Human Services. Moreover, Head Start and Even Start entrance criteria exclude many children who would potentially benefit from participating, including children of the working class. Other state and local programs, including Title I, vary in availability as well as quality. Thus many children who would directly benefit from participating in high-quality early childhood education are not offered the opportunity to do so.

Given the uneven quality of Even Start and Head Start programs and their equivocal impact on children's literacy outcomes, we can learn more about which elements of early childhood intervention yield stronger outcomes if we examine model programs with documented success serving children at risk for academic failure. These include the Abecedarian Project, the Perry Preschool Project, and the School Development Program. Reviewing these programs provides insights as to how we might define "high quality" and ultimately how we might structure effective early childhood programs on a national scale.

Elements of Successful Early Childhood Programs

Clearly, if we are to improve literacy in America, federally and state-funded preschool intervention programs should be expanded so that all children who might benefit can participate. However, it is not enough to say that children should have access to "high-quality" early childhood care and education. What do we mean when we say "high quality?" One of the dilemmas when designing effective early childhood programs is the shifting definition of program quality, which is closely tied to definitions of child success. Although Head Start was "not successful" when the definition of child success was IQ score, in many cases, programs were effective in improving families' lives when success was defined in ways more in line with the broader focus of Head Start. And so it is with early childhood programs in general. Depending on the focus of the researchers and stakeholders, program quality and child success are defined very differently. By examining research results for programs that have proven effective in promoting long-term academic success for children at risk for learning failure, we can sharpen our definition of "high quality" and pinpoint why these high-quality programs are effective in improving literacy.

Model Programs: High/Scope Perry Preschool, Abecedarian, and the School Development Programs

High/Scope Perry Preschool Project. This program and study began in 1962 and enrolled 128 children (5 were lost to follow-up) from low-income African American families who were judged to be at risk for academic failure based on low IQ scores (Barnett, Young, and Schweinhart 1998). Children were matched on key characteristics and then randomly assigned to treatment (high-quality preschool education program) or control (did not attend the program) groups. Children in the treatment group started the preschool program at age four and attended for one or two years before they began kindergarten. The Perry Preschool offered two and one-half–hour morning classes five days a week during the school year. Additionally, teachers visited the children and parents at home once a week in the afternoon for ninety minutes. Classroom staff members were certified public school teachers, and the child/staff ratio was low (6:1). The curriculum, which evolved over the years of the study, was "child centered and explicitly focused on supporting children's cognitive development through individualized teaching and learning" and was based on "Piagetian theory" (Barnett, Young, and Schweinhart 1998, 171). Overall, children who participated in the High/Scope Perry Preschool Project were less likely to be referred to special education and to be retained a grade. Treatment and control group differences in IQ scores diminished over time, but differences in achievement levels in school and student motivation levels persisted—children in the treatment group displayed stronger school achievement and higher motivation than did children in the control group through the age of nineteen years (Barnett, Young, and Schweinhart 1998).

Abecedarian Project. The Abecedarian Project was designed as a prospective experiment on the effect of intensive early childhood education for children at risk for academic failure (risks included poverty, ethnic minority status, ESL, and so on) (Ramey and Campbell 1984; Campbell et al. 2001). One hundred eleven children and their families were randomly assigned to treatment and control groups (that is, no treatment). The study began in early infancy and extended through the preschool years (a total of five years). The intervention was delivered at a university-based childcare center that was open eight hours per day, five days per week, fifty weeks per year. Child/teacher ratios were low (3:1 for infants and 6:1 for children), there was intensive teacher training, and staff turnover was low. The infant program was designed to promote cognitive, language, perceptual-motor, and social development through interactions with caregivers and access to educational toys and materials. As children left infancy, there was increasing emphasis on language and preliteracy skills coupled with positive and caring interactions with teachers and staff. Additionally, the curriculum was "individualized" for each child. There was also a strong research emphasis at the center (Campbell et al. 2001).

Nutrition was an important component of the infant program; all of the babies (in both the treatment and control groups) received iron-fortified formula for the first fifteen months so that the effects of nutrition on cognitive development could not bias the results. Social work services and free diapers were also provided to all families (treatment and control), and many children in the control group attended other childcare centers. The point was to keep the services provided to the treatment and control group families as similar as possible except for the center-based educational component of the project. Children were then followed through early adulthood. Recent results (Campbell et al. 2001) show that children who received the intensive center-based educational program (treatment group) made greater gains on a number of academic indicators when compared to children in the control group who did not attend the center. Comparing how cognitive skills changed over time for the two groups is revealing. During the first four years of life, the cognitive skills (for example, vocabulary, language, problem solving) of children in the treatment group grew much more quickly than did the cognitive skills of children in the control group. Once children reached age six, the rate of cognitive growth for the two groups was very nearly the same, but the children in the treatment group had significantly stronger skills, and their advantage was still evident at twenty-one years of age. Children in the treatment group also had stronger reading and math skills at age twenty-one years than did children in the control group.

Researchers state that these persistent advantages over time are related to the early cognitive boost children in the treatment group received during infancy by participating in an intensive and high-quality center-based program (Campbell et al. 2001). They also note that children lived in communities dedicated to providing "adequate housing, low-cost medical care, and public transportation" (239). Moreover, the public schools that many of the children attended were generally "good," and special education support was provided as needed.

The School Development Program. The School Development Program was designed to "rebuild learning communities by connecting the significant adults [parents and teachers] in children's lives through a collaborative process of systemic reform and school improvement" (Haynes and Comer 1990, 501). The program focuses on children's cognitive, physical, social, emotional, behavioral, moral, and speech and language development using three mechanisms: (1) school planning and management teams; (2) student and staff support teams; and (3) parent programs. This program has been in effect for over twenty-five years and supports children and families just before and during the elementary school years. In this way it differs from the other model programs in that it begins later in children's lives, but it lasts throughout elementary school and uses a systemic approach rather than a direct intervention approach.

The school planning and management team is responsible for shaping the social and academic climate of the school and functions as the central management and organizing body. Members of the team include the school principal, teachers, school support staff, parents, and, in some schools, students and members of the wider community. This team establishes goals and oversees their implementation in four major domains: "student achievement, social climate, staff development, and community relations" (Haynes and Comer 1990, 502).

The student and staff support teams address classroom and individual student problems and are designed to prevent potential problems from developing into crisis situations. This team also works with the wider community and garners needed community resources.

The parent program involves parents in social activities, parent-teacher conferences, volunteer work in the school, and as members of the school management team and is designed to enhance collaboration between parents, teachers, and the wider community. Researchers note that several conditions must exist if parents are to be successfully involved in their children's school: (1) trust; (2) preplanning; and (3) empowerment (Haynes and Comer 1996). Community involvement is also a critical component of the School Development Program.

Research findings indicate that the School Development Program can have an important positive effect on students' achievement, behavior, self-esteem, and overall adjustment (Cauce, Comer, and Schwartz 1987; Haynes and Comer 1990; Haynes, Comer, and Hamilton-Lee 1988, 1989). After the intervention parents felt more connected to their child's school, and some were motivated to obtain their high school equivalency degree (Haynes, Comer, and Hamilton-Lee 1989). Teachers reported more satisfaction with their work, and children rated the school climate as more positive after implementation than before. These effects may last into high school (Haynes, Comer, and Hamilton-Lee 1988, 1989). It is important to note, however, that because there was no control group, these positive effects may have been a result of something other than the School Development Program (such as more money to schools). Nonetheless, overall, the results are encouraging and suggest that focusing on multiple sources of influence (teachers, parents, principals, support staff) on children's literacy development may be especially beneficial.

A Closer Look at Key Components of High-Quality Programs

Research evidence reveals that there are multiple effects of early childhood programs that directly and positively impact children's language and early literacy (Barnett, Young, and Schweinhart 1998; NICHD-ECCRN 2002a, 2004). These changes contribute to long-term effects directly through enhanced learning skills and indirectly through the motivation and teacher/parent expectation benefits garnered by the child's early academic success (Lazar et al. 1982). When children at risk for academic failure attend high-quality early childhood education/intervention programs, the early boost in social, language, and literacy skills appears to directly affect their long-term prospects for school success. But exactly how are these effective preschool programs supporting children's development?

Using our model programs as a guide in combination with other research on effective preschool interventions such as the Home-School Study (Dickenson and Tabors, 2001), there are at least five shared elements of successful programs: (1) strong support for parents; (2) intensity; (3) beginning earlier rather than later in the child's life; (4) well-qualified teachers; and (5) a rich linguistic environment and a strong focus on emergent literacy.

Strong support for parents. In every model preschool program and in successful Even Start and Head Start programs, an intensive center-based program for children was coupled with support for parents through home visits, parent education, and parent involvement. Indeed, parenting and support for parents are such important topics that we devote the next chapter to them.

Intensity. The effects on cognitive skills for children in the Abecedarian Project were sustained over the long term, whereas the effects for children in the Perry Preschool were not (although there were other lasting benefits). Researchers associated with the Abecedarian Project propose that this sustained effect is because the program began its intervention during children's infancy and continued it through the first few years of school. Moreover, they argue, the program was available to children all day, five days per week. In contrast, the Perry Preschool intervention was a half-day program for one or two years. One of the criticisms of Head Start programs is that they are not intensive enough to effect long-term improvement in children's school success; the days are too short and the curriculum not rigorous enough. Researchers examining the Even Start programs observed that the programs that provided intensive center-based services for children in addition to parent support were more successful than programs that relied on once-a-week home visits. Thus, for children at-risk, access to more time in high-quality preschool interventions appears to be important if the services are to have a positive effect on children's literacy development and long-term school success.

Beginning earlier rather than later. Consider also that the programs with the greatest benefit-cost ratios (Abecedarian, Chicago Title I) began their interventions when children were babies. Again comparing the Abecedarian and the Perry Preschool projects, note that long-term improvements in cognitive skills (for example, language and literacy) were observed only for the program that began intervention while children were infants. Hart and Risley (1995) observed that parenting and how much parents talked to their children in the first two years of life were associated with stronger vocabulary growth and later school success. Young children are developing social skills, are learning to talk, and are becoming competent users of social skills and language across a variety of settings during the first years of life (Gleason 1997). It may be that strong support for parents coupled with a rigorous preschool intervention for children may support more rapid development of these critical social and language skills, which, in turn, support literacy development and school success. Research-supported theories of language development (Locke 1993; Mayberry, Lock, and Kazmi 2002) suggest that early linguistic experiences are crucial for children's long-term language development. During the first years of life, children's neurological system may be "experience expectant" for learning language. In other words, very young children are learning their language more quickly than older children because their brains are designed to do so. Indeed, merely adequate exposure to the language being used all around them permits toddlers to become capable communicators. However, children will develop stronger language skills when they participate in richer linguistic environments at home (Hart and Risley 1995; Huttenlocher et al. 2002) and at school (Dickinson and Tabors 2001; Huttenlocher et al. 2002). This may be one reason the cognitive advantage persisted for children in the Abecedarian Project, which started shortly after birth and lasted most of the day, five days per week, fifty weeks per year, whereas the cognitive advantage did not persist for the Perry Preschool participants, who did not begin until age four and attended only in the mornings during the school year.

There is less research evidence for the importance of early intervention for self-regulation (ability to attend, to persist on tasks, and so on) and social skills (self-regulation, interactions with adults and peers, and the like), but early access to preschool may affect these important precursors of academic success. We discuss self-regulation and social skills more fully in chapter 5.

Well-qualified teachers. Another characteristic of effective preschool programs was the training teachers received. In general, programs with certified teachers demonstrated lasting effects on children's development (for example, model programs), whereas programs that did not hire well-trained staff (for example, some Even Start and Head Start programs) did not (see also Dickinson and Tabors 2001). This is an important topic that we will discuss more completely in chapter 7.

Rich linguistic environment and support for emergent literacy. One of the most powerful forces promoting stronger literacy skills in the model programs involved the linguistic environment of the center or classroom and included teacher-child interactions, teacher responsiveness, and teachers' styles of interactions with children. In these studies (Smith and Dickinson 1994; Dickinson et al. 1992; Dickinson and Smith 1994; Dickinson and Tabors 2001; Buzzelli 1996; Campbell et al. 2001; Barnett 1995), verbal interactions (conversations and instruction) between the teacher and students were consistent predictors of children's early literacy and communicative competence. Additionally, these programs enhanced children's language and prereading skills and contributed to children's reading skills in later grades. Some directly targeted preliteracy skills (for example, the Abecedarian Project).

For example, children in Head Start and Title 1 preschool classrooms where teachers used more *wh*-questions (who, what, where, when, why) than yes-no questions or imperatives (that is, commands such as "Be quiet" and "Sit down") tended to achieve higher scores on measures that predict later reading success (Connor 2002). Classroom transcripts revealed that when teachers used *wh*-questions, they tended to elicit more cognitively challenging talk from children, including predicting, inferring, and enriching vocabulary, than when they used yes-no questions or imperatives. In classrooms where teachers interacted with preschoolers using more *cognitively challenging talk* and *rare words* (more advanced vocabulary), children demonstrated stronger vocabulary and reading comprehension skills in first grade and beyond compared to children in classrooms where the teacher-child interactions were proportionally more didactic and directive (telling rather than explaining) (Dickinson and Tabors 2001). The frequency of such interactions was strongly predictive of children's later literacy (Dickinson and Tabors 2001; Gleason 1997).

As we will discuss in chapter 5, there is strong evidence that children's language and literacy skills are strongly related (Loban 1976; Snow, Burns, and Griffin 1998). For example, metalinguistic awareness, the ability to consciously manipulate the phonological, semantic, and syntactic aspects of language, is strongly predictive of later reading (Tumner, Nesdale, and Wright 1987; Rayner et al. 2001). Children with stronger metalinguistic awareness tend to be stronger readers. In particular, phonological awareness is related to reading in important ways and, when explicitly taught, leads to stronger reading (Rayner et al. 2001; Bradley and Bryant 1983). Thus, enhancing children's language skills, including metalinguistic awareness, early in life appears to support their literacy skills later in life, although this relation is complex. Effective preschool programs take this into account.

Particular aspects of language at different ages predict children's reading skills (Scarborough, Charity, and Griffin 2002). For example, for babies, articulation (that is, how precisely they make the sounds of speech) most strongly predicts later reading skill. However, for preschoolers, vocabulary and grammar are the strongest predictors. Only later, in kindergarten and first grade, is phonological awareness a strong predictor. Again, the underlying process of language acquisition appears to be important. Altogether, for preschoolers, linguistic environments that enrich their vocabulary and use of more sophisticated grammatical structures tend to support literacy development (Huttenlocher et al. 2002).

Although research is just emerging on the specific *hows* and *whys* of which elements of literacy to teach young children, over the last decade *what* children need to learn has been fairly well established (Rayner et al. 2001), and we will discuss this more thoroughly in chapter 5. Children who begin first grade with strong skills in the following areas experience greater success learning to read than do children with weaker skills: (1) letters and letter-sound correspondence; (2) phonological awareness, including rhyming, phonemic segmentation, and blending; (3) emergent reading; (4) emergent writing; (5) an understanding of the purposes of literacy; (6) vocabulary and oral language skills (Storch and Whitehurst 2002). Notice that our model programs included specific focus on all of these elements.

For example, in a nationally representative sample, children who began kindergarten already knowing their letters were stronger readers by the end of first grade (Catts 1997)—an important advantage that should follow them through school (Entwisle, Alexander, and Olson 1997; Campbell et al. 2001). Phonological awareness, one of the most important predictors of children's later reading ability, is a skill that can be taught and when explicitly taught, it promotes stronger reading skills (Bradley and Bryant 1983). Pretending to read storybooks, called emergent reading (Sulzby 1985; Snow, Burns, and Griffin 1998) and pretending to write, also called emergent writing or invented spelling (Shilt 2003), are also positively associated with children's early literacy, as is dialogic reading. Dialogic reading—where teachers or parents interact with children in cognitively challenging ways, ask questions about what is being read, relate what is happening to their own experiences, and predict—can be effectively taught to parents and teachers. When taught, dialogic reading leads to stronger early literacy skills (Whitehurst et al. 1994; Storch and Whitehurst 2002). As we discussed, a rich linguistic environment that promotes vocabulary growth and oral language skills is a common component of all high-quality early childhood intervention programs.

As can be seen in model programs, each of these elements of literacy can be taught through playful activities, such as pretend story writing, word and rhyming games, shared storybook reading, number games, puzzles, and poetry. Children who begin school at a disadvantage, with low vocabulary skills and without experience with letters, reading, and word games, may especially benefit from explicit focus on such activities. For example, children who begin prekindergarten with smaller vocabularies in general achieve stronger early literacy skills when their teachers talk more frequently about letters, letter sounds, and rhyming; play word games; and encourage children to write their names. However, such talk appears to be less important for children with strong vocabulary skills. For these children, more frequent focus on metacognitive aspects of literacy such as talk about storybooks, authors, and the purpose of reading and writing, coupled with opportunities to interact with books independently, appears to be related to stronger early literacy skill growth (Connor 2002). As we will discuss in chapter 6, this specificity of learning is apparent throughout children's school career. Children with differing skill levels benefit most from instruction tailored for their specific strengths and weaknesses. Thus, monitoring children's progress during their early years may be an important but little-understood element of high-quality early intervention programs.

Opportunities for Children from Different Cultural and Linguistic Backgrounds

Children may come to school with the discourse practices of their heritage discourse community, which may differ in important ways from the discourse practices of the school classroom (Heath 1983). Preschools can offer an opportunity for these children to learn English, if they speak another language at home. It may also help children from minority ethnic groups learn the kinds and ways of talking that are generally preferred in schools, including use of Standard American English (SAE) and the more formal interactions that occur in classrooms. Given the opportunity, preschool children are able to adopt school ways of talking over the course of the school year (Kantor et al. 1992). Some educators (for example, Delpit 1995) suggest that explicitly teaching classroom discourse routines, such as responding to and using *wh*-questions and using conventional grammar (SAE), may be more effective in supporting children's later success in school than ignoring or accepting forms of English (for example, African American Vernacular English) that may work against their ongoing academic achievement (Charity, Scarborough, and Griffin 2004). There is emerging evidence that African American children who are more familiar with the English spoken at school (that is, SAE) are better readers than are children who are less familiar with SAE (Charity, Scarborough, and Griffin 2004). This does not mean that children must "give up" their culture. Rather, the goal is to help them learn both systems well—school discourse as well as the discourse and languages associated with their home culture (Tabors 1997; Delpit 1995).

The years before formal schooling begins are important for children for whom English is a second language. The formal designations for children who are learning English vary across states and include ESL (English as a second language), ELL (English-language learners), and NEP (not English proficient). Bilingual education and how we should educate ESL children are, not surprisingly, highly controversial topics. Research results are unclear as to the most effective way to serve these students, although it is evident that we, as a nation, are not serving them well. Preliminary results indicate that early preschool experiences that are literacy focused (that is, focused on letters, reading, phonological decoding, writing) yet follow a predictable routine (for example, calendar time) appear to support ESL children's literacy development (Connor 2002). However, the role of early childhood educational experiences has not been well researched, and the effects of specific programs (for example, immersion versus bilingual-bicultural) are not well known (Hacsi 2002b), although it appears that providing children access to their native language while also providing specific instruction in English may be more effective in the long run than taking a "sink or swim" approach (Hacsi 2002b; Tabors 1997; Rodriguez et al. 1995).

In summary, early childhood care and education programs can have a sustained positive influence on children's developing literacy, especially for those children at risk of academic failure. Effective programs reach out to families and the community and have strong parent outreach and adult educational components. And these activities and services are individualized for students and their families. Effective programs are intensive and begin early in life. They are sufficiently funded and provide a safe environment with properly trained teachers and staff, appropriate child-staff ratios, and infrequent staff turnover. The most effective programs offer a rich linguistic environment and introduce children, in explicit ways, to school ways of speaking, rare words, and cognitively challenging talk (that is, predicting, inference). They offer children specific opportunities to strengthen developing literacy through focus on letters and letter-sound correspondence, rhyming, and word games that support phonological awareness as well as opportunities to write. The specific needs of children for whom English is a second language or who are less familiar with Standard American English are addressed. Adequate monitoring systems are in place.

Unfortunately, the very children most likely to benefit from participating in effective early childhood programs—children living in poverty, children from minority families, children with more difficult home situations, ESL children, and other children at risk—are the least likely to participate in such programs (Peisner-Feinberg and Burchinal 1997). Establishing consistent nationwide research-based standards—including individualized goals to support children's developing literacy across all childcare settings—coupled with access to programs for all children who would potentially benefit and carrying these strategies into elementary school as direct interventions and as part of systemic reform involving schools, parents, and the larger community will be important for improving literacy in America.

4

Parenting

Parents are the most important influences in children's lives, but little is known about how to intervene effectively with parents to enhance child development.

R. G. St. Pierre and J. I. Layzer

Parenting skills are learned. Unfortunately, few of us are explicitly taught to parent, so we end up repeating some of the mistakes our parents made.

Parenting 101

Repeatedly throughout the past two chapters, parenting has surfaced as a critical element of literacy development, either for transmitting the effects of race/ethnicity and socioeconomic status more directly to children or for enhancing the benefits of preschool interventions. However, while compelling evidence converges on the importance of parenting, this conclusion has not been readily embraced by the media and policy makers. They tend to highlight very distal, "top-down" educational influences like per-pupil spending, student-teacher ratios, and vouchers. Ironically, while parents are rarely implicated in public discussions about literacy problems in America, retailers and popular parenting magazines barrage parents with messages that highlight their importance for supporting their children's intellectual growth and general well-being. Whether it is enriched baby formula (Retsinas 2003) or *Baby Mozart* videos, parents are commercially inundated with goods and services that promise to enhance their young child's physical, cognitive, and social development.

So what are we to believe regarding the role of parenting in children's lives? Outside the public eye, a great deal of research has been conducted to determine: (1) the extent to which parenting uniquely affects literacy skills compared to other environmental factors or children's genetic predispositions; (2) the behaviors, beliefs, and strategies used by parents to promote children's literacy development; and (3) the degree to which interventions can successfully improve parenting as a means of advancing at-risk children's language and literacy growth. The present chapter will directly confront these mixed issues. We will conclude that parenting is a critical, underexploited resource in our drive to improve literacy, but that it is no easy task to improve parenting skills.

Before we embark on this review, we should also note that while mothers and fathers may play unique and complementary roles in their parenting styles, evidence documenting the influence of father involvement on children's literacy development has received much less scientific attention, due in part to the difficulties of obtaining data from fathers (Cabrera et al. 2000; Coley 2001). Consequently, the majority of references to parents throughout this chapter are based primarily on research conducted with mothers, although many of the key maternal parenting practices that promote literacy development would be expected to generalize to other, nonmaternal caregivers (Chase-Lansdale et al. 1999).

Does Parenting Matter?

Scientists agree that research conducted before the 1980s overemphasized the importance of parenting for children's development (Collins et al. 2000; Cowan and Cowan 2002). Parents were assigned a major role in evolutionary, psychodynamic, and attachment theories of development. However, traditional methods of past research, such as obtaining mothers' reports of parent *and* child behaviors at only one point in time, could not help us understand whether parents were affecting children, children were affecting parents, or parents and children were affecting each other. This line of parenting research has been strongly criticized by behavior-geneticists who attempt to separate nature (genes) from nurture (environment) by comparing twins, siblings, or children before and after adoption (Plomin 1990; Rowe 1994). These researchers maintain that children's genetic and biological traits significantly influence, and perhaps even drive, the tone and content of parent-child interactions. Behavior-genetics studies typically find that environmental influences contribute substantially less to individual differences in child outcomes than do genetic factors. From this recurrent pattern of results, behavior-geneticists have posited that: (1) children's development can withstand great variability in parenting practices and emerge essentially unimpeded; and (2) other socializing forces, particularly peers, wield considerably more long-term impacts on the manifestation of personality traits, such as individuals' adaptation to the norms of different social settings (Harris 1995; Rowe 1994).

While these concerns were warranted for past developmental research, the increased scientific rigor employed in the last decade (for example, complex statistical analysis of data gathered from multiple methods and informants) has rendered these criticisms less viable. Moreover, the findings revealed by these technical and methodological advances continue to point toward the centrality of parenting for children's development. Accumulating evidence has demonstrated that the expression of children's genetic or biological makeup will largely depend on the home environments to which they are exposed (Maccoby 2002). For example, in a French study of late-adopted children (ages three to five) with below-average IQ's, children adopted into families of higher socioeconomic status exhibited appreciable gains in IQ (approximately nineteen points) by eleven to eighteen years of age (Duyme, Dumaret, and Tomkiewicz 1999). In contrast, the IQ's of children adopted into lower SES families improved by an average of eight points. Clearly, when children with similar genetic characteristics are compared, environmental inputs emerge as fundamentally critical for shaping development.

It has also become increasingly evident that "parenting" is an incredibly complex skill that changes across time as children traverse developmental transitions (for example, speaking first words, entering kindergarten, or pubertal onset). The behavior-genetics approach to studying parenting—namely, isolating a particular point in time and creating one parenting trait that aggregates a number of aspects of parenting—masks the tremendous individual variation that transpires across time, contexts, and developmental periods. In future research, "rather than pit genes versus parenting, or even parents versus peers, it [will be] more fruitful to examine *how* parenting exerts an influence on a child" (Dodge 2002, 219).

Does Parenting Contribute to Individual Differences in Literacy?

One method of determining whether parenting practices uniquely impact child development is to conduct intervention studies. This approach compares at least two groups of parents (treatment and control) with similar background characteristics to examine whether: (1) the interventions actually change parents' behavior; and (2) changes in parenting skills and/or economic resources are linked to corresponding gains in child well-being. Over the last several decades, researchers have tested numerous intervention strategies that varied widely in where they were conducted (at home, childcare center, or both), who was the target group (for example, medically at risk or low income), and other important features (the children's ages, the durations and intensity of the program; for a review, see Brooks-Gunn 2004). Two major intervention strategies that include parents as service recipients are family-focused early childhood education (ECE) programs that combine center-based childcare with home-based services and parent-focused home visiting programs.

Family-Focused ECE Programs

As reviewed in chapter 3, the combination of center-based education programs for children with parental involvement and training has proven to be one of the more effective strategies for enhancing children's cognitive skills, particularly among at-risk populations. In truth, it becomes difficult to pinpoint the source of short-term gains in cognitive development displayed by children receiving center-based care in large-scale interventions like the Infant Health and Development Program (IHDP), because families were offered weekly home visits during the child's first year of life that continued, albeit less frequently, throughout the toddler years (Brooks-Gunn 2004). Conversely, comparisons of programs that provide center-based care *and* home visiting versus home visiting alone (for example, the Abecedarian Project and Project CARE, respectively) reveal that no treatment effects on cognitive outcomes emerge for children who do not attend center-based care (Campbell and Ramey 1994). Findings such as these suggest that interventions without a child-based component may face substantially greater challenges for improving child well-being (Magnuson and Duncan 2004).

Parent-Focused Home Visiting Programs

Other programs have been designed to provide adults with social support, case management assistance to connect families with community services, and education about parenting and children's development as a direct means of improving families' socioeconomic and psychological resources (Gomby, Culross, and Behrman 1999). By offering a more comprehensive array of services, these interventions aim to enhance children's cognitive, social, and physical development *indirectly* by improving parenting skills (for example, literacy-related interactions). A recent review of national home visiting programs concluded that none of the interventions demonstrated significant treatment effects on all—or even the majority of—outcomes; indeed, many programs failed to produce even one positive effect (Gomby, Culross, and Behrman 1999). The Home Instruction Program for Preschool Youngsters (HIPPY) (Baker, Piotrkowski, and Brooks-Gunn 1998, 1999) and Parents as Teachers (PAT) (Owen and Mulvihill 1994) interventions revealed some positive treatment effects for children's cognitive and social skills, but the findings were inconsistent and modest in size (Gomby, Culross, and Behrman 1999). Many of these adult-based programs did not substantially increase parents' human capital (for example, educational attainment), which may be one reason why gains in children's academic achievement or behavior were generally so elusive (Magnuson and Duncan 2004).

Overall, the short- and long-term impacts of these multifaceted, labor-intensive interventions on parent behaviors and children's literacy development have been surprisingly small. However, before concluding that the worth of these interventions, relative to the costs, is minimal, or that parenting practices are impervious to environmental inputs, it is necessary to recognize that, for a number of reasons, these treatment effects are probably underestimated. First, intervention efforts that address the diverse needs of at-risk populations commonly encounter families that are hampered by chronic adversities. In the Comprehensive Child Development Program (CCDP) (St. Pierre and

Layzer 1999), case managers were trained to assist parents and other adults in the family in meeting their long-range parenting, economic, housing, and employment goals. However, the pressing needs facing the program families challenged the original service delivery plans.

In the first year of the CCDP, case managers' ability to engage families in the orderly, long-term planning required for the program was hindered by the need to resolve frequent family crises. Inadequate and unstable housing arrangements, lack of food or heat, substance abuse, and legal problems all made it difficult for adult family members to gain control over their lives. In many cases, paraprofessional case managers found it difficult to move beyond crisis intervention to help families develop and work toward more long-term goals (St. Pierre and Layzer 1999, 138).

Furthermore, while it has not been easy to detect broad improvements for families, certain subgroups have been shown to exhibit significant gains from program participation (Liaw and Brooks-Gunn 1994). Families who were poor, or nonpoor but experiencing multiple familial risks (for example, single parent, less than a high school education, unemployed head of the household), showed significant treatment effects, whereas nonpoor children with few familial risks did not appear to benefit from the intervention. Among three-year-olds in the IHDP, gains in IQ scores were greatest for children who received the least amount of parental language or literacy promotion at home (Bradley, Burchinal, and Casey 2001). In other words, the children with multiple risk factors impinging on their early development profited the most from intensive intervention efforts containing child-based services. These results echo the findings reviewed in the previous chapter that the benefit of more childcare experience on children's literacy outcomes was most evident for low SES families with low family literacy environments (Christian et al. 2000).

Another issue that is receiving increased attention is the "dosage" of the treatment—namely, the degree to which parents actively use the services in the offered programs (Brooks-Gunn 2004). Despite the best-laid plans conceived and implemented by researchers, clinicians, and social workers, parental enrollment and participation in intervention programs is ultimately voluntary, making receipt of services highly variable across families and programs. In national home visiting programs, enrolled families received only about half of their scheduled home visits, regardless of the number originally planned, because they were either unwilling or unable to obtain the intended services (Gomby, Culross, and Behrman 1999). These low treatment dosages are particularly problematic for parent-focused home visiting programs that are designed to improve child well-being primarily via changes in parental functioning. When eligible families are divided according to their degree of participation, significant benefits emerge for children whose parents maintained greater involvement, even if the intervention program did not demonstrate an overall treatment effect for the entire sample (Brooks-Gunn, Burchinal, and Lopez 2001).

In addition, recent reviews of early childhood intervention programs (Brooks-Gunn, Berlin, and Fuligni 2000; Magnuson and Duncan 2004; Brooks-Gunn 2004) exclude smaller, locally based, experimental studies that focus more narrowly on enriching a singular aspect of parental literacy promotion, like shared book reading. Using videos and/or several weeks of home visits to train parents in more elaborate, descriptive, and engaging book-reading styles has resulted in measurable gains in children's oral language skills across many different samples that vary in socioeconomic status (Lonigan and Whitehurst 1998; Payne, Whitehurst, and Angell 1994; Reese and Cox 1999; Senechal and LeFevre 2001).

Finally, recent reviews also omit mention of successful national health campaigns or Medicaid policies to alter parenting behaviors. Large-scale efforts targeting children's physical health and well-being have been somewhat effective in modifying certain parenting practices. Mothers are now seeking out prenatal care earlier and more frequently, and trends in tobacco and alcohol use during pregnancy have declined in the nation as a whole (Bradley and Corwyn 2004).

Future Directions in Intervention Research

Clearly, more research into the impact of parenting interventions is needed, and the burgeoning evidence points to several considerations for future research and intervention efforts. One immediate question is: how much treatment is enough? Although parental take-up of services and implementation costs are important considerations, perhaps the education and training components of these programs require greater intensity and longer durations to effect long-term changes in parent behaviors and child functioning. For example, while the CCDP (St. Pierre and Layzer 1999) offered an impressive array of economic, educational, psychological, and social services to adults, in contrast, involved parents received parenting-skills training from a home visitor for a maximum of thirteen hours per year (half an hour biweekly), which may be insufficient to promote and sustain meaningful improvements over time. A second critical question is determining which component(s) of the intervention programs are promoting the greatest benefits. The intervention research to date has primarily tested a "black-box" method of evaluation, whereby a variety of services are delivered and overall treatment effects are reported without elucidating which programmatic features are the most potent (Berlin, O'Neil, and Brooks-Gunn 1998).

One methodological approach to address these concerns is evaluating randomized experiments that vary the intensity, duration, and type of services offered to better inform policy makers of the most practical and cost-effective means of supplying programs to children and families (Magnuson and Duncan 2004). In fact, Whitehurst and colleagues (1994) have demonstrated that teaching parents more sophisticated book-reading strategies (dialogic reading) can be implemented within a relatively short amount of time and for very modest costs.

Last, parenting for literacy development is a more complex process than simply engaging with children in cognitively stimulating learning activities. Early childhood interventions that focus primarily on this one aspect of parenting may be inadvertently limiting their effectiveness. In the following section, we will examine more specialized parenting behaviors that differentially promote emergent literacy and oral language skills. Additional dimensions of parenting, such as the degree of emotional warmth and sensitivity exhibited by parents in responding to their children as well as how they establish and maintain control and discipline, will also be explored for their direct and indirect contributions to early literacy development.

What Do We Mean by "Parenting"?

As an overarching framework, parenting practices could be placed into one of two categories, didactic or social (Bornstein 1989), meaning that parents are providing some form of instruction or socialization. Didactic parenting behaviors involve cognitively stimulating activities, such as shared book reading, and are expected to directly enhance literacy development. Socialization characteristics include affective and relational aspects of parent-child interactions, such as warmth, sensitivity, and responsivity. These latter behaviors predict children's social and emotional skills but are less commonly examined in studies of cognition or literacy (for example, phonological awareness or word decoding). However, growing evidence strongly suggests that these cognitive and social processes are inextricably linked. A child's ability to regulate his or her behavior and attention, like sitting still while a book is read aloud or working independently to complete a task, shapes how he or she engages in and benefits from learning opportunities (Li-Grining, Pittman, and Chase-Lansdale, in review; Kurdek and Sinclair 2000). Therefore, while parenting practices could affect children's literacy development directly, parental behaviors could also indirectly contribute to literacy acquisition via their effects on children's social development. Accordingly, we will adopt a broad conceptualization of "parenting for literacy development" that incorporates the instructional content, affective and relational quality, and overall structure of parent-child interactions. Three parenting dimensions emerge as most pertinent for early literacy: the home learning environment, warmth and responsivity, and control/discipline.

Home Learning Environments

Efforts to identify key parenting behaviors that promote or hinder literacy development have concentrated primarily on the learning activities and supports that parents provide in the home. In large national data sets, measures of "cognitive stimulation" or "home learning" have predicted preschoolers' IQ and vocabulary comprehension (Berlin and Brooks-Gunn 1995; Bradley et al. 1993; Johnson et al. 1993; Sugland et al. 1995) and elementary school students' reading, mathematics, and vocabulary skills (Smith, Brooks-Gunn, and Klebanov 1997). These parenting measures were obtained from experimenter observations that recorded a range of literacy-promoting behaviors: using standard English grammar and complex vocabulary and sentence structure; encouraging knowledge of the alphabet, numbers, colors, and shapes; subscribing to newspapers and magazines; and providing children with books and educational toys. Not only do these measures significantly predict children's language and literacy skills, these parenting behaviors also mediate, or transmit, the influence of more distal, socioeconomic indices, like income, onto children's cognitive functioning (Linver, Brooks-Gunn, and Kohen 2002; Raviv, Kessenich, and Morrison, in review).

One limitation of this home inventory is that it combines parents' diverse efforts to promote language or literacy skills into a global "cognitive stimulation" or "learning" scale, which may mask more specific correlations. Increasingly, researchers have attempted to dissect these component properties and focus more explicitly on the unique influence of specific parental behaviors on language and emergent literacy skills. Although there is some disagreement about which prereading skills should be considered dimensions of "emergent literacy" (Mason and Stewart 1990; Whitehurst and Lonigan 1998), most scientists distinguish oral language (for example, vocabulary and listening comprehension) from emergent literacy (for example, letter-sound correspondences and print knowledge) skills since different parental behaviors differentially contribute to growth in each of these domains (Senechal et al. 2001).

Language-promoting behaviors. The vocabularies of mothers and toddlers often appear quite related in both size and composition (Hart and Risley 1995; Hoff-Ginsberg 1991). For example, if mothers frequently label and describe objects and events in children's surroundings, their children usually display larger vocabularies (Della Corte, Benedict, and Klein 1983; Hart and Risley 1995; Nelson 1981). Preschoolers' vocabulary growth is also enhanced if mothers speak using many different words (Hart and Risley 1995) and provide enough information during conversations for children to acquire the meanings of new words (Tabors, Beals, and Weizman 2001). The overall amount and complexity of parental speech children are exposed to are also predictive of individual variation in children's vocabulary and complex grammar acquisition (Huttenlocher et al. 1991, 2002).

Not only are the size and content of mothers' and toddlers' vocabularies comparable, *how* mothers talk to their children is as important for their vocabulary development as *what* they say. When mothers speak to toddlers primarily to control and direct behaviors rather than to elicit conversation and describe features of the environment, their children tend to acquire smaller vocabularies (Hart and Risley 1995; Hoff-Ginsberg 1991). Transcripts of language samples collected during daily activities in professional, working-class, and welfare families revealed: "The richer the parent's utterances to the child were in initiations, imperatives, and prohibitions, the less rapid was the child's vocabulary use, and the fewer were the child's general accomplishments as estimated by the Stanford-Binet IQ test. We saw the powerful dampening effects on development when relatively more of the child's interactions began with a parent-initiated imperative ('Don't,' 'Stop,' 'Quit') that prohibited what the child was doing" (Hart and Risley 1995, 147).

Moreover, the strategies mothers use to initiate and maintain social interactions with their young children are strongly connected to subsequent vocabulary growth. If a child is playing with a ball, a parent could offer descriptive information about the ball, such as "That's a ball," "It's red," or "It bounces." Parents' efforts to talk about and explore the objects that their children are already looking at greatly helps advance their vocabularies (Tomasello and Todd 1983). When a mother tries to redirect her toddler's attention away from the ball to a different toy, it is more difficult for the child to make the switch in his or her mother's speech to a different object in the environment. In other words, the child may not know which toy the parent is now describing. Consequently, children learn fewer labels for objects, which limits the overall size of their vocabularies. Mothers with more education typically maintain longer periods of joint attention on an object with their child and are more responsive to toddlers' utterances and actions, whereas less educated mothers more often try to direct their child's attention and control their behavior (Hart and Risley 1995; Hoff-Ginsberg 1991).

In addition to all the opportunities for language stimulation during daily activities and playtimes, parents can enhance children's language development by reading books with their preschoolers. Shared book reading is a far richer and more nuanced activity than is generally recognized. Book reading can be relegated to a list of daily tasks, like teeth brushing, where parents simply go through the motions and read the text verbatim, or parents can generate a more enriching experience by asking open-ended or probing questions, adding descriptive information to the text or illustrations, and elaborating on the storyline (Haden, Reese, and Fivush 1996; Scarborough and Dobrich 1994; Senechal and LeFevre 2001; Reese and Cox 1999). In randomized experiments, book-reading styles that involve labeling and describing the illustrations or encouraging and assisting children's storytelling abilities significantly bolster children's vocabulary development (Lonigan and Whitehurst 1998; Whitehurst et al. 1988). These language benefits from shared book-reading interactions apply to children from low-income and working-class families (Lonigan and Whitehurst 1998; Payne, Whitehurst, and Angell 1994; Reese and Cox 1999) as well as to children from more affluent backgrounds (Debaryshe 1993; Whitehurst et al. 1988).

Literacy-promoting behaviors. The way parents talk to and engage their child throughout the day holds profound implications for that child's language development. However, parenting for literacy development could be considered even more deliberate and intentional because it requires parents to take the time to instruct children about fundamental reading and writing skills. When parents explicitly teach their children how to name and print letters and words, children's print knowledge (Senechal et al. 1998) and elementary school students' word decoding and reading comprehension skills improve (Senechal and LeFevre 2002). In addition, parenting strategies such as reading to their children and themselves, providing print exposure (books, magazines, or newspapers), and limiting the amount of time their children view television are associated with higher reading, vocabulary, and general knowledge at kindergarten entry (Griffin and Morrison 1997), second grade reading competency (Griffin and Morrison 1997; Scarborough, Dobrich, and Hager 1991), and even eleventh grade reading comprehension (Cunningham and Stanovich 1997).

Nevertheless, while these home literacy activities predict pre-schoolers' oral language skills and school-age children's academic achievement, there is surprisingly little connection between shared book-reading experiences and preschoolers' emergent literacy development (Scarborough and Dobrich 1994). Informal literacy experiences that do not incorporate explicit prereading instruction do not appear to be sufficient to foster emergent literacy skills such as alphabet knowledge or letter-sound correspondences (Evans, Shaw, and Bell 2000; Senechal and LeFevre 2002; Whitehurst et al. 1994). Unless parents point out and name the letters of the alphabet while reading or demonstrate how the sounds of the letters combine to form words, simply reading a book aloud will not in itself give children the skills necessary to "sound out" and decode words. However, there is some indication that these home literacy activities and print exposure may indirectly promote emergent literacy skills through their impact on children's phonological awareness, listening comprehension, and vocabulary development (Fritjers, Barron, and Brunello 2000; Senechal et al. 1998).

In summary, parents' language and literacy promotion are potent, proximal sources of influence that can substantially enhance or depress children's cognitive development. Not only are dramatically significant effects detected among very young children, these early parenting practices are strongly associated with children's later academic achievement as well. Notably, more fine-grained analyses of diverse parenting behaviors have uncovered a high degree of domain-specificity, such that "stimulating" parenting behaviors differentially predict emergent literacy and vocabulary skills.

Parental Warmth and Responsivity

It is fairly easy to see how shared book-reading interactions could be used to boost children's vocabulary development and knowledge of letter names and sounds. However, as stated earlier, book reading can be much more than an instructional activity. The emotional tone during this time can range from warm and loving to cold and detached. The affective climate in which these learning opportunities are nested could also shape children's approach to learning, motivation, and social competence. In the extant literature, observations of parental

warmth, such as open displays of affection, physical or verbal rein-
forcement, and sensitivity to children's requests and feelings, have been
significantly associated with preschoolers' literacy and language skills
and later school performance (Berlin and Brooks-Gunn 1995). For example, the affective quality of mother-child interactions at three years
of age exerted a long-term influence on a variety of outcomes: cognitive ability at age four, school readiness skills at ages five and six, IQ
scores at age six, and vocabulary and mathematics performance at age
twelve (Estrada et al. 1987). These authors proposed that the affective
characteristics of parent-child interactions shape children's cognitive
development in three ways: (1) by increasing parents' willingness to initiate and assist their children with problem-solving tasks; (2) by enhancing children's social competence, such as their ability to solicit and
effectively use parental supports; and (3) by encouraging children's ex-
ploratory tendencies, which reinforces their motivation and persistence in challenging tasks.

Likewise, mothers' sensitivity to children's developmental progress (for example, responsiveness, positive regard, and nonrestrictive-
ness) during the first two years of life predicted cognitive and language
skills for children in preschool (NICHD-ECCRN 1998; Tamis-
LeMonda et al. 1996), kindergarten, and first grade (Coates and Lewis
1984; Kelly et al. 1996). Specifically, when mothers offer relevant and
timely responses to their infants' vocalizations, explorations of objects,
and play behaviors, toddlers reach major language milestones earlier
(for example, expression of first words and production of fifty words)
(Tamis-LeMonda, Bornstein, and Baumwell 2001). In addition, more
responsive mothers of six- to twelve-month-old infants reduce the
length of their utterances so their child can better comprehend their
speech (Murray, Johnson, and Peters 1990). If unusual or rare words
are spoken, responsive parents provide sufficient information for their
preschoolers to better deduce the meanings of these new words (Beals
1997). For example, at-risk groups of children, such as those with high
medical risk (Landry et al. 1997) or less advanced early language skills
(Baumwell, Tamis-LeMonda, and Bornstein 1997), have experienced
great benefit when mothers consistently interacted with them in a
highly responsive manner; over time, the cognitive gaps between these
at-risk children and their less at-risk peers significantly narrowed.

Most noteworthy in these studies are the robust effects of parental socialization on social *and* cognitive domains that are evident prior to kindergarten entry. Not only have patterns of social behavior and cognitive functioning been established before children experience a formal schooling environment, but the affective quality of parent-child relationships seems to sustain the long-term stability of these effects.

Parental Control and Discipline

While the "warmth," or affective climate of the home is an important component of parenting, setting and maintaining rules, standards, and limits establishes parental authority and also creates a supportive, structured context for children's literacy development (Hartup 1989; Chase-Lansdale and Pittman 2002). For example, in our shared book-reading vignette, this interaction also provides the opportunity for parents to encourage children to resist squirming and fidgeting and sustain their attention until the story is finished, even as they may become fatigued or bored. The influence of parental control on children's social competence, and particularly on their self-regulation abilities, will promote or impede subsequent cognitive growth. Cooney (1998) uncovered this indirect association in an investigation of alphabet recognition, reading, and vocabulary comprehension skills at kindergarten entry. Parents' use of controlling or disciplinary practices did not directly predict literacy outcomes; instead, these parenting behaviors significantly predicted children's social functioning (for example, cooperation, independence, and responsibility), which in turn contributed to their academic performance. While more research is necessary to substantiate causality, there appears to be an important, albeit complex, connection between parental rules, standards, and limits and children's early literacy development.

In summary, several major conclusions emerge from our review of parenting. First, parenting for literacy development is not a simple or unidimensional endeavor. Effective parenting for language and literacy acquisition is a complex, multifaceted process, which is made even more complicated when the unique characteristics of each child are taken into account, as we will discuss in the following chapter. Second, parenting interventions to date have incorporated a wide array of

social, educational, and psychological services, but the parenting training has not been broad enough to effect long-lasting improvements in
child well-being. We argue that parenting for literacy development involves more than teaching parents to provide enriching learning opportunities. Instead, interventions should address three critical dimensions of parenting: home literacy and language promotion, warmth
and responsivity, and control/discipline.

Mixed Messages from Schools Regarding Parental Involvement

Claims about the importance of parenting have been delivered not
only by researchers; schools are increasingly advocating for more involved and responsive parenting as well. Parental involvement in
schools used to include signing report cards, volunteering for a school
function, or sending a snack for the class. However, as schools face
greater accountability for children's academic successes and failures,
several school districts have started holding a wider range of community members responsible, including parents. For example, school officials in New Haven, Connecticut, have developed a "shared accountability plan" that includes issuing parent report cards to monitor
parents' involvement in their children's education. "Parents will be
graded on a point system. To get a passing mark, they must be sure
their children attend school. They'll be required to volunteer at least
once per marking period, and show up for at least one school event"
(National Public Radio 2002). The education consultant hired by the
New Haven school district maintained: "What takes place in a school
is critical, but it's not sufficient. And what happens between three in
the afternoon and seven in the morning is at least as important as what
happens in the school day." The superintendent claimed that truancy,
in particular, would be closely watched. As a last resort, negligent parents would be reported to the Department of Child and Family Services or court authorities because "education cannot take place if a
child is not in school."

Other school districts have sought the support of community
employers to enable and encourage parental involvement during the
school day. An unexpected model for this approach is the Department

of Defense (DoD) school system. The DoD services a student body that is about 40 percent ethnic minority, experiences high rates of poverty (approximately 50 percent of students qualify for free or reduced-price lunch), and reports a transience rate that is comparable to rates in inner-city schools (35 percent) due to military reassignments to other bases. Nevertheless, the DoD schools have achieved an incredible feat: the test-score gap among African American, Hispanic, and White students is the narrowest in the country, and performance discrepancies across SES groups are difficult to detect (Smrekar et al. 2001). There are several demographic differences between DoD parents and parents in civilian school districts that should be noted. Single-parent families are much less common (6.7 percent) than occur nationally (27 percent). In addition, every child in the DoD system has at least one employed parent, and the enlisted personnel, who compose 80 percent of school families, have high school diplomas. While the family characteristics and student achievement patterns may, on the surface, appear military-specific, DoD school officials, teachers, and parents attribute the children's academic successes to a potentially transferable component of their educational system: parental involvement.

A recent episode of *60 Minutes* highlights the academic accomplishments of students in the Pentagon schools and the factors that enable parents' high degree of involvement (CBS News 2002). Soldiers are given time off to volunteer in the schools. If parents do not get involved, the school superintendent can notify commanding officers as an impetus for parents to visit their child's classroom. In fact, the Fort Campbell superintendent maintained: "When I was in the public schools, and I had one of the largest industries in America right out my back door. . . . I—without hesitation—have called on several occasions their supervisors and asked them to help me get the parents into the school . . . [and] it worked" (12). Not only are parents encouraged to get involved, the DoD schools have deliberately fostered a welcoming environment to sustain parental participation. As one teacher described it: "I think we really have an underlying attitude. If you want to just come on in and sit for 15 minutes and go eat lunch with your child, that's fine, we're not going to question it. Go ahead and go. I think that is unique" (13).

Parent response to this schooling environment has been remarkable. DoD schools are available only to personnel residing in military housing. The families interviewed on *60 Minutes* opted to stay on the base and live in smaller homes, rather than purchase a larger home off base and accrue equity, so their children could remain enrolled in the DoD school system (CBS News 2002). Parents' favorable view of the schools has also led to more stability in the military's workforce. A parent disclosed, "I was going to get out of the military, I really was. But because my daughter is doing so well and stuff, I would rather sacrifice and stay here. . . . My daughter made the A and B honor roll twice. She has never done that, never" (14).

It remains to be seen whether school-industry partnerships in civilian school districts can be similarly implemented to facilitate parental involvement in the schools. In addition, researchers continue to develop and evaluate programs that are designed to encourage and strengthen parents' involvement in their child's schooling, such as the School Development Program, which we discussed in chapter 3 (Comer and Haynes 1991). Modest empirical evidence has demonstrated that parents' active participation in classroom and school activities and monitoring of their children's school performance are associated with higher achievement for elementary school students (Porche 2001).

In summary, we recognize that there is a fine line between recognizing the importance of parents for children's development and blaming parents—our goal is to emphasize the former point. As stated in chapter 1, many American students are performing just fine. For those who are struggling, increased literacy and language promotion; warmth and sensitivity; enforcement of rules, standards, and limits; and parental involvement in the school system should yield meaningful benefits for children's early cognitive and social development.

In addition, we would be remiss not to acknowledge that any relationship between individuals is a "two-way street." Children bring an array of cognitive, socioemotional, and behavioral characteristics with them to every interaction. Consequently, parents are not simply acting upon their children; parents also react to their children's predispositions and abilities in a variety of ways. In the following chapter, we will explore the relation between unique individual differences in children and the variability that is readily apparent in American children's early literacy skills.

5

The Role of Children in Literacy Development

Girls are on a tear through the educational system. In the past 30 years, nearly every inch of educational progress has gone to them.

Thomas G. Mortenson

Ready for kindergarten means more than ABCs.

Smart Start

One of the most important policy goals to emerge in the last decade is that all children will arrive at school "ready to learn" (No Child Left Behind [NCLB] Act). But what exactly does "ready to learn" mean? What knowledge and skills are important prerequisites for children's success in school? Throughout the past chapters we have discussed the influence of cultural, socioeconomic, preschool, childcare, and parenting on children's early literacy development. In this chapter, we weave the pieces together to present the complexity of skills that constitutes school readiness, including both cognitive—language and early literacy skills—and social-emotional skills, such as behavior, temperament, and self-regulation.

Unfortunately, too many of America's children are not "ready" for the transition into a formal schooling environment, either socially or academically. Among a national sample of almost 3,600 teachers, over one-third maintained that *about half of their class or more* began kindergarten socially and emotionally unprepared for the demands of the classroom (Rimm-Kaufman and Pianta, 2000). Considering that these teachers managed classrooms with an average of twenty-two students, this estimate translates into a staggering number of children. Teachers reported that at least half of the students in their class had "difficulty following directions" (46 percent), "difficulty working independently" (34 percent), and "difficulty working as part of a group" (30 percent) when they began school. Other pressing problems included students' "lack of academic skills" (36 percent), "disorganized home environment" (35 percent), or "lack of any formal preschool experience" (31 percent). Note that these teachers identified as many social-emotional skills as they did academic and cognitive skills.

It is clear that being ready for school is a two-way street. While children need to have developed a functional level of a number of cognitive, language, literacy, and social skills, in parallel the schools must be ready to help the children they receive. Hence any real discussion of readiness to learn must acknowledge the reciprocal interplay of the child's level of function and the schools' instructional activities. We will discuss these interactions more fully in chapter 6. Here we will begin to lay out the child factors associated with school success.

As researchers investigate the construct of school readiness, they include both cognitive and social-emotional skills. For example, standardized assessments of school readiness usually assess general social interaction, cognitive skills, and concrete academic concepts such as identifying letters, numbers, colors, and parts of the body (Stipek 2002). Accumulating research reveals that children's profile of literacy and social competence in early elementary school is highly predictive of academic achievement in junior high (Hansen 2001; Martin, Olejnik, and Gaddis 1994) and high school (Cunningham and Stanovich 1997), as well as whether students will drop out of high school (Shepard and Smith 1988a). Consequently, children's ease with the transition to school (Entwisle and Alexander 1993) and their cognitive and social/behavioral skills at kindergarten entry have meaningful implications for their later educational and vocational success. We will discuss these factors and why they might be related to students' success in school.

Ask any parent of more than one child, and they will confirm that their children are very different and have been since the day they were born. "Oh, yes," they will say, "Jack was born a worrier; Kate showed her temper the first time I changed her diaper; Kari was an easy baby right from the start; I swear, Jess was born talking." Children bring unique characteristics and propensities with them to the learning process, which interact with their experiences at home and at school and shape their literacy learning experiences. Some children learn to read as easily as they learned to talk, while others struggle to relate letters to sounds or to understand what they have read. Underscoring all of this is an appreciation of the active role that children play in their own learning through their interactions with parents, teachers, and peers as they gain key school readiness skills.

The bulk of our discussion will focus on the vital role of oral language, literacy, and self-regulation skills. Nevertheless, there are a number of issues of particular concern to parents and teachers that are important to consider initially. The first is entrance age. Each year we receive calls from parents trying to decide whether or not their child with a fall birthday should begin kindergarten or spend another year in preschool. They are worried either that their child is not ready for the rigors of school or that the child is ready for school and time's a-wasting. Another issue is gender. What role does gender play with regard to school success? Are boys less ready for school than girls? Are girls at a disadvantage, especially in math? We will begin this chapter discussing these vital topics. We will then move to a discussion of IQ and general cognitive ability as well as the critical cognitive skills—language and academic skills—that are related to students' success in school. We will then discuss social-emotional aspects of school readiness, focusing particularly on children's social skills, temperament, and self-regulation.

Entrance Age

A child's age at kindergarten entry is often a source of concern for parents and teachers. Older kindergartners have experienced almost a year more of language and literacy exposure than their younger classmates and may be more socially mature. National surveys indicate that 9 or 10 percent of parents delay their child's entrance to kindergarten, especially if they are among the youngest in their classroom (that is, if their birthday falls close to the school cutoff date) (Cosden, Zimmer, and Tuss 1993; May and Kundert 1995; National Center for Educational Statistics 1999). Earlier research may have unduly influenced parents' fears by suggesting that younger children were at greater risk for poor academic performance (Breznitz and Teltsch 1989; Davis, Trimble, and Vincent 1980), grade retention (Langer, Kalk, and Searls 1984), and special education referrals (DiPasquale, Moule, and Flewelling 1980; Maddux 1980).

More recent investigations have used a variety of methods to evaluate how young children perform in school compared to their older peers. Researchers have compared: (1) children who entered school when eligible with children who delayed entrance for one year; (2) the oldest and youngest children in the same grade; and (3) same-age children in different grades. This last technique has provided the most rigorous strategy for distinguishing effects of experiencing a year of schooling from maturational (age) effects. However, across all of these methods, any early discrepancies that favored older children in kindergarten significantly diminished by second or third grade (McClelland, Morrison, and Holmes 2000; Morrison, Griffith, and Alberts 1997; Stipek and Byler 2001). Overall, younger children benefit from formal instruction as much as do their older peers and are able to match the performance of older classmates within a relatively short amount of time.

While these studies persuasively demonstrate that entrance age, in and of itself, is not a useful predictor of early academic achievement, two issues remain unresolved. First, although the early effects of entrance age appeared short-lived, the long-term effects have not been adequately examined. It is possible that despite substantial reductions in entrance age gaps during early elementary school (Stipek 2002), the influence of age on cognitive and social domains may reemerge as schooling requirements become more complex and student-managed (Crosser 1991; DeMeis and Stearns 1992). A recent analysis of approximately 14,000 children from the National Education Longitudinal Study (NELS) offered encouraging evidence that the early narrowing of the entrance age gap is maintained throughout formal schooling. For example, no significant differences emerged between younger and older kindergartners across a range of long-term educational and social outcomes, such as high school dropout incidence, college attendance, behavior problems, and arrests (Arnold and Painter 2002a, 2002b). Second, it is also still not clear whether entrance age is an independent risk factor, or whether the risk is produced when being young at school entry is combined with other child factors, such as weaker cognitive skills or social immaturity. For example, Shepard and Smith (1988b) uncovered the largest discrepancies between older and younger students who were in the lowest twenty-fifth percentile of cognitive ability. Nevertheless, while some questions remain to be addressed, chronological age at school entry does not appear to be an important source of school readiness.

Gender

Gender differences in verbal and mathematics abilities have been tracked for decades. Early reviews in the 1970s indicated that discrepancies detected at young ages were generally small, whereas consistently significant sex differences that favored boys in verbal, mathematics, and spatial abilities did not often emerge until ten or eleven years of age (Maccoby and Jacklin 1972, 1974). In contrast, later evidence revealed girls' advanced verbal ability and that their mathematics and memory performance was comparable to that of boys (Entwisle and Baker 1983; Stevenson et al. 1976). By the end of the 1980s, the size of the gender differences in math and verbal skills had substantially declined. Not only did the gender gaps in academic achievement narrow, but disparities in math performance actually began to favor females (Hyde, Fennema, and Lamon 1990; Hyde and Linn 1988).

So now that the women who entered the workforce and pursued professional degrees in the 1970s and 1980s are sending their own sons and daughters to school, what has happened to the gender gap? According to 2003 NAEP data, female students in fourth and eighth grades outscored male students in reading by an average of seven to eleven points (National Center for Educational Statistics 2003b). In contrast, the mathematics gap is much smaller, with boys scoring higher than girls by only two or three points (National Center for Educational Statistics 2003a). Furthermore, the magnitude of these gender gaps has remained fairly consistent since the early 1990s.

It is important to keep in mind that these national data reflect academic achievement but not necessarily school performance. Girls' achievement, especially in math and science, was once a major educational concern, but researchers and educators are now arguing that a "new gender gap" has emerged in American schools: "'Every time I turn around, if something good is happening, there's a female in charge,' says

Terrill O. Stammler, principal of Rising Sun High School in Rising Sun, Md. 'Boys are missing from nearly every leadership position, academic honors slot, and student-activity post at the school. Even Rising Sun's girls' sports teams do better than the boys'" (Conlin 2003).

This new achievement disparity continues after high school as well. For more than ten years, women have surpassed men in earning postsecondary degrees (for example, bachelor's or master's degrees), and current projections anticipate a widening of the gap in men's and women's educational attainment over the next decade (National Center for Educational Statistics 2002). So how early do these gender differences appear? Female toddlers exhibit greater rates of vocabulary production (Huttenlocher et al. 1991; Reznick and Goldsmith 1989) and language complexity, expression, and comprehension (Bornstein 1998). However, these differences are usually small in size (Hyde and Linn 1988) and diminish by twenty to twenty-four months of age (Huttenlocher et al. 1991). In preschool measures of emergent literacy, generally significant gender discrepancies are not found (Chaney 1994; Senechal 1997) or weakly favor girls (NICHD-ECCRN 2000).

Some researchers are currently arguing that rather than gender per se, disparities in social maturity or the socialization practices that girls and boys experience may place girls at an advantage in both the classroom and the workplace. James Garbarino, professor and author of *Lost Boys: Why Our Sons Turn Violent and How We Can Save Them*, contends that "Girls are better able to deliver in terms of what modern society requires of people—paying attention, abiding by rules, being verbally competent, and dealing with interpersonal relationships in offices" (Conlin 2003). It is important to recognize that in and of itself, focusing on gender may not be terribly illuminating in helping us understand the growing divergence among boys and girls in school success. In a sense, gender, like SES, is a distal factor that operates through more proximal sources of influence, like parenting, or children's social maturity and self-regulation.

Cognitive Skills and IQ

Another commonly recognized characteristic of children that greatly contributes to literacy acquisition is their intelligence, an attribute that goes by many names (for example, IQ or cognitive competence). In a classroom it is readily evident that some children are able to learn and apply new information with greater ease and accuracy than their peers. Efforts to somehow measure or quantify these abilities are generally constrained by children's language development. In other words, if we want to examine the influence of children's intelligence on the variability in children's literacy skills at kindergarten entry, the earliest we could administer a standardized IQ test would be around age two, when children are better able to produce answers to questions. In response, psychologists have also used more global mental and psychomotor scales, such as the Bayley Scales of Infant Development (Bayley 1969, 1993), to assess major areas of infants' and toddlers' cognitive development, such as sensation, perception, memory, and language (Bornstein and Lamb 1992). Scores on the BSID at two years of age have been useful for detecting language delays (Siegel et al. 1995) and are strongly associated with later academic and language skills during the preschool and elementary school years (Bachman and Morrison 2002; Olson, Bates, and Kaskie 1992). In recent decades, cognitive researchers have devised several techniques to obtain indicators of infants' cognitive development at very young ages, presumably when performance would better represent biological traits than would environmental experiences. For example, infants' abilities to distinguish new from familiar sounds or pictures during the first year of life predicts cognitive scores two to eight years later (McCall and Carriger 1993).

Not only are there age issues to consider when assessing children's intelligence, but researchers continue to disagree about the aspects of intelligence to include in standardized tests (Sternberg 1997). Most IQ tests contain verbal (vocabulary, comprehension, general information) and quantitative (arithmetic, problem-solving, spatial reasoning) components that can be aggregated to form a global score. However, Gardner (1983) has argued that each individual possesses multiple intelligences that include musical, bodily-kinesthetic, interpersonal, and intrapersonal domains in addition to the more traditional intelligence domains of linguistic, logical-mathematical, and spatial skills. Despite the controversy surrounding the content of IQ tests, children's verbal and quantitative abilities in preschool and early elementary school do predict a variety of later academic outcomes, such as grades and standardized test scores of reading and mathematics (Kaplan 1993; Martin and Holbrook 1985; Morrison and Connor 2002; Plomin and Neiderhiser 1991) and even likelihood of high school dropout (Jimerson et al. 2000). Further, IQ scores are often among the most predictive of factors for academic competence, over and above measures of SES, parenting practices, and children's social and behavioral skills (Mantzicopoulos 1997; Pellegrini et al. 1987).

Nevertheless, it is important to reiterate that while our culture reifies intelligence as a heritable trait, IQ scores do not solely reflect genetic characteristics but are also responsive to environmental experiences. For example, adopted children's IQ scores increase substantially more if they are adopted into families of higher SES (Duyme, Dumaret, and Tomkiewicz 1999), and years of school attendance, independent of chronological age, positively affect IQ scores (Stelzl et al. 1995).

Moreover, using IQ to predict school success is like using a sledgehammer to carve an ice sculpture. You get quick results, but they won't be nuanced, detailed, or very appealing. Instead, we propose examining the many and multifaceted aspects of cognitive development captured in IQ scores, including language, literacy, and self-regulation. Additionally, converging research reveals that children's social skills are critical for school success, and consideration of these skills is missing in any discussion of IQ. All of the abilities and skills we associate with IQ are most certainly interrelated and interact with each other and the child's environment. For example, children's vocabulary, a key aspect of IQ, is clearly a universal human trait (Locke 1993). Yet vocabulary and oral language development in general are shaped by the child's environment. How much parents talk with their child and the complexity of their language predict their child's vocabulary and use of complex grammar (Hart and Risley 1995; Huttenlocher et al. 2002). This, in turn, affects the child's literacy development (Snow, Burns, and Griffin 1998).

Language

Our ability to use language to communicate feelings, ideas, emotions, and plans is a unique human ability that affects every aspect of our lives. It is the medium by which we learn and teach. It is like the air, something vital that we tend not to think about. By three years of age, most children have figured out how to use language for relatively sophisticated purposes, as any parent knows. Toddlers negotiate nap time, they express frustration, they even begin to deceive and manipulate. By four and a half years, children are masters at communicating, ready to maneuver through the complexities of home, community, and school interactions. Yet when we think about what is entailed in learning a language, these feats are as remarkable as they are universal. Children do not learn to talk for the sake of becoming users of language; they master communicating for the sake of being part of their family and social community (Locke 1993). And they will become reasonably proficient communicators unless they meet with neurological, physical, or environmental disaster, and even then they may compensate magnificently. Think about deaf children. They cannot hear spoken language and so may not learn to speak. However, they can learn to talk with their hands, using either sign language (Lane, Hoffmeister, and Bahan 1996) or made-up home signs that have much of the structure found in languages across the world (Goldin-Meadow 2002). They even learn to use spoken language with the less than optimal auditory information provided by hearing aids and cochlear implants.

As we discuss children's language throughout this book, we will divide it into pieces—sounds or phonemes, vocabulary, semantics (the meaning of what is said), morphemes (the pieces of language that carry meaning, like "-ed," which marks past tense, or "-es," which marks plurals), syntax (the ways in which we order words, use pronouns and verbs, and structure sentences), and pragmatics (the ways in which we use language, such as how we take turns talking, decide who gets to talk, and use language that is appropriate for the setting—for example, we don't swear in front of our grandmothers). But it is important to keep in mind that we don't compartmentalize language in real life; language is all of one piece, and using it is largely unconscious. When we are conscious of using language and can manipulate it (the deft skill of punsters, the rhyming ability of rappers), this is called metalinguistic awareness. It turns out that metalinguistic awareness is critical to the process of learning to read and may provide a salient link between language and reading. Additionally, language, as the medium of learning and teaching, is a critical component of literacy.

There are also important social and pragmatic aspects to language that have implications for children's learning. For example, children who do not learn the rules about how to talk in the classroom (for example, keep their questions and answers to the point, don't interrupt other speakers, tell stories with a beginning and an end) have tremendous difficulty negotiating the school environment both on the playground and in the classroom. They have problems interacting with peers and teachers alike (Craig 1995) and may be at a disadvantage during class discussions and during peer learning opportunities.

As toddlers, children display different patterns of expressive language development. Some children exhibit a dramatic increase in their spoken language skills, often referred to as a "vocabulary burst," which is generally an increase in their use of object labels to name the features of their environment (Nelson 1973; Resnick 1992). In contrast, other toddlers show steady but gradual gains in the amount of spoken words they produce. Among these children, their expressive or productive vocabularies contain a more even mix of nouns, verbs, and adjectives. This variation has been linked to differences in mothers' speech patterns (Hoff-Ginsberg 1991; Nelson 1973) but may also reflect variation among children in the types of words they extract from all the language that surrounds them (Resnick 1992).

For example, Beals (1997) obtained language samples from families' mealtime interactions in an effort to connect parental language characteristics with children's vocabulary development. Rare or uncommon words were identified in their conversations, and the transcripts were reviewed to determine the kinds of contextual or linguistic supports parents provided that aided children's ability to infer the meanings of these novel words. Among this low-income sample of three-year-olds, who were collectively exposed to over 1,600 rare words, children explicitly asked parents for the meanings of these new words only nineteen times. This astonishingly low incidence of asking questions about the language spoken to and around them suggests that children may rely quite heavily on context to ascertain word meanings. However, if children have limited vocabularies already, inferring the meanings of words from language in their environment may be very difficult. There is also evidence that children rely on syntax to help them understand the meaning of words (Gleitman and Gillette 1999). For example, we can figure out that *glax* is a verb rather than a noun when we read the sentence, "She went glaxing yesterday but didn't find a thing." We can even infer that when we go glaxing we are looking for something based on the information in the sentence. Thus children with an immature or incomplete grasp of English grammar (for example, children for whom English is a second language) will have more difficulty learning new words.

Links between Language and Literacy

Since the early 1970s, the relation between children's ability to communicate effectively and their success throughout their school career has received considerable scientific attention. In general, children who achieved at the highest academic levels were consistently rated by their teachers as students who used language with "notable skill and power" (Loban 1976, 145). Further, children who started kindergarten with stronger oral language skills became the most proficient readers and writers by high school (Loban 1976). Our knowledge about the links between language and literacy increased substantially during the 1980s and 1990s.

Phonological awareness, the ability to consciously manipulate the component sounds within words, emerged as a key skill for successful reading. Thus children who could, for example, respond "cow" when asked what word is left in "cowboy" without "boy" or who could blend onsets (first sound "b") and rimes (the rest of the word "in"; answer "bin") were consistently better readers than were children who could not do these tasks (Catts et al. 1999; Rayner et al. 2001).

To accurately decode and read a word, children must be able to separate the word into meaningful chunks or units of sounds. For example, words can be divided into syllables (*wagon,* /wa-gon/), onsets and rimes (*show,* /sh-ow/), and phonemes, which are the smallest units of sounds (*grin,* /g-r-i-n/). Identifying these different types of sounds in words generally promotes reading ability (Chaney 1998; Stahl and Murray 1994; Wagner et al. 1997). Locating the phonemes in a word is one of the strongest positive predictors of reading acquisition (Mann, Shankweiler, and Smith 1984; Nation and Hulme 1997; Share et al. 1984), although it is also one of the most developmentally challenging phonological awareness tasks for young children (Chafouleas et al.

1997). Children's awareness that sounds are put together to form words, and that words can be separated into smaller sounds, especially when linked to letters, greatly facilitates the development of their early reading skills.

Emerging research indicates that other aspects of metalinguistic awareness are also intricately linked with children's developing literacy. Children's morphosyntactic awareness (for example, that "nation," "national," and "nationalistic" all share the same root or that "The boy ran the couch" does not make any sense) is related to reading comprehension (Carlisle 2000; Snow 2001). We will delve into these aspects of language and literacy more fully in chapter 6.

However, the links between language and literacy are proving to be more intricate than the simple relation between letters and sounds. This is largely because language develops. Children coo and gurgle as infants, then they begin to babble (*bababa dada*) at about six months. Sometime around their first birthday they say their first real word, and then they begin to combine words. For the first five years of life, their average sentence increases by one word each year. By the age of three years, children are competent communicators, although they may appear to be more linguistically sophisticated than they really are. By five years of age, children have mastered all but the most complex syntactic structures (such as passive voice—"The dog was pulled by the boy"). It is quite likely that the language skills most closely tied to later reading success may vary depending on the child's age (Scarborough 2001). For example, the strongest predictors of whether children would develop reading disabilities were how accurately they pronounced words and the complexity of their sentences when they were twenty months of age. However, by the time they were forty-two months, vocabulary predicted more strongly than did pronunciation. By five years of age, only phonological awareness differentiated between children with reading difficulties and those without.

Emergent reading, children's early interactions with reading and writing text, is also proving a key "readiness" skill. Before children learn to read and write conventionally, they pretend (Teale and Sulzby 1986). You may have seen a young child at the library pick up a book and "read" it, using the intonation, prosody, and syntax that we find in storybooks. The child may have memorized the book and may be able to "read" it nearly verbatim. This is emergent reading, which may be related to the ways parents interact with children at home (Senechal et al. 1998) as well as opportunities at preschool. Emergent reading helps children learn the narrative structure of stories and the complex grammar found in written text (Dickinson and Tabors 2001; Snow and Tabors 1993; Sulzby 1985), which appear to support literacy development, specifically reading comprehension (Snow 2001). Children's pretend writing, also called invented spelling, is associated with early literacy development as well (Shilt 2003).

Of course, knowing letter sounds without recognizing letters and knowing how to tell a story without being able to read words doesn't guarantee that children will learn to read successfully. Just as important as children's awareness of the sounds within words is their familiarity with the names and sounds of the letters in the alphabet (Treiman 2000). Children's knowledge of the alphabet when they enter kindergarten is one of the best predictors of learning to read successfully (Snow, Burns, and Griffin 1998). Letter knowledge predicts more advanced phonological awareness (Wagner et al. 1997) and word decoding skills throughout elementary school (Lonigan, Burgess, and Anthony 2000).

The interplay among language, literacy, and social skills can perhaps best be appreciated in the common practice of shared book reading between parents and children. As we saw in chapter 4, shared book reading is one of the most successful methods that parents can employ to enhance their children's language and emergent reading skills. Nevertheless, Scarborough and Dobrich (1994) have pointed out that not all children enjoy this activity; a small percentage of children complain and squirm when parents try to read stories to them. This tendency may be linked to children's particular temperamental characteristics (very active children or children with attention difficulties may not want to or be able to sit still). Other children may not enjoy reading, or their parents may not make shared book reading a warm and engaging activity. These preschoolers' dislike of book reading will have implications for their language development and for their approach to learning reading skills in elementary school as well. Conversely, other children derive great pleasure from books and will independently seek out books to look at or ask adults to read to them.

It is this "child effect," or recognition of the role children play as drivers of their development, that may be absent in literacy research. Children's development of early reading habits is associated with their later familiarity with popular books and stronger comprehension skills in high school (Cunningham and Stanovich 1997). Likewise, the more book titles elementary school children recognize (an indicator of the "print exposure" children have sought out or received from parents), the greater their growth in vocabulary, spelling, and reading comprehension skills (Echols et al. 1996). Children's oral language abilities, as well as their approach to learning language and early reading skills and self-regulation, may notably influence the amount of print exposure they obtain and the reading habits they develop.

Social Skills and Temperament

While not all reading or educational researchers include children's social skills in theories or models of literacy acquisition, reports from kindergarten teachers (for example, West, Hausken, and Collins 1995), as well as parents' decisions to delay kindergarten entrance for their young boys (Stipek 2002), strongly suggest that social maturity and behavior problems are serious concerns for parents and teachers. Anecdotally, in the course of our research, teachers often volunteered to us their frustrations with the seemingly large proportion of children who began kindergarten "looking like preschoolers." In fact, several schools have resorted to rather severe disciplinary measures for very young children to curb problem behavior and prompt parental involvement.

A new policy has required principals in the Philadelphia schools to report all "serious incidents," resulting in the suspensions of thirty-three kindergartners (Rimer 2002). Children received suspensions for hurting other children or school employees, "includ[ing] a student who stabbed a classmate with a pencil, another who punched a teacher who was seven and a half months pregnant in the stomach . . . [and] one girl who bit her teacher's hand and kicked her." While this vignette may seem somewhat extreme, it illustrates just how widely the range of disruptive and problem behaviors extends among very young elementary school students. As schools enact new regulations to confront these challenges, more severe disciplinary tactics, like suspending kin-

dergartners, are used as yet another deliberate means of not only managing problem behaviors but coercing parents' involvement in their
children's classroom performance. One Philadelphia school official
who oversees discipline commented: "Part of what the suspension al-
lows us to do is get the attention of the parent. . . . It's not about pun-
ishing the kid or hammering the kid. Clearly, at age 5 or 6 this is a par-
ent-education issue. How do we bring parents in to support social
school skills?" (Rimer 2002).

Social Behaviors That Promote School Success

Under the broad heading of social skills, researchers have distinguished
two primary components of children's behavior that influence academic performance: interpersonal skills, which involve the quality of
social relations with peers and adults, and learning-related social skills,
such as the degree of independence, responsibility, and self-control
children exhibit in the classroom.

Children's ability to maintain positive peer relations is associated
with both social and academic benefits during their early schooling experience. Stable peer relationships facilitate better school adjustment
during children's transition from preschool to kindergarten (Ladd and
Price 1987). Kindergartners' ability to form new friendships with their
classmates during the first two months of school yielded significant
gains in their academic skills by the end of their first year. In contrast,
children who were rejected by their peers at the beginning of kindergarten displayed lower academic performance during the course of the
year. This relation between the quality of peer interactions and academic achievement is evident later in elementary school as well. For
example, the third graders identified as academically successful were
also able to sustain positive relationships, and their peers reported liking them more than the academically struggling students (Green et al.
1980).

A great deal of research attention has also been devoted to children's social competence in the classroom, or "learning-related behaviors" (Alexander, Entwisle, and Dauber 1993). The classroom environment places a number of social demands on children. They are
required to sit still, raise their hand before speaking or leaving their

desk, work cooperatively in groups, and wait their turn. Children are also expected to complete worksheets and projects independently, which necessitates that children focus their attention and stay on-task to finish their work in a timely manner with the pace of their classmates. Moreover, given time and class-size constraints, teachers are rarely able to provide the assistance needed to more directly manage the behaviors of children struggling with these skills (Martin 1989).

Children with poor learning-related social skills score significantly lower than their peers in reading, math, vocabulary, and general knowledge at school entry and the end of second grade (McClelland, Morrison, and Holmes 2000). Likewise, behaviors such as sustaining participation and attention while restraining restlessness are significantly associated with higher test scores and report card marks in first grade (Alexander, Entwisle, and Dauber 1993). Moreover, the relation between academic and social competence persists throughout school (Malecki and Elliott 2002; Welsh et al. 2001). Adolescents rated highly by teachers and peers as exhibiting "socially responsible behaviors," such as complying with social rules and role expectations, cooperating, and showing respect for others, also perform significantly higher on measures of academic achievement than their peers with less social maturity (Hansen 2001; Wentzel 1991a, 1991b, 1993).

The precursors of adaptive or problematic classroom behaviors are evident during the prekindergarten years in children's early temperamental characteristics and their ability to regulate their emotions and behaviors.

Temperament

A young child's temperament is thought to reflect the early origins of personality characteristics. Temperament can be broadly defined as "constitutionally based individual differences in emotional, motor, and attentional reactivity and self-regulation . . . [that] demonstrate consistency across situations, as well as relative stability over time" (Rothbart and Bates 1998, 109). A number of attributes fall under this construct, such as persistence, distractibility, activity level, attentional control, emotionality, and reactivity. The majority of research in this area has linked early temperamental characteristics in infancy with children's later social competence (see Kagan 1998; Rothbart and Bates 1998 for reviews). However, there are several reasons to expect that problematic temperamental profiles could have serious consequences for school performance. For example, distractible, nonpersistent children could be easily sidetracked by their own thoughts or movements or by peers' actions in the classroom. The difficulties this type of child experiences when following directions and completing assignments would certainly be expected to lower grades and test scores (Martin 1989). In addition, teachers may be more inclined to remove disruptive children from the classroom, which would decrease the amount of instruction these children receive (Martin 1989). Conversely, shy or inhibited children may face a different set of challenges in school settings (Henderson and Fox 1998). For example, inhibited kindergartners tend to be quieter, more subdued, and spend more time isolating themselves rather than interacting with peers (Garcia-Coll, Kagan, and Reznick 1984).

A smaller but growing body of research has connected temperamental characteristics to early language and literacy development. Bloom (1998) has noted earlier signs of language learning among children who exhibit more neutral affect (that is, are not easily excited or distressed), presumably because these children are not distracted by their own movements, like arm flailing or kicking, and are better able to sustain their attention on the speech and activities around them. In addition, toddlers' persistence, adaptability, and positive mood at thirteen months were related to advanced language production at twenty months of age (Dixon and Smith 2000). Parents' or kindergarten teachers' assessments of persistence and attentional control predict performance on school readiness scores (Schoen and Nagle 1994) and intellectual and academic scores at four years and second grade (Palisin 1986). Furthermore, children who are able to sustain their attention, while maintaining low levels of activity and negative emotionality, show more advanced literacy and numeracy skills in kindergarten (Coplan and Barber 1999) and higher reading and mathematics achievement in first grade, even after accounting for the influence of IQ (Martin and Holbrook 1985).

Although studies may focus on different aspects of temperament, converging evidence points to the importance of children's early temperamental characteristics for language and literacy acquisition.

Self-Regulation

Increasing attention in school readiness research is being focused on children's self-regulation skills, which develop during the preschool years (Rothbart and Bates 1998). Self-regulation (sometimes called executive functioning) reflects children's ability to exert cognitive and emotional control, such as focusing their attention, monitoring their emotions, and restraining impulsive behaviors (Calkins and Fox 2002; Eisenberg et al. 1995; Kochanska et al. 1996). One classic test of these competencies is to allow children to choose between receiving a more valuable treat or prize later (about fifteen minutes) or a less valuable treat at any time during the waiting period (Mischel, Shoda, and Rodriguez 1989). Their facility with managing their behaviors and delaying gratification until the end of the task is indicative of their general ability to self-regulate in a variety of environments. Furthermore, if preschoolers are able to distract themselves by redirecting their attention away from the tempting treat in front of them, they not only score as more regulated, but teachers rate their social competence highly, and they experience more acceptance by their peers than do children who struggle with this task (Raver and Bancroft 1999). Not surprisingly, these skills are highly related to literacy and numeracy development in the preschool years (Li-Grining, Pittman, and Chase-Lansdale in review) and social competence in early elementary school (Eisenberg et al. 1995; Murray and Kochanska 2002). In fact, preschool abilities to delay gratification have shown associations with cognitive skills in adolescence (Shoda, Mischel, and Peake 1990).

Individual differences in self-regulation appear to stem, at least in part, from variation in parenting practices. Parents' expressions of encouragement, support, and guidance as children engage in tasks enhance their mastery of self-regulation (Grolnick and Ryan 1989; Stright et al. 2001). Moreover, compelling evidence has demonstrated that distal factors like SES (Meich et al. 2001) and environmental risk (Lengua 2002), as well as more proximal parenting practices (Brody and Flor

1998; Eisenberg et al. 1995), transmit influence on children's academic and social competence via their effects on children's self-regulatory skills.

Taken together, children's academic success is inextricably linked to the social maturity they exhibit in the classroom, whether in peer interactions or when individually completing tasks. Children who lack the skills to focus their attention and curb their impulsivity, activity, or negative emotionality will face greater challenges adjusting to the demands of the classroom environment and handling the independence and responsibility that increase with each grade.

Self-Regulated Learning: Motivation and Persistence

Motivational processes, a key component of self-regulation, are also at play to engage children in learning activities and foster persistence when tasks become more challenging. Motivation involves students' values and beliefs when approaching school tasks, such as their self-efficacy beliefs, attributions, and goal orientation (for review, see Eccles and Wigfield 2002; Linnenbrink and Pintrich 2002). Essentially, if students feel efficacious, or capable of successfully finishing a task, they also tend to work harder, enroll in more challenging courses, and persevere when faced with difficult assignments. Note that this is more specific and directly tied to task performance than a general sense of self-worth or self-esteem. Similarly, as children encounter failures in their schoolwork, the source of their poor achievement can be attributed to a stable, individual characteristic, like intelligence, or they can link their performance to modifiable behaviors such as low effort or not asking for assistance. Over time, as children build up a history of academic successes and failures, their goals when assigned a task may range from deliberately trying to improve their competence and understand the material (mastery goal), to attempting to gauge their self-worth and ability level by competing with peers (performance goals), or minimally satisfying the requirements with little investment or interest (work-avoidant goals) (Kamins and Dweck 1999; Linnenbrink and Pintrich 2002; Meece and Miller 1999). In reading research, intrinsic motivation is positively associated with enhanced reading comprehension and more reading for enjoyment among students, above and beyond the contribution of cognitive skills (Cox and Guthrie 2001; Wigfield and Guthrie 1997).

Clearly, children's cognitive and behavioral skills are related to their academic motivation and engagement in learning. Students who have experienced a sense of mastery in the past when learning challenging material may be more likely to persist with other demanding tasks and try a variety of cognitive strategies to accomplish their academic goals (Linnenbrink and Pintrich 2003). Children may also begin to seek out additional learning experiences outside of school for personal enjoyment or interest (Cox and Guthrie 2001). These interrelations are more evident among older children because adolescents have developed metacognitive skills that enable them to better self-evaluate and monitor their learning and performance (Eccles, Wigfield, and Schiefele 1998). For example, adolescent students may periodically stop reading a textbook to test their memory for the passage they just read, or they may reread a text and apply various cognitive strategies if they are having difficulty understanding what they are reading. Adolescents can also recognize the value of acquiring academic skills and knowledge and may put forth a great deal of effort even when the tasks do not seem particularly interesting or important to them (Eccles, Wigfield, and Schiefele 1998; Linnenbrink and Pintrich 2002).

However, children's motivation and self-efficacy also appear linked to environmental influences, especially the feedback they receive from parents and teachers. For instance, when students solve a difficult math problem, they could be praised for their prolonged efforts and use of different methods to solve the problem or be told, "You are so good at math." In other words, instructors could focus on the process of children's learning or on a global trait or talent of the child (Kamins and Dweck 1999). But what happens the next time a child attempts to solve a challenging math problem and fails? If he or she previously received process-oriented feedback, then the student is more likely to attribute the failure to a lack of effort or a problem with the strategy they selected. Conversely, if a child's past praise or criticism were person-oriented, then the student will tend to internalize the failure and believe that he or she is simply not capable of successfully mastering certain kinds of math problems. As this learned helplessness continues, students often disengage from academic pursuits and avoid asking for assistance in the classroom (Ryan, Pintrich, and Midgley 2001).

Experimental studies have been modestly successful in changing students' achievement attributions and increasing their engagement. For example, in one intervention study, students were given fewer simple, teacher-directed tasks and were instead assigned more complex reading and writing assignments that required longer completion times and peer collaboration. At the end of the experiment, students reported less task avoidance and were also less motivated by the final grade or outperforming their fellow classmates (Meece and Miller 1999). Furthermore, when students were given process-oriented feedback about their effort or strategy use, they were significantly less likely to display helpless responses or negative personal attributions about their performance than children who received evaluative feedback that was connected to their traits or abilities (Kamins and Dweck 1999). Although it remains unclear how these motivational processes develop among younger children in the preschool and early elementary years, children's early school experiences are likely to contribute to their later self-efficacy beliefs, attributions, and academic goals.

Thus we see that children themselves are an important part of the equation when considering their literacy development. They are active agents in this process. The language, temperament, self-regulation, motivation, and other characteristics they bring to learning contribute significantly to their success or failure in school by influencing how they respond to learning opportunities and by shaping how parents and teachers may respond to them.

III

Once Children Get to School

6

The Classroom
Teaching and Learning

These reforms express my deep belief in our public schools and their
mission to build the mind and character of every child, from every
background, in every part of America.

President George W. Bush

Forget the Fads—The Old Way Works Best.

Newsweek

Teaching children how to read, write, and do math may be one of the
most difficult but important endeavors facing a literate society—especially if that society has decided that literacy is a right and not a privi-
lege (No Child Left Behind Act, www.ed.gov). Although the characteristics children bring to each classroom must be recognized (see
particularly chapter 5), the contribution of variability in how and what
we teach children cannot be ignored. Just as there are key parenting
practices that contribute to children's early literacy development (see
chapter 4), the instructional practices of teachers are also powerful
agents of child development. Accumulating evidence documents striking variation in the amount and kind of instruction being offered to
children in our schools. Beyond instruction, variation in teachers' facility organizing the school day and efficiently managing transitions
between activities significantly influences the amount of time available
for effective instruction (Cameron, Connor, and Morrison 2004; Taylor et al. 2000).

Further, what is regarded as meaningful instruction also varies
substantially among classrooms. Some teachers provide a literature-
rich environment with books well displayed and available to children.
They offer students many opportunities to read and write indepen-

dently and encourage their development as literate members of the classroom community (Dahl and Freppon 1995). Other teachers focus on the basic skills children need to read—letter knowledge, phonological awareness, phonics, and how to decode words they do not know (Foorman et al. 1998). Such foundational skills are critical to children's literacy development (Snow, Burns, and Griffin 1998). The contrast of these two approaches epitomizes the "Reading Wars"—whole language, or meaning-based instruction, versus phonics, or code-based instruction. In this chapter, we will discuss the roots of the reading wars and then examine how these historical debates might be better understood in light of the significant variability in amounts and type of instruction found across America's classrooms, the specificity of the effects of schooling, and how the effectiveness of instruction varies according to the individual characteristics children bring with them to the classroom.

A Century of Reading Wars

The reading wars are not a recent controversy. The history of reading instruction is characterized by contention and division. Indeed, it has been argued that the reading wars reflect a larger debate in the field of education that finds its early roots in romanticism and the traditional versus progressive movements (Loveless 2001). The debate is mirrored in the content areas of math and science but is most salient in reading. Until the early 1800s, reading instruction in the United States had been accomplished using the Webster speller (introduced in 1782) and then the McGuffey readers, which incorporated both alphabetic and phonics methods while extolling the virtues of honesty, thrift, and kindness. Then, in 1832, John Miller Keagy introduced the whole-word method (Ravitch 2001; Davis 1987). Proponents of the method, also advocates of romanticism, stated that learning to read should not be "tiresome drudgery" (as exemplified by the McGuffey reader) but rather should be "as natural as learning to talk" (Ravitch 2001)—this statement should sound familiar to those familiar with contemporary whole language approaches (Goelman, Oberg, and Smith 1984). In the 1930s, the Dick and Jane series, using the whole-word method, gained widespread popularity through the 1950s, until *Why Johnny Can't Read* (Flesch 1955) was first published. Coupled with rising criticism of public education, this book reached the national best-seller list and further charged the bitter debate—the book was touted by the general press as the solution to reading problems but was rejected by educators and educational researchers as based on opinion rather than science (Ravitch 2001).

In 1967, Jeanne Chall published her seminal book, *Learning to Read: The Great Debate* (1967), which had been commissioned by the Carnegie Corporation of New York. This research was supposed to settle the debate once and for all. However, as Chall soon discovered, comparing reading methods' efficacy was quite difficult. No one method completely eliminated children's reading failure, and teachers frequently used a combination of methods. Even when new methods were introduced, the old survived. Chall observed that phonics survived in the 1930s because some teachers "got out their old phonics charts, *closed the doors,* and hoped the supervisor or principal would not enter unannounced" (7). Nevertheless, when she reviewed the available research, Chall determined that an early emphasis on decoding was critical for children's reading success.

But bubbling underneath the surface throughout the 1970s was the notion that learning to read was like learning to talk or that it was a "psycholinguistic guessing game" (Goodman 1970). These ideas formed the foundation of the whole language approach. Its proponents suggested that learning to read was a natural process; children needed only to be exposed to "authentic" text and coached by their teacher to enable them to succeed (Goodman 1984; Dahl and Freppon 1995). Educators' enthusiastic response to whole language was, in part, a reaction to the overemphasis on script, drill, and workbooks that was typical of the 1970s and early 1980s (Ravitch 2001). Whole language approaches deemphasized the basal reader, tended to empower teachers, and favored using interesting books and instilling a joy for reading. Nevertheless, researchers in the 1990s rediscovered what Chall had found in the 1960s—that many children needed explicit decoding instruction if they were to become successful readers (Langenberg 2000). And so the reading wars were reignited and raged once more throughout the 1990s and into the new millennium.

Learning to Read versus Learning to Talk

Skills that come easily to children, like talking, are not embroiled in such political debates—at least not on such a grand scale. Why might this be? Perhaps because language is a common human characteristic found within every human society—and reading is not (Liberman 1997). Given a marginally acceptable linguistic environment, adequate hearing, and cognitive wherewithal, all children learn to talk—there appears to be a "language instinct" (Pinker 1994). That is not to say that the linguistic environment doesn't matter. Most certainly it does. Otherwise, all of us would speak the same language and all children would have very similar language abilities. But in fact, as we discussed in chapters 4 and 5, children show appreciable variability in the language abilities with which they begin school, and a large part of this variability can be traced to the home linguistic environment (Hart and Risley 1995). Nevertheless, babies babble, toddlers talk, and three-year-olds carry on conversations. The same robust development is not evident for literacy. There *are* children who learn to read and do math almost regardless of instruction. Most children, given adequate instruction, do become literate members of society. Unfortunately, too many children (by some estimates 30 percent) fail to reach functional levels of literacy (National Center for Educational Statistics 2003b). Some are learning disabled, fewer have language or other communication challenges, but a great many receive instruction that is simply not effective for them. It is the latter group of children who are invariably at the heart of the reading wars and have been for the last century.

Variability in Amount of Instruction

At least part of the reason that instruction may not be effective for many children is that they do not receive enough of it. As early as the 1970s, studies revealed startling disparities in the amount of instruction children received throughout the school year, which had an effect on how much children learned (Durkin 1987; Brophy 1979). Although the lengths of the school day and year placed upper limits on the amount of time available for student learning within each day, the efficient use of time varied greatly among classrooms. In one study, 36 percent of American first graders' days were spent in nonacademic activities (Stevenson 1992). In contrast, only 15 percent of the school day in China was spent in nonacademic activities. Results for fifth graders mirrored these results.

Not only are there cross-cultural differences, there are differences between classrooms within the same school district (Meyer, Linn, and Hastings 1991; Pressley et al. 1998). For example, in one study, the amount of time spent in nonacademic activities varied from as much as an hour and a half to as little as forty minutes in first grade classrooms in a midwestern city (Connor, Morrison, and Katch 2004). This translates to a staggering 6.4 hours per week, or 230 hours per school year, of disparity in the amount of instruction children in the same school district received. These differences were consistent across subjects— teachers who spent more time in language arts also spent more time in math and science. And they were consistent from year to year— amounts of academic instruction time teachers provided in one year predicted the amount of instruction time teachers provided the next year.

We conjecture that a number of factors contributes to the variability in the amount of instruction children need. Teachers' skill managing the course of the school day and maintaining the engagement of their students is clearly one important factor. However, the students in the classroom also contribute to the learning environment in important ways. As we discussed in chapter 5, children's self-regulation and work-related skills are directly related to their academic achievement. Children who are better able to attend to and engage with learning activities make it easier for teachers to increase the amount of time dedicated to instruction. In contrast, children who act out, wander about the classroom, and do not pay attention may act to reduce the amount of effective instruction provided to all of the students in the classroom.

Specificity of Schooling Effects

However, understanding how much instruction children need may not be enough to ensure learning because converging evidence reveals that the effect of schooling is highly specific (Christian et al. 2000). Although it is going too far to say that children learn only what we teach them, it is fair to say that the impact of instruction does not generalize across domains (for example, decoding, comprehending, counting, math concepts) as much as has been portrayed by broad developmental theories. These theories (like Piaget's) portray children as progressing through a series of developmental stages that affect their literacy skills in a broad and uniform manner (Piaget 1960). As we stated before, cross-cultural research indicates that American children spend much less time in math instruction than do their Japanese and Chinese peers (Stevenson 1992), which may explain much of why American children achieve lower math scores.

One way to examine the specific effect of schooling on cognitive development is to examine skill growth for children who just make or just miss the rather arbitrary birthday cutoff date school districts set for school entry. Thus the children are the same age—but half the children start kindergarten, while the other half start first grade. In this way schooling versus maturational (or more general developmental) effects on children's growth can be examined separately. If both groups demonstrate similar rates of growth in a particular skill, then that skill is most likely a product of maturation—or other age-related factors. On the other hand, if children in first grade demonstrate greater rates of skill growth than their age peers in kindergarten, then that skill is most likely a product of schooling (Morrison and Connor 2002).

Using this method, research has clearly shown there is not a systematic schooling effect for some skills, whereas for other skills, there is a distinct schooling effect—schooling *is* critical for growth. The timing of these effects varies systematically across grades as well. These patterns in several studies are presented in table 6.1. Schooling effects are evident for alphabet recognition, word decoding, phonemic (individual sounds within words) awareness, general knowledge, addition, short-term memory, sentence memory, and visuospatial memory. On the other hand, schooling effects are not evident for receptive vocabulary, conservation of number and quantity, addition strategies, and narrative coherence. Children demonstrate similar rates of growth in these skills regardless of whether they are in kindergarten or first grade. These findings are observed with different children in different schools and in some cases, different countries (Christian, Bachman, and Morrison 2001). What happens when we look at this broad range of skills for children within one school district? Indeed, we see the same effects.

Table 6.1. Summary of School-Related and Age-Related Effects from "School Cutoff" Investigations

Grade	School-Related Effects	Age-Related or Nonschooling Effects
Language and literacy skills		
K and I	Alphabet recognition[1,2]	Receptive vocabulary[1,2,3]
K and I	Word decoding[1,2,4]	Subsyllabic segmentation[2,5]
K and I	Syllabic segmentation[2,5]	
I	Phonemic segmentation[2,3,5]	
I	General information[1,2]	
K	Emergent literacy[4]	Narrative coherence[6]
K and I	Components of narrative[10]	
Mathematical skills		
K and I	Addition[7,8]	Conservation of number[7]
K and I	Standardized math I	
I	Addition strategies (Japan)[8]	
General cognition		
K	Short-term verbal memory[5]	Knowledge of syntactic constituents[9]
I	Sentence memory[9]	
K and I	Production and memory[10]	
K and I	Visuospatial memory[11] (matching)	
K and I	Visuospatial memory[11] (explicit)	
K and I	Visuospatial memory[11] (implicit)	
I, 2, 3, 4	Executive function[12]	

1. Morrison, Griffith, and Frazier 1996.
2. Christian et al. 2000.
3. Bowey and Francis 1991.
4. Crone and Whitehurst 1999.
5. Morrison, Smith, and Dow-Ehrensberger 1995.
6. Frazier, Morrison, and Trabasso 1995.
7. Bisanz, Morrison, and Dunn 1995.
8. Naito and Miura 2001.
9. Ferreira and Morrison 1994.
10. Varnhagen et al. 1994.
11. Massetti and Morrison 1997.
12. McCrea, Mueller, and Parrilla 1999.

Christian et al. (2000) examined skills across domains (reading, general information, math, and so on) for eighty-nine children attending the same school district while taking into account the influence of their cognitive abilities and their parents' education. There were kindergarten but not first grade effects for letter naming. There were kindergarten and first grade effects for basic reading skills, including word decoding. There were first grade effects only for general information, mathematics, and phonemic segmentation (identifying the individual sounds in words).

These results are particularly revealing if we consider the three phonological awareness tasks that, as we will discuss, strongly predict reading success. These tasks were quite similar and differed only in the level of segmentation the child was asked to complete—syllabic, subsyllabic, and phonemic. For the syllabic segmentation task, children were asked to say the number of syllables in a word. For example, *banana* has three syllables, ba-na-na. In the subsyllabic task, children were asked to identify the onset and rime (*br* and *eak* for *break*). For the phonemic task, children were asked to count the number of individual sounds in a word. For example, *fast* has four sounds, /f-a-s-t/. As similar as these tasks were, being in kindergarten or first grade made a difference for children's performance. For syllabic segmentation, neither first grade nor kindergarten had an effect on growth in these skills. For subsyllabic segmentation, both first grade and kindergarten affected growth. In contrast, first grade but *not* kindergarten had an effect on phonemic segmentation. So here are three highly similar tasks that schooling affected very differently. Why might this be?

Linking Instruction with Children's Learning

In light of the specificity and timing of schooling effects, what is taught and what constitutes meaningful instruction are important to consider. As we have shown, the type of instruction provided, as well as the amount, varies substantially among classrooms nationwide as well as within school districts. There is accumulating evidence that we can explain the specificity and timing of schooling effects by understanding both the amount and type of instruction children receive.

Beyond the Reading Wars

As we will discuss in the next chapter, what educators teach children is guided partly by their personal experiences and by what they perceive to be important. Research indicates that, indeed, based on the goals of the educator, both whole language and phonics can be considered effective. If the teacher's goal is to instill a love of reading, then whole language is the preferred approach. In head-to-head comparisons, children in whole language classrooms tended to have more positive attitudes toward reading than did children in phonics or skill-based classrooms (Dahl and Freppon 1995; Foorman et al. 1998). However, positive attitudes toward reading do not ensure proficient reading. Research also clearly reveals that children in skill-based classrooms tended to be better at decoding text, especially if they began the school year with less knowledge of the alphabet and of the association between letters and sounds (Foorman et al. 1998). However, children in both types of classrooms did equally well, on average, on standardized tests of reading. Clearly, children benefit from both meaning-based (whole language) and skills-based (phonics) instruction. Based on this emerging evidence, educators have been calling for *balanced instruction* (Rayner et al. 2001; Taylor et al. 2000; Snow, Burns, and Griffin 1998).

Clearly, balanced instruction is an important advance. However, is it the final answer to improving literacy in America? Perhaps not. Legend has it that a successful principal was once asked how he had taken a failing school and turned it around. His reply: "We stopped teaching children the way we feed chickens. When we feed chickens," he continued, "we scatter grain in front of them and they are expected to eat it. We used to teach children the same way. We scattered the information in front of them and it was up to them to take it and use it. But that meant that some children grabbed more and some didn't get any at all. A better way, we discovered, was to figure out what each student needed and to make sure he or she got it."

New research supports the principal's notion of how to teach children. Children learn to read in different ways and at different rates. As a result, different patterns and types of instruction are more effective for them (Connor, Morrison, and Katch 2004; Foorman et al.

1998; Juel and Minden-Cupp 2000). It turns out that children respond best to instruction when teachers are cognizant of the skills their students bring to the classroom and design their instruction accordingly. This is called *individualizing instruction*.

Learning to Read

An appreciation for the potential import of individualizing instruction can be gleaned from an understanding of how children become literate. Research over the past decades has revealed important insights into this process (Neuman and Dickinson, 2001; Rayner et al. 2001; Connor, Morrison, and Katch 2004), and the fundamental role skilled reading plays in literacy is writ large. The basic process of reading includes mapping the language we speak onto written text and grasping the underlying meaning. Excellent readers do this fluently without conscious attention to letters or even words (Magliano, Trabasso, and Graesser 1999; Stanovich 1994). Yet without a complete grasp of how the sounds we speak map onto the letters we see, and how the words and sentences composed of these letters then map onto the language we speak, children may not learn to read. This metalinguistic knowledge is learned primarily when explicitly taught (Schribner and Cole 1978), although a few children may grasp the concept implicitly (Goodman 1984). There is some evidence that parents may be making these metalinguistic concepts more salient for their children through storybook reading as well as through the word and letter games they play with their children (Senechal et al. 1998). Other children gain the concepts in kindergarten or first grade when explicitly taught (Bryant, Maclean, and Bradley 1990). Children without metalinguistic awareness have tremendous difficulty learning to read (Vellutino et al. 1996). Most current research focuses on phonological awareness, which is the understanding that words are composed of phonemes or sounds (Rayner et al., 2001). However, emerging research suggests that morphological and syntactic awareness may also be important for reading comprehension (Carlisle 2000; Rego and Bryant 1993). Morphosyntactic awareness is the understanding that *-ed* at the end of a verb makes it past tense, and the common root in *criticism* and *critique* indicates that the words have similar meanings that are related to the word *critic*. Children's vocabulary and prior knowledge are also critical ingredients for proficient literacy (Neuman and Dickinson 2001; Snow, Burns, and Griffin 1998). Just as important, children need to learn to relate these metalinguistic skills to actual written text—sounds map onto letters, sound combinations map onto words, and morphemes carry meaning in written words.

In addition to decoding words, which relies on phonological awareness and understanding that letters map onto sounds, fluent reading and comprehending what has been read are also important aspects of successful reading. There are children who can read individual words beautifully but do not understand what they have read. New findings on the foundations of reading comprehension are emerging. Especially for young children, oral language and early literacy are intricately woven. There is evidence, however, that the associations between oral language and early reading may be fairly specific (Connor 2002). Certain skills, such as letter/word identification, vocabulary, and phonological awareness, appear to predict later decoding skills (Catts et al. 2001); but others, such as complex language and the ability to tell and understand stories, predict later reading comprehension (Connor, Craig, and Washington 2001; Snow and Dickinson 1990). According to the RAND group: "Reading comprehension is the process of simultaneously extracting and constructing meaning through interaction and involvement with written language. Comprehension has these elements: the reader, the text, and the activity or purpose for reading. These elements define a phenomenon—reading comprehension—that occurs within a larger sociocultural context that shapes and is shaped by the reader and that infuses each of the elements" (Snow 2001, xiii).

Complex oral language tasks (including narrative tasks) that predict reading comprehension appear to be somewhat distinct from the essentially word-level measures (such as phonological awareness, letter/word identification, and vocabulary) that predict decoding. These tasks assess mastery of more mature morphosyntactic forms, language comprehension, and pragmatic use of literate language. For example, to do well on a pretend storybook reading task, children must be familiar with the kinds of discourse that Western society associates with storybook reading, such as the more mature grammar and distinct prosody and structure of storybook language. These complex linguistic and pragmatic abilities may be very important skills for emerging readers to master because they appear to provide a foundation for developing reading comprehension skills later on. Watson (2001) suggests, "Oral language may have a broad-based influence on the acquisition of competence that is necessary to succeed in the institutions of a literate culture. It gives children an understanding of how to recruit their knowledge in ways that are relevant to text-based understanding" (52). Further, if one considers the RAND definition (Snow 2001), then complex language skills and pragmatic mastery of literate communication may provide the foundation for developing reading comprehension skills. Just as with phonological awareness, these metalinguistic skills must be mapped onto written text—the child should learn that combinations of words and morphemes in sentences and paragraphs carry the meaning of ideas, and comprehension of these ideas is enhanced by an explicit understanding of the rule-based patterns of story organization and grammar. Pragmatically, children also should learn how to read and write thoughtfully, considering the message and how it is delivered, as well as their thoughts and reactions to what they read and write. However, as we illustrated in chapter 5, children enter school varying tremendously in their oral language abilities—including their use of narrative structures and complex grammar and their notion of what the acts of reading and writing should mean.

Dimensions of Teaching

Because children arrive at school varying widely in their grasp of critical foundational skills (phonological awareness, complex language, vocabulary, narrative skills, alphabet knowledge, decoding skills, language ability), knowing what children know and hence what they need to learn is important when designing effective instruction (Rayner et al. 2001; Connor, Morrison, and Katch 2004). However, to understand the interaction between child characteristics and instruction, a more complex view is needed of exactly what instruction is.

Just as parents vary on important dimensions of parenting, teachers differ in important dimensions, including warmth/sensitivity, control/discipline, and instruction (see figure 6.1). Each dimension

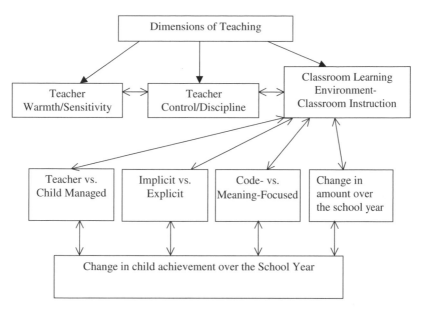

Figure 6.1. Dimensions of teaching.

has potentially important implications for children's learning. Teachers' regard for their students, their responsiveness to student questions and interests, and the emotional climate of the classroom all contribute to student achievement (Green et al. 1992; Torgesen et al. 1999; Snow, Burns, and Griffin 1998). Further, as we will discuss in more depth at the end of this chapter and in chapter 7, teachers' ability to manage and control their students' learning and behavior in the classroom also predicts student achievement (Brophy and Good 1986). In this chapter, we focus most closely on the act of instruction itself.

A quandary in the code-based (phonics) versus meaning-based (whole language) debate is that many teachers use aspects of both types of instruction but in varying amounts (Chall 1967; Taylor et al. 2000; Juel and Minden-Cupp 2000; Connor, Morrison, and Katch 2004). One-dimensional descriptions of literacy instruction tend to oversimplify what is actually happening in classrooms. A different way to think about instruction is in terms of multiple dimensions of instruction within the larger dimension (see figure 6.1). Recent research points to four crucial dimensions of instruction: (1) explicit versus implicit;

(2) code- versus meaning-focused; (3) teacher-managed versus child-managed; and (4) change in amount of instruction over time (Connor, Morrison, and Katch 2004; Juel and Minden-Cupp 2000; Taylor et al. 2000; Rayner et al. 2001). These dimensions of instruction operate simultaneously, as can be seen in figure 6.1 and in the example provided in table 6.2 for decoding instruction.

Explicit versus implicit instruction. The first dimension focuses on whether instruction is explicit or implicit in promoting growth of a particular skill, such as word decoding or reading comprehension. For example, Foorman et al. (1998) grouped classrooms along the explicit-implicit continuum, focusing on decoding skill instruction (that is, direct code, embedded code, implicit code). Specifically, if word decoding is the targeted skill, then instructional activities, such as teaching phonological awareness or teaching letter-sound correspondence, would be considered explicit because the children's attention is primarily directed to components of word-decoding strategies. In contrast, activities like defining words, in which the child's attention is more directly focused on word meaning, could still influence word-decoding skills in an implicit or incidental fashion.

As defined, explicit decoding instruction encompasses much of what has been described as code-based instruction, including teaching of phoneme-grapheme correspondences, phonological awareness (for example, onset-rime or subsyllabic segmentation, blending phonemes, segmenting phonemes), and letter names and sounds. Implicit decoding instruction includes meaning-based activities such as teachers reading to students, discussions about books, teachers and students reading together, and students reading and writing independently. Note that if reading comprehension had been the outcome of interest, different sets of instructional activities would have been defined as explicit or implicit. The definition of explicit versus implicit relies entirely on what we are trying to teach children—decoding, comprehension, math, science, and so on.

Code- versus meaning-focused instruction. For reading, instruction may focus on word-level activities (for example, alphabet, letter-sound) or higher-order activities (for example, reading comprehension, vocabulary). Yet again, observations of classroom instruction reveal that teachers provide both types of instruction, albeit in differing proportions (Connor, Morrison, and Katch 2004). For example, a teacher might focus on teaching the correspondence between letters and sounds in a particular word (code-focused activity) before she discusses what the word means (meaning-focused), whereas another teacher might focus solely on discussing the meaning of the word or encourage children to figure out the meaning on their own as they come across it in the books they are reading.

Teacher-managed versus child-managed instruction. The third dimension refers to the degree to which instructional activity and the child's attention are primarily under the direction of the teacher (for example, when the teacher is explicitly instructing the children in word-decoding strategies) or primarily controlled by the child (such as in sustained silent reading). Rayner et al. (2001) described methods of instruction that included this dimension, such as prescriptive (teacher-managed) and responsive (teacher-managed moving toward child-managed). This dimension should not be confused with instructional styles such as "child-centered" and "teacher-directed" (Bredekemp and Copple 1997). Child-centered activities, such as discussions about books, would be considered teacher-managed, whereas teacher-directed activities, such as completing worksheets, would be considered child-managed.

For example, in the following exchange between the teacher and her students, the teacher is managing the interaction:

> TEACHER: The next line says "id." What is that word /l/ / I d /?
> CLASS: Little?
> TEACHER: No.
> CLASS: Lid.
> TEACHER: Good! /l I d/.

Sustained silent reading, where children select a book of their choice and read either silently or quietly with a partner, is an example of a child-managed activity.

Change in amount of instructional activities over the school year. The fourth dimension addresses the *timing* of when a particular type of instruction is provided. Timing might be across grades—we would expect first grade teachers to spend more time on basic decoding compared to fourth grade teachers. But timing within grades also appears to influence children's literacy development. One provocative finding in the Juel and Minden-Cupp (2000) study revealed that some teachers changed their instructional emphasis over the course of the first grade school year. For example, one teacher began the year with a strong focus on explicit, teacher-managed decoding instruction that tapered off as the year progressed and as children mastered basic skills. In this class, children with weaker fall reading skills (that is, children in the low reading group) achieved stronger spring decoding scores than did children in the low reading group in other classrooms. Thus changing the emphasis of instruction in response to children's changing abilities appears to be an important dimension of instruction both within and across grades.

The Effect of Dimensions of Instruction for First Graders

In a recent study (Connor, Morrison, and Katch 2004), we directly examined the nature and impact of these instructional domains on decoding growth in first grade students. We observed their classrooms during the fall, winter, and spring of the school year and recorded the amount of time teachers spent in various language arts activities. These activities were then coded according to the dimensions of instruction (teacher- versus child-managed, explicit versus implicit decoding). The dimension of code- versus meaning-focused divided in exactly the same way as explicit versus implicit, so the two dimensions were combined (see table 6.2). The change in amount over the school year of each variable was noted as well.

Surprisingly, the overall number of minutes teachers provided of language arts instruction had no direct influence on children's decoding skill growth. Rather, the effect of amount and type of instruction depended on the skills with which the students began first grade—that is, there were "child by instruction interactions." Children who started first grade with weaker decoding and vocabulary skills achieved greater decoding skill growth when they were in classrooms where the teacher provided more time in teacher-managed explicit decoding activities (TME) (for example, teaching letter-sound associations), especially at the beginning of the year. However, these children also learned to de-

Table 6.2 Instructional Activities Comprising Each Dimension of Instruction: Teacher- versus Child-Managed and Explicit versus Implicit Decoding

	Teacher-Managed	Child-Managed
Explicit or Code- Focused	Alphabet activity Letter sight-sound Initial consonant stripping Word segmentation	Spelling
Implicit or Meaning- Focused	Vocabulary Teacher read aloud Student read aloud, choral Teacher-managed group writing Writing instruction Teacher model writing Discussion Conventions of print Listening comprehension	Student read aloud, individual Sustained silent reading Reading comprehension activity Student independent writing Student group writing

Source: Connor, Morrison, and Katch 2004.

code better when the teacher started the year with smaller amounts of child-managed implicit instruction (CMI) (such as sustained silent reading), but increased the amount over the school year.

The exact patterns of instruction children received had a dramatic impact on their growth in first grade. As depicted in figure 6.2, two children who started first grade with identical vocabulary and decoding scores (half a year below grade level) showed dramatically different rates of decoding growth depending on whether they received a more or less effective instructional pattern. As can be seen, the child exposed to a more effective instructional regime achieved a decoding score increase of almost two grade equivalents. In contrast, the other child, receiving a less effective instructional pattern, demonstrated only limited growth in decoding scores, or less than half a grade equivalent. The children's fitted spring decoding scores differed by more than two grade equivalents.

Children who began the year with strong vocabulary and decod-

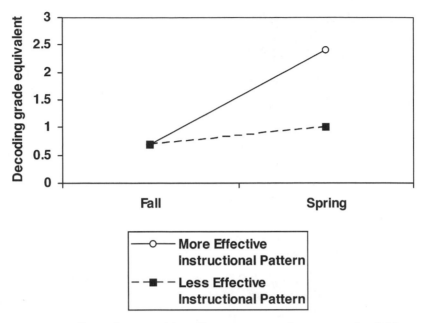

Figure 6.2. Effects of more and less effective patterns of instruction for children who began the school year with low vocabulary and low decoding scores. (*Source:* Connor, Morrison, and Katch 2004.)

ing skills achieved greater reading growth when they were in classrooms where the teacher provided more time in CMI all year long (for example, sustained independent silent reading). Amount of TME had little effect at all on their reading scores. Although these children's decoding skills improved regardless of the pattern of instruction, children who received the more effective pattern of instruction were, by the end of the year, about half a grade ahead of their peers who received the less effective pattern of instruction.

Even more intriguing, some children started first grade with strong vocabulary but weaker decoding skills. For these children, high amounts of CMI instruction all year long in combination with high amounts of TME instruction led to greater decoding skill growth. Comparing more and less effective patterns of instruction yielded a full grade difference in reading skills by the end of the year (see figure 6.3). For children with weaker vocabulary but stronger decoding skills, less CMI in the fall but more in the spring and less TME led to greater decoding skill growth. Contrasting more and less effective patterns of

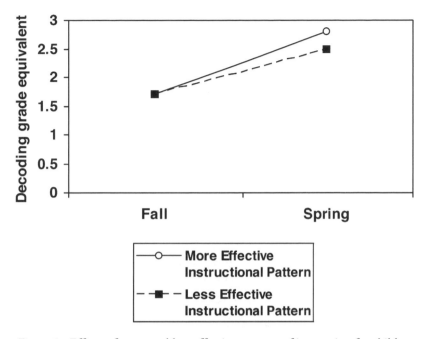

Figure 6.3. Effects of more and less effective patterns of instruction for children who began the school year with high vocabulary and high decoding scores. (*Source:* Connor, Morrison, and Katch 2004.)

instruction revealed more than one grade equivalent difference in spring decoding (see figure 6.4).

The impact of these child by instruction interactions are more dramatic when we consider what happens to actual students. David and Patrick (not their real names) began first grade with vocabulary skills that fell below expectations for children their age (see figure 6.5). They knew only a few letters of the alphabet and could not read the simple words that many of their classmates could decode easily. Overall, David's teacher provided 10.4 minutes of TME per day and 11.8 minutes of CMI per day in the fall, increasing to 31.0 minutes of CMI per day in the spring. Patrick's teacher provided only 3.5 minutes of TME per day but 26.8 minutes of CMI per day in the fall, increasing to 38.2 minutes of CMI per day in the spring, which is a fairly steady amount. Thus, according to the model, David was receiving a more effective pattern of instruction than was Patrick and would be expected to achieve greater growth in decoding scores by the spring than Patrick.

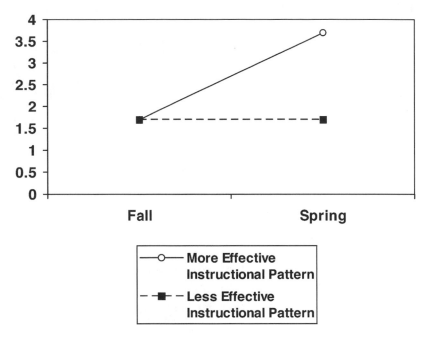

Figure 6.4. Effects of more and less effective patterns of instruction for children who began the school year with low vocabulary and high decoding scores. (*Source:* Connor, Morrison, and Katch forthcoming.)

This was indeed the case. David achieved an observed gain of fourteen points compared to Patrick, who gained only six points. Although David started first grade with a decoding score well below Patrick's, his spring decoding score was higher than Patrick's (see figure 6.5). Note that neither child achieved grade-appropriate decoding scores by the spring of his first grade year (grade-equivalent = 1.9). Both children needed substantially more time participating in TME instructional activities and/or lower CMI amounts in the fall, increasing more as the year progressed.

The ongoing importance of classroom instruction is illustrated by following David into second grade. Here, on average, children with lower fall decoding scores achieved greater decoding skill growth when they received higher amounts of TME. Unfortunately, David received less than a minute per day of TME and, as depicted in figure 6.5, his decoding skills stagnated. By the end of second grade, his reading skills were seriously delayed.

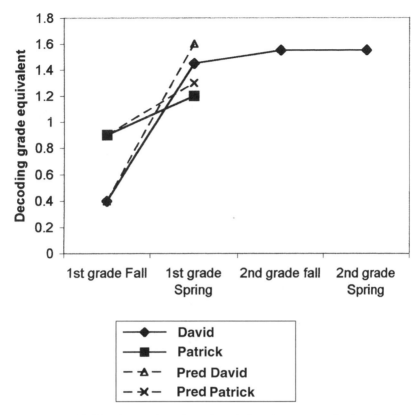

Figure 6.5. Children's actual and predicted decoding scores during the first grade. Closed shapes represent actual scores (David; Patrick). Open shape represents fitted spring decoding scores (Pred David; Pred Patrick). David and Patrick both had low fall vocabulary scores relative to the mean for the sample. Based on their fall vocabulary and decoding scores, David was in a classroom with a more effective pattern of instruction for him, and Patrick was in a classroom with a less effective pattern of instruction for him.

Not surprisingly, we find child by instruction interactions for reading comprehension growth as well. Third graders with lower reading comprehension skills in the fall achieved greater reading comprehension skill growth in classrooms with greater amounts of time spent in teacher-managed explicit reading comprehension activities, but less time in *child*-managed explicit reading comprehension activities. In contrast, children with *stronger* fall reading comprehension skills achieved greater reading comprehension growth when they were in classrooms with *more* time spent in child-managed explicit reading comprehension activities but *less* in teacher-managed (Connor, Morrison, and Petrella 2004).

Providing Individualized Instruction—Can It Be Done?

These dramatic results clearly imply that by understanding children's strengths and weaknesses and mapping them to appropriate kinds of instruction, teachers can be more mindful of how their practices will affect each student in their classroom. The dilemma, of course, is that individualizing instruction inserts a level of complexity into designing and implementing effective classroom instruction, especially if teachers' classrooms include many students with very different skill levels, cultures, and languages. However, it can be done. A recent series of studies (Taylor et al. 2000; Westat 2001; Wharton-McDonald, Pressley, and Hampston 1998) examined common elements of schools that "beat the odds" with important insights for individualizing instruction. These studies consistently identified four characteristics of schools that effectively supported reading outcomes for children at risk for academic failure. These indicators were: (1) time on task and individualized instruction; (2) ongoing use of child assessment to guide classroom practice; (3) use of small groups for instruction; and (4) effective teachers. We discuss each in turn.

Time on task and individualized instruction. Across studies (Taylor et al. 2000; Westat 2001; Wharton-McDonald, Pressley, and Hampston 1998), a consistent finding was that the more time children spent learning to read, the better they read. This is not a new or surprising finding. Efforts toward individualized instruction were also a hallmark of effective teachers and schools. Wharton-McDonald, Pressley, and Hampston note that the effective teachers in their study used "some mixture of direct skills instruction and 'authentic' whole-language-type activities" (111). If time on task is coupled with individualized instructional approaches, then the chances of a particular child experiencing effective instruction increases. For example, had Patrick's teacher provided more time in language arts instruction and used more equal amounts of TME and CMI, our estimates predict, Patrick's spring decoding score would have reached grade level. However, had the additional time been spent in CMI, he might have demonstrated less growth in decoding. In fact, Wharton-McDonald and her colleagues observed that the most effective teachers in their study "provided individualized instruction and review for students who needed it" (114).

Ongoing use of child assessment to guide classroom practice. In schools that beat the odds, children achieved greater growth in literacy skills in the schools that incorporated some form of systematic internal assessment of students' ongoing progress. One principal related "that the teachers had learned how to confront [assessment] data, to keep data in front of them, to use data to identify specific strategies to help struggling readers, [and] to provide support in the implementation of strategies" (Taylor et al. 2000, 141). Given the observed interactions between children's fall vocabulary and decoding skills and TMI and CMI amount and change, such assessment feedback must be considered crucial in designing and monitoring effective classroom practices. Individualized instruction can be implemented effectively only if there is a good grasp of children's strengths and weaknesses. Implicit in this school's attitude was that assessment was a tool for creating more individualized and effective instructional practices that changed as children's skills changed.

Unfortunately, externally administered test results are typically not delivered in a timely fashion, nor are they frequent enough to be used to guide instructional practices. Further, many teachers have negative beliefs about testing and have limited training and experience designing and administering assessments that might be useful in guiding practice (Gellman, Guarino, and Witte 2001). Professional development and preservice education programs that provide training in assessment and psychometrics may offer opportunities to promote individualized instruction indirectly by helping teachers appropriately monitor their students' literacy development. We discuss this more fully in the next chapter.

Use of small groups for instruction. One of the most difficult aspects of individualized instruction is implementation. One promising strategy is the use of small groups based on children's abilities. In schools that beat the odds, a common element among effective teachers was the use of small-group instruction (Wharton-McDonald, Pressley, and Hampston 1998; Taylor et al. 2000). Taylor et al. noted:

"In all of the most effective schools, the basis for forming small groups was perceived [student] ability. . . . Even so, the teachers in the most effective schools were very aware of the need to make sure that the groups were flexible, that students moved to another group when their performance (as measured by the internal school-based monitoring system) merited movement. The importance of school-wide monitoring cannot be underestimated in this regard" (146). Thus small groups combined with monitoring students' progress may be an effective method of providing individualized instruction.

Nevertheless, one of the great barriers that we confront in education is the number of children who come to school without the self-regulation skills needed to succeed in small groups. As we discussed in chapter 5, children vary widely in their ability to sit still and sustain their attention to the task at hand. Thus understanding the role of self-regulation and its sources of influence will be crucial.

Effective teachers. "Teachers who obtained high [student] achievement were masterful classroom managers. They managed not only student behavior—preventing misbehavior before it could occur—but time, activities, student interactions, and outside resource people as well. Their management efforts clearly involved both planned and impromptu decisions. . . . The high-achievement teachers were consistently well prepared. They knew what they wanted to teach, their lessons were well planned, and they always had their materials ready and close at hand" (Wharton-McDonald, Pressley, and Hampston 1998, 120).

Further, effective teachers followed predictable patterns of activities but remained flexible and would pursue other topics that were relevant. And they would provide mini-lessons when needed. In other words, effective teachers were able to provide substantial amounts of time in relevant activities. Further, they were able to use ongoing assessment to monitor students' progress and were able to tailor instruction to children's needs through flexible small-group instruction and mini-lessons. "The most effective teachers . . . managed, on average, to engage virtually all of their students in the work of the classroom" (Taylor et al. 2000, 158). Effective teachers were better able to provide individualized instruction. Less effective teachers "struggled to complete morning routines and begin instruction . . . explaining that their morning was 'chaotic' often attributing this to some unexpected change in routine" (Wharton-McDonald, Pressley, and Hampston 1998, 120). Unfortunately, in these studies, only about one-half of the teachers in schools that beat the odds were identified as effective. The percentage was lower, about 30 percent, in less effective schools. We will focus more carefully on teachers and their training in the next chapter.

Looking for the Silver Bullet?

The most sophisticated educational research being done today tries to establish the causal effect of various school-, curriculum-, and classroom-level interventions on children's learning. New calls for research encourage the use of randomized studies following models provided by medical researchers. Underlying all is the notion that we will find a silver bullet—the perfect curriculum or the high-quality program that will meet the needs of all children. The problem is that many of these studies examine distal factors rather than the proximal factors of children and teachers interacting in the classroom. At the level of individual child outcomes, school- and classroom-based programs that are considered high quality for one child (that is, positive outcomes) may be considered poor quality for another (negative outcomes). For example, substantial amounts of CMI for a first grade child with high vocabulary and high decoding skills may promote optimal development, whereas the same amount of CMI for a child with low vocabulary and low decoding skills may be detrimental to progress. Further, an effective program for first graders would probably not be as effective for third graders. Thus there doesn't appear to be a quick fix or a silver bullet that will prevent academic failure. Rather, systematic application of research that takes into account the specificity of schooling effects, the strengths and weaknesses children bring to the classroom (and the effect of ongoing parenting), the multiple dimensions of instruction, and the complex system that they create will be critical to improving literacy in America.

We have seen how variable teaching contributed to variability in children's outcomes. At this point we need to ask: What produces this variability in teachers? In the next chapter we will look at who our teachers are and how we prepare them for teaching.

7

Teacher Qualifications, Training, and Knowledge

We give our teachers a great responsibility: to shape the minds and hopes of our children. We owe them our thanks and our praise and our support.

President George W. Bush

Teachers themselves agree that their preparation has been inadequate and the current system of in-services is inadequate. They're desperate for help.

Judith A. Renyi

Chapter 6 highlighted the striking variation in amount and types of instruction being offered to children and its direct effect on their learning. We also discussed effective instruction and the skills of effective teachers—and how crucial these skills and abilities appear to be. In this chapter we ask, do we have the teachers we need to provide effective instruction? Unfortunately, as a nation, the answer is we do not, uniformly—yet, as in other areas of education, there is contention and misunderstanding. Some experts say the teachers we have now are just what we need; it is only that they are undervalued and underpaid (Darling-Hammond and Youngs 2002; Crosby 2002). Others recognize weaknesses in the teaching profession and observe that we need tighter regulations and more rigorous credentialing procedures (Wang and Walberg 2001). There are those who claim that these very procedures prevent highly qualified persons from entering the profession; teacher education doesn't make a difference, only verbal skills and knowledge of content areas do (Kanstoroom and Finn 1999). Some view teaching as a craft (Shavelson and Towne 2002); others view it as a profession analogous to medicine (U.S. House of Representatives 2002). Unfortunately, the research base for analyzing this crucial issue is under-whelming, with opinion largely provided in books, rather than in peer-reviewed journal articles, and too often based on personal experience, politics, and conflicting research studies. In this chapter, we review the research that is available and discuss strategies that have supported teachers' development as professionals both before they begin to teach as well as after they enter the classroom. We also discuss why, as a na-tion, we seem to be unable to keep highly qualified teachers in the pro-fession overall and with the students who need them the most.

Not only is good research on the effects of teacher quality and training sparse, but accumulating evidence reveals that teachers do not use research to guide their practice (Littlewood 2001). Rather, they rely on their personal and childhood experiences and the advice of other teachers. However, as we discussed in chapter 6, teaching children how to read, write, and grow as literate members of society is a highly tech-nical endeavor—one that is not intuitively grasped or naturally occur-ring. An understanding of the foundational skills children must ac-quire and how to instill these skills and to make the transition from "learning to read to reading to learn" may be found only in rigorous re-search. In this chapter, we will discuss the need to improve rapport and foster greater ongoing interaction between researchers and teachers, including the need for higher-quality educational research.

Who Is Teaching?

There is evidence that the teaching profession does not attract the most qualified students. Research reveals that for students who in-tended to major in education, the mean SAT score in 1998 was 964, fifty-two points lower than was the average for all college-bound se-niors (Palmaffy 1999). The SAT for students actually pursuing a degree in education was slightly higher. Still, education majors were more likely to be in the bottom quartile and less likely to be in the top quar-tile of their class than any other major (Henke et al. 1996). And this may be important because teachers' verbal aptitude scores are related to their students' achievement (Ehrenberg and Brewer 1995; Ferguson 1991; Ferguson and Ladd 1996; Ferguson 1990).

Compounding this situation is that young adults who do pursue a degree in education frequently receive training that inadequately prepares them for the complex and demanding job of teaching children. Nor are they adequately supported once they enter the classroom (Kauffman et al. 2002). Alarmingly low percentages of American teachers feel "very well prepared" to face the challenges of teaching (Lewis et al. 1999):

- Only 48 percent of teachers feel very well prepared to implement new teaching methods.
- 54 percent of teachers teach children with limited English proficiency or who are culturally diverse. 71 percent teach children with disabilities. However, only 20 percent of teachers feel very well prepared to meet the needs of these children.
- Only 28 percent of teachers feel well prepared to use student performance assessments to inform instruction.
- Only 36 percent feel very well prepared to implement state or district curriculum and performance standards.
- Only 20 percent of teachers feel well prepared to integrate educational technology into classroom instruction.

Yet an overwhelming percentage of America's teachers hold a bachelor's degree, and nearly half hold a master's degree (Lewis et al. 1999). Further, 93 percent of elementary school teachers hold a regular or advanced teaching credential, with an additional 6 percent holding provisional, probationary, or temporary certificates (DOE 2002).

Why don't teachers feel prepared? They have attended college. They have completed coursework and internships to obtain teaching credentials. They have practiced in classrooms under the supervision of mentor teachers. Professional development is frequently a negotiated or legislated opportunity. What is going on? Some experts have suggested that colleges of education do not provide the teaching and learning experiences that educators need to become effective teachers (Kanstoroom and Finn 1999). Studies have shown that even experienced teachers have insufficient knowledge of language elements and are unprepared to teach foundational reading skills (Moats 1994). Whatever the case, there is a clear consensus that we need more qualified teachers in the classroom (No Child Left Behind Act, 2002). In the next section, we take a closer look at teacher qualifications and how well these qualifications predict children's literacy development.

Teacher Qualifications

There is accumulating evidence that teachers' credentials, experience, and years of education do make a difference in children's achievement (Darling-Hammond 2000; Connor et al. in review). Although some argue that the process of credentialing tends to discourage more qualified persons from becoming teachers (Kanstoroom and Finn 1999; DOE 2002), clearly teachers' training and qualifications, as they pertain to teacher quality, deserve attention. Yet as we have discussed in the previous chapters, if we are to improve literacy in America, then an examination of more proximal factors—such as teachers' practices, how they learn them, and what affects them—may be more worthwhile. As we saw with instruction, "quality" is not a one-dimensional construct. Rather, what might be considered high-quality instruction for one child might be poor quality and ineffective for another. A more useful notion of teacher qualification might be teacher effectiveness, which would relate to the specific child outcomes of interest: reading, writing, communication skills, engagement, motivation, higher-order thinking, and so on, which are all child outcomes that are important in a literate society.

Across disciplines, there is converging evidence that teachers' practices are related to student achievement (Connor, Morrison, and Katch 2004; Brophy and Good 1986; Taylor et al. 2000; Wharton-McDonald, Pressley, and Hampston 1998; Stigler and Hiebert 1999). We presented several examples in chapter 6. Additionally, "effective teachers appear to be effective with students of all achievement levels" (Wright, Horn, and Sanders 1997, 63).

However, the factors that predict effective teaching are less apparent. In the mid-1960s, the Coleman report indicated that teachers' verbal ability was related to students' academic success. The effect of teacher education, experience, and credentials was much less evident (Coleman et al. 1966; DOE 2002; Kanstoroom and Finn 1999). More recently, converging evidence indicates that specific teacher qualifications are related to students' achievement (Darling-Hammond and Youngs 2002). These include teachers':

- general academic and verbal ability;
- subject matter knowledge;
- knowledge about teaching and learning as reflected in teacher education courses or preparation experiences;
- experience;
- certification (16; see also Darling-Hammond 2000).

Teacher Education

Undoubtedly, the quality of the higher education training and professional development teachers receive is critical to improving classroom practices (Kanstoroom and Finn 1999; Darling-Hammond and Youngs 2002; Wang and Walberg 2001). Research reveals that the type and amount of college education teachers receive is related to student achievement for both content area and student learning (Monk 1994; Darling-Hammond and Youngs 2002; Wenglinsky 2000; Greenwald, Hedges, and Laine 1996). For example, Wenglinsky (2000), using information on students across the nation (NAEP), observed that, on average, eighth grade students performed better on math assessments when their teachers had a major or minor in math. Teacher training in how to teach higher-order thinking also contributed to student math achievement; training in how to provide "hands-on science" contributed to stronger science scores. In a separate study, students who had teachers with master's-level degrees demonstrated stronger academic outcomes than did students who had teachers with fewer years of education (Ferguson 1991). Further, looking at results of many different studies that examined school resources and their effect on student achievement revealed that, across studies, teachers' educational levels positively predicted student outcomes (Greenwald, Hedges, and Laine 1996). All of these studies related years of teacher education directly to student outcomes.

It is clear, however, that based on what we know about who the most effective teachers are, efforts on the part of universities and colleges to attract highly qualified students to the teaching profession are important. Next, colleges should provide these highly qualified students rigorous educational programs that instill a substantial knowledge base along with an understanding about how to continue to hone teaching expertise and broaden their knowledge base after graduation.

Teaching Credentials

States require teachers to be credentialed in order to ensure that the teachers in classrooms are qualified to teach. In general, current state credentialing standards include passing a proficiency examination on knowledge about teaching, learning, and subject matter. Minimum college-level grade point averages in content area and education coursework may be required. Typically, student teaching or other direct experience with teaching is required, and there may be a probationary period, although this varies, as do the specific requirements, from state to state (Darling-Hammond and Youngs 2002). A number of studies have linked teachers' credentials to stronger student achievement (Goldhaber and Brewer 1999, 2000; Greenwald, Hedges, and Laine 1996). For example, using information on students in another large national study (NELS), overall, high school students with credentialed teachers demonstrated stronger outcomes than did students with probationary or emergency credentialed or uncredentialed teachers (Goldhaber and Brewer 2000). The effect of having a credentialed teacher was larger for math than for science. Also, students from lower SES families were less likely to have a fully certified teacher. Similar results were found for middle school students (Hawk, Coble, and Swanson 1985). More studies at the district and state levels reveal similar associations between teacher credentialing procedures and student outcomes (Darling-Hammond 2000). However, just as in the studies about the effect of teacher education, all of these studies treated what happened in the classrooms like a black box, so it is not clear how having a credential affected teachers' practices.

Experienced Teachers

Everybody assumes that the more years of experience teachers have, the more effective their teaching will be. Concerns about keeping teachers in the discipline as well as in the classroom make this assumption implicitly. But there is not much research about the effect of years of teaching experience on student academic outcomes. The studies that look at the effect of teachers' years of experience on students' achievement reveal that experience might contribute to student outcomes (Goldhaber and Brewer 2000; Rivkin, Hanushek, and Kain 2001; Greenwald, Hedges, and Laine 1996; NICHD-ECCRN 2002b). A study using information on students and teachers across the nation (NAEP) (Goldhaber and Brewer 1999, 2000) did not find a significant relation between teachers' years of experience and their students' achievement levels. A meta-analysis, which compared results from many studies examining school resources and their effect on student achievement, revealed that students whose teachers had more years of experience were more likely to have stronger academic outcomes, but this effect was very small (Greenwald, Hedges, and Laine 1996, 17).

Relating Teacher Qualifications to Classroom Practice

Unfortunately, the research just described takes teacher variables, such as years of experience, and relates them directly to student achievement. In this way, we are left to infer that teacher credentials, experience, and education shape teachers' instructional practices, which in turn impacts students' learning. This happens because research that actually observes teachers teaching is time consuming and costly. It is much easier to treat instruction like a black box or to ask teachers what they do on questionnaires. Of course, all of us tend to report what it is we want to accomplish rather that what we actually do, and teachers are no different (Dickinson and Tabors 2001). Because observation is time and resource intensive, studies that do use classroom observation tend to include relatively small numbers of classrooms, which makes generalizing their findings to practice, and to our nation as a whole, difficult.

Fortunately, a few studies are emerging that do include classroom observation for significant numbers of children and teachers in classrooms (Stigler and Hiebert 1999; NICHD-ECCRN 2002b; Connor, Morrison, and Katch 2004; Connor, Morrison, and Petrella 2004). For example, the NICHD Early Child Care Research Network includes first grade classroom observations for almost 900 of its participants. This study also includes teachers' credentials, education, and years of experience as well as a variety of child outcomes. Using these data, we can begin to gain some sense of how teachers' qualifications affect their practices, which in turn affect children's learning. For example (NICHD-ECCRN 2002b), teachers' total years of experience were not related to their teaching practices. However, teachers with more years of experience teaching first grade devoted a greater proportion of the day to academic activities, but this effect was small. Teachers with more years of education provided more emotional support and also devoted more time to academic activities. But this study did not directly relate teacher qualifications and practice to student achievement. The authors did note that student engagement in academic activities and positive peer interactions were related to teacher practices, and we might infer that student engagement would be related to stronger academic outcomes.

More recently, we used these data to examine the effect of teacher qualifications on teachers' literacy practices and, in turn, the effect of these practices on first graders' decoding outcomes (Connor et al. in review). This study included over 780 first grade public school classrooms. In the model (see figure 7.1), each arrow indicates the direction of the effect. Solid lines indicate significant effects; dotted lines nonsignificant effects. The numbers by each arrow are the standardized path coefficients, which range from negative 1 to 1. The higher the absolute value, the stronger the effect is.

We discovered that teachers with more years of education tended to interact with their students in warmer and more responsive ways, and this predicted children's language growth in first grade. None of the teacher qualifications predicted time spent on academics, yet students whose teachers spent more time in academic activities showed greater reading growth. Not surprisingly, since this was first grade, most of the academic time was spent in language arts instruction. But children affected classroom practices as well. Children who had lower decoding skills in kindergarten were less likely to be in classrooms that were judged to be high quality and with teachers who were warmer and more responsive. The social inequity is even clearer when we examine the association between family SES and teacher qualifications. Chil-

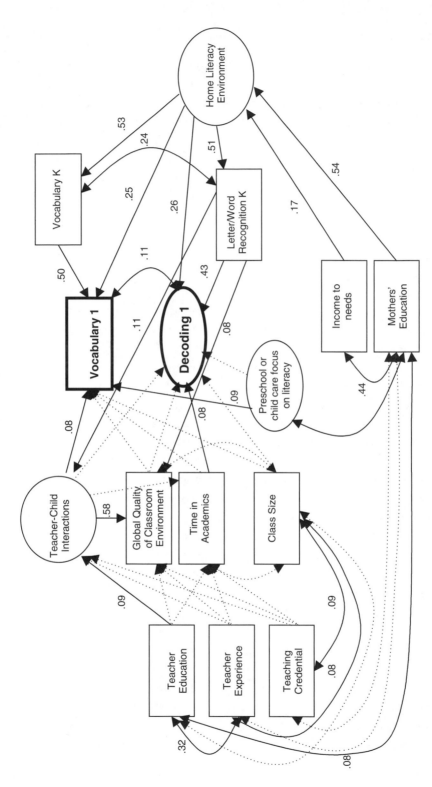

Figure 7.1. X^2 (136) = 330.30, p < .001, TLI = .995, CFI = .997, RMSEA = .043, which suggest the model fits the data well. Teacher experience was positively correlated with teachers' years of education. Ninety-seven percent of teachers had credentials.

dren whose mothers have fewer years of education are less likely to have well-educated and experienced teachers. This may reflect the nationwide trend revealed in other studies that less effective and less qualified teachers tend to teach in schools where children are more at risk, such as high-poverty schools (Wang and Walberg 2001).

It seems that teacher qualifications do, through their effect on teacher practice, impact student learning. But qualifications alone do not explain many of the differences in how teachers teach, the amount of time they devote to academic activities, and how they teach literacy. All of the effects in our model were very small, especially the effect of teacher education on classroom practice. The effect of classroom practice on students' learning was larger but still small. Thus without a very large sample, we would not have been able to detect these effects at all.

There is growing evidence that school resources alone, including teacher qualifications, do not have a very big effect on students' achievement (Shavelson and Towne 2002). Clearly, resources are important but not sufficient. How the resources are used to affect student achievement is just as important, if not more so (Cohen, Raudenbush, and Ball 2002, 2003). There are other issues to consider as well: the abilities that the teachers have may not be reflected in their credentials and education; the quality of the education they receive, the support they receive from their principal and district, the amount and quality of professional development they receive, and other factors that we haven't considered may be important as well.

Notice that based on our model in figure 7.1, teachers' experience, education, and credentials did not directly affect children's decoding skill growth. Teachers' qualifications affected children's learning through their classroom practices. Thus teacher qualifications are a distal variable, much like sociocultural factors. As we have revealed throughout this book, we may be more successful improving literacy in America if we consider proximal factors more carefully, such as teacher practices, and then determine how to instill these skills, attitudes, and aptitudes in the people who are teaching our children.

Figure 7.1 indicates that teachers are only part of a system that impacts students' learning. This system includes children, families, and homes; daycare and preschool experiences; teachers and classrooms; and resources in both school (teacher qualifications) and home (family income and parent education). Impacting just one part of this system may be necessary for improving literacy in America, but it will not be sufficient. As we have stated in previous chapters and will say again, there are multiple sources of influence on children's developing literacy, and to improve literacy in America will require multiple strategies.

Getting More Effective Teachers into the Classroom
Defining Teaching

Young adults entering the teaching profession need to learn the skills and strategies that support students' learning much the way medical students need to learn the skills and strategies of effective medical practice. Notice that we call teaching a *profession,* but whether teaching is truly a profession is currently being debated. Although some researchers strive to compare the teaching field with the medical profession (U.S. House of Representatives 2002), others claim that there is no similarity because "doctoring rests on a solid foundation of specialized professional knowledge that is scientifically buttressed by reliable reputable research. . . . Unfortunately this is not the case in education" (Finn and Kanstoroom 2001, 158). Indeed, some educational researchers state that teachers can't be held accountable for children's learning because children must be accountable for their own learning (Frymier 1998). Yet as we showed in chapter 6 and in this chapter, teachers' instructional practices do make a difference in children's learning.

Teaching may be perceived as an art or a craft (Shavelson and Towne 2002), in which case training should take experienced teachers' practical wisdom and share it with younger teachers. More time spent teaching should lead to stronger teaching and better student outcomes. A substantial body of scientific evidence and years of teacher education, ipso facto, become less important

It has also been suggested that teaching is a cultural activity, one that is learned over long periods of time through participating in the activity. "It is something one learns to do more by growing up in a culture than by studying it formally" (Stigler and Hiebert 1999, 86). If it is viewed as a cultural activity, then, it makes sense that teachers would rely largely on childhood, family, and classroom experiences rather than preservice education or professional development (Littlewood 2001). Teachers' cultural script for instruction begins when they enter school as children. They carry these scripts with them throughout their school career and then into their own classroom once they become teachers. In this way, methods of teaching may be very stable across generations and across the country (Stigler and Hiebert 1999). It may be that in order to help teachers become more effective, these largely unconscious cultural scripts need to be carefully and systematically examined. Regardless of the debate, supporting highly qualified teachers through mentoring, effective professional development, and attention to research may help teachers be more mindful of their educational practices and how to improve them.

Research and the Classroom

Another way to improve classroom practices is to systematically examine classroom instruction through rigorous research. However, if good research is to find its way into the classroom, the classroom teacher must use this research. Unfortunately, many teachers do not use research to guide their practice (Littlewood 2001). "One of my more discouraging experiences as an educational researcher was hearing the overwhelming groan emitted by a theater full of practicing teachers when the invited speaker from the National Center on Education Statistics (NCES) was introduced. I realized then that research was not important to them. At best it was irrelevant; at worst it was a tool to attack their validity and professional credibility" (Connor 2000).

   If teachers don't use research, how do they design their practice? Here is a list, in order of frequency, reported by exemplary teachers (Littlewood 2001). Teachers rely on:

   - childhood experiences at home and in the classroom, both positive and negative;
     - classroom experience;
     - professional experience;
     - parenting experiences;
     - teacher education.

Notice that research is not even listed, and their formal education is placed last. In studies, teachers were less likely to rely on research and more likely to rely on information from other teachers and personal experiences when working to improve their practice (Boerst 2003; Kaestle 1993).

Why don't teachers rely on research findings to guide their practice? Reasons may be found in the history of educational research. Although other sciences, such as physics, are hundreds of years old, the notion that education could be studied scientifically emerged only at the beginning of the twentieth century (Shavelson and Towne 2002; Lagemann 2000). Beginning as a branch of psychology, which was still considered part of philosophy, educational research focused primarily on aspects of the school curriculum: reading, mathematics, and social studies. From its inception there was skepticism that a science of education was valuable. Faculty in the arts and sciences did not respect scholars who focused on education. A noted academic observed, when "Professor Hanus [Harvard's first scholar of education] came to Cambridge, he bore the onus of his subject" (Lagemann 2000, 72).

Although the field has grown, until very recently there continued to be a lack of public support for research on education. Scholars offer several reasons for this. First, research on education has been viewed as of poor quality, without the rigor needed to answer important questions of policy and practice (Kaestle 1993; Lagemann 1996, 2000). The silver bullet mentality that there should be an education pill that cures academic woes is unrealistic. Even in medicine, complex conditions require complex solutions that are not the same for each and every person (National Research Council 2001). Perhaps the most important reasons lie in the historical divide between researchers (mostly men who have never taught in a classroom) and teachers (mostly women). "Operating in different worlds, researchers and practitioners did not develop the kinds of cross fertilization that are necessary in fields where research and practice should develop reciprocally" (Shavelson and Towne 2002, 15).

Our experience in the medical profession finds full professors at medical schools who maintain a clinical practice with no indication that their research undermines their practice or that their practice undermines their research. Our experience in education is that former teachers do not continue to teach once they begin their lives as researchers. Of course, until recently most physicians practicing and researching have been men, which has never been the case for education.

Indeed, it seems that there is an implicit assumption among education researchers that teachers cannot or will not use scientific research findings to guide their practice. Rather, teachers should turn to descriptions and interpretations of research spoon-fed by publishers of textbooks, scripted uniform curricula, and watered-down articles in flashy magazines.

This assumption is clearer when we review our list of factors related to teacher effectiveness above. The ability to understand and implement findings from educational research is not listed. There is no indication from this study that teachers mentioned research at all during their interviews. When the expectation is included in a study (Boerst 2003), we find that, overwhelmingly, teachers do not use research to guide their practice. There seems to be absolutely no expectation that practicing teachers will keep up to date on the findings of current research or use these findings to improve their practice. Imagine: if a pediatrician did not stay current with research, she might still be prescribing aspirin for children (which is related to Reyes syndrome) or telling parents to place their infants on their stomachs to sleep (which is related to sudden infant death syndrome).

But if educational research is to be effective, it must find its way into the classroom, which means that the crucial reciprocal interactions between researcher and practitioner must be strengthened. One way to do this would be to include in teacher education requirements how to read research articles, how to understand the strengths and limitations of various research methods, how to assess and use standardized tests, and how to conduct their own research. Action research (where teachers conduct research in their own classroom), although generally dismissed in research circles, may be an important movement toward instilling an understanding of why research is important (Martella, Nelson, and Marchand-Martella 1999).

Why is research important for teachers? First of all, education cannot be considered a credible discipline, with the prestige and remuneration that comes with it, unless the findings of research are incorporated into practice. As long as teachers rely solely on practical wisdom and others to interpret the research base for them, research will be used inappropriately to guide policy and practice. For example, in the moves toward "accountability," politicians have mandated child-achievement testing to determine teacher success (Olson 1999), even though there is accumulating evidence that child factors—such as the skills that children bring with them to the classroom, home and community environment, and prior classroom experiences—explain much more of the variability in children's academic achievement. Had teachers been savvier with regard to these findings, they could have pointed out the obvious flaws in judging school and teacher efficacy based on tests such as the fourth grade NAEP (National Center for Educational Statistics 2001b).

Let's take this a step further. What if in our model in figure 7.1 we had failed to take into account that children's kindergarten decoding score explained most of the variability in decoding at the end of first grade and that children with stronger kindergarten decoding scores tended to be in higher-quality classrooms where the teachers were more sensitive and responsive? Using this model, it is clear that a large part of the teachers' effectiveness was related to who was in their classroom. Without this important information, teachers in high-poverty schools, where children frequently enter the classroom with weaker decoding skills, would look like they were less effective than teachers in higher SES schools when, in fact, almost all of the differences in students' achievement could be explained by children's entering skills. A teacher in a high-poverty school might not be less effective; his students just have further to go.

Another important reason for teachers to be discerning consumers of educational research is because research in education is accumulating critical amounts of knowledge about children's learning (Shavelson and Towne 2002), which promises to change teaching as we know it. Further, recent policy has called for scientifically rigorous research and may actually put in place adequate funding and support for this effort. We don't really know yet the most effective ways to teach individual children. Thus, understanding the implications of new research for changing practice will be critical. Further, teachers should play an important role in identifying important research questions. But without true dialogue between researchers and teachers, critical issues may be overlooked. As research becomes more relevant to understanding and appreciating the complexities of the classroom, teachers may be more willing to listen to advice from researchers.

Altogether, teaching is an important and demanding profession that requires understanding of the children being taught and how best to teach them. Unfortunately, some teachers are poorly equipped to teach effectively. Examining teachers' practices in the classroom and how to effect substantial change in the cultural system of teaching may be a more fruitful policy than focusing on distal variables such as teacher credentials. Rigorous preservice education, ongoing effective professional development, changing teachers' facility with research, and fostering greater ongoing interactions between researchers and teachers offer strategies to improve teacher efficacy, educational research, and, ultimately, our children's opportunities to learn.

IV

Historical Perspective

8

The "Perfect Educational Storm"

Late October and November are months with weather in rapid transition in the eastern U.S. To the west, large fresh cold air masses from Canada begin to envelope the Midwest on a regular basis. To the east, the Atlantic Ocean is slower to lose its stored summer heat than the continent, and hurricanes sometimes form over the warm waters. An enormous extratropical low [created] havoc along the entire Eastern Atlantic Seaboard . . . on October 30, 1991. Labeled the "perfect storm" by the National Weather Service, the storm sank the swordfishing boat Andrea Gail.

National Climatic Data Center

The evidence that we have reviewed thus far points to a number of forces shaping the state of literacy in America's children. In particular, parenting emerges as a critical, if not sole, factor responsible for the levels of variability seen in children before school entry. In school, variability in instructional practices as well as in teacher qualifications and preparation contributes to the maintenance and even the magnification of achievement differences as children progress through the elementary school years. One final question that we would like to address is quite simply, "How did we arrive at the situation?" An accumulating store of historical scholarship and data argues persuasively that significant changes in both parenting and teaching over the last half century have unwittingly conspired to come together to contribute to the current situation. We have termed this historical convergence the "perfect educational storm." The phrase is borrowed from a recent popular book by Sebastian Junger titled *The Perfect Storm*. The novel depicts the devastating impact of the rare, unusual convergence of three separate weather systems off the coast of the northeastern United States,

Nova Scotia, and Newfoundland. The coming together of these independent climatological conditions yielded a storm of calamitous proportions that wreaked havoc on the area and its inhabitants. In our
view, a similar educational storm with serious negative consequences
for some children's educational achievement has been created by a series of historical forces in the worlds of parenting and teaching over the
last half century.

To be sure, we are not claiming that the current crisis has been
created exclusively by historical shifts in parenting and teaching. As we
set forth in the beginning chapter, some children have always struggled
to learn in school. But despite growing public awareness and mounting concern, in spite of substantial increases in public spending on education in America, the problems persist and may have worsened recently. It is our contention that some countervailing historical forces
must be at work.

The Social and Psychological Climate at Midcentury

To better appreciate these historical trends and their impact, it would
be useful to describe the circumstances in which children and families
were developing in the years following the Second World War. As historians have documented, the 1950s initiated a period of unparalleled
prosperity in the United States. Rapid and substantial economic expansion fueled the growth of a larger middle class. Simultaneously, the
postwar baby boom created a large cohort of children who gradually
began to exert more economic and social clout. Perhaps most influential for the children of the time was a series of scientific, medical, and
technological advances that seemed to herald the creation of a qualitatively different society from earlier years—and with it, new attitudes
and hopes for the future. The introduction and mass distribution of
commercial television into American society in the 1940s and 1950s
yielded a significant leap forward over the old technology of radio.
Technological advances in design materials like structural steel, alu-
minum, glass, and plastics began to show up in new architectural de-
signs. The buildings of the 1950s were taller, sleeker, more streamlined,
fresher, and cleaner looking than their dumpy brick and concrete predecessors. In the mid-1950s automobiles changed their design radi-

cally. The old models, characterized by dark single colors, bulky round contours, and drab interiors, were abandoned; cars rolling off the assembly lines in the 1950s sported sleek lines, eye-catching chrome, bright multicolored exteriors, and numerous creature comforts inside. A corresponding revolution occurred in the world of music with the emergence of rock and roll. Here too, a distinct shift with the past was seen, with the older, softer, elegant acoustic music of the 1940s giving way to a more vibrant, forceful, down-to-earth electronic form. Clearly, the advent of stereo sound and other electronic advances in the music industry reinforced the impact of rock-and-roll music and further distanced it from earlier eras.

A seemingly unending series of scientific and medical advances further nurtured the growing belief that a new, qualitatively different era in the history of humanity was dawning. The discovery and mass distribution of the polio vaccine began the process of eradicating one of the most devastating childhood disorders. Advances were beginning to be seen in the fight against cancer, a disease that in earlier epochs was viewed as a death sentence. The commercial introduction of the birth control pill was universally seen as a significant scientific advance of international proportions in the fight against population explosions and unwanted pregnancies. It clearly laid the foundation for and contributed significantly to changes in sexual behavior and other aspects of personal relationships.

The Psychological Impact

The variety and intensity of these scientific, medical, technological, and cultural changes had a profound psychological impact on many of the children and young adults growing up during that era. A deep sense of optimism, idealism, self-empowerment, maybe even entitlement, began to take hold of some in this new generation. They were healthier, wealthier, held higher educational aspirations and loftier occupational goals. They grew up with the sense that the world they inhabited—and were, in fact, creating—would be far better than in any previous era of human history. Though history would demonstrate this attitude to be naive and simplistic, an infectious air of optimism, idealism, positivity, and possibility gripped this new generation and began to insinuate itself into all facets of life. Attitudes toward the work environment began to change discernibly. A job was no longer seen as something one was forced to do in order to put bread on the table, as in the period following the Depression, but rather something that one should enjoy doing. Likewise, prevailing attitudes about marriage came under critical scrutiny. Noting the significant numbers of their parents who remained in unhappy marriages simply out of obligation or for the children's sake, a new generation rejected the hypocrisy inherent in such a scheme that put obligation above personal happiness. They gradually began to look more favorably upon alternative arrangements like living together and sexual intimacy before marriage. The blanket condemnation of divorce seen in earlier generations was softened, and even attitudes toward children out of wedlock, earlier labeled as "illegitimate," turned more sympathetic. Finally, grounded in a firm sense of economic well-being and surrounded by abundant evidence of the positive effects of modernization, this generation began to gradually notice discrepancies in the attainment of the "American dream." With increasing awareness and rejection of the generations of racism and discrimination, young Black and White Americans allied to demand equal rights. Likewise, it became increasingly clear that similar levels of discrimination against women in education, employment, and other areas had to be reversed. Finally, attitudes toward children and eventually toward child rearing began to change in similar ways. Lingering notions from earlier generations, like "Spare the rod and spoil the child" or "Children should be seen and not heard" came to be regarded as outmoded, even destructive, and disrespectful to children. Rejecting the more punitive and authoritarian practices of their parents, increasing numbers in this generation vowed to make parenting a more positive and enjoyable experience. They might even be friends with their children, a relationship their parents would never have dreamed of fostering.

The same straightforward optimism found its way into the world of school and teaching. People began to question whether traditional attitudes toward education, prevalent in the 1950s, that emphasized a rigorous curriculum, hard work, and respect for the authority of the teacher and the school, constituted the best way to educate children (Ravitch 2000). They wondered whether a more open environment, in which children had much greater say in what and how they would be taught, and in which teachers were seen more as coaches than as authority figures, would prove more effective. Clearly, such classrooms would be more enjoyable for children, and subject matter taught this way would be more fun. Like other aspects of society, educational practice might be fundamentally restructured to create happier, more motivated and engaged students.

Demographic and Social Trends

The psychological changes wrought by these historical shifts gradually began to reshape the social and economic landscape. Beginning in the early 1960s and accelerating rapidly through the last three decades of the twentieth century, a series of major changes in our society substantially altered the nature of work, families, relationships, child rearing, and education. Yet as we hope to show, many of the claims about the negative impact of these changes (for example, working women) have been shown empirically to be false. Hence it will require careful scrutiny to discern the real changes that have occurred that truly affected children's development. While many changes occurred in American society over that time, we will focus on seven major changes most relevant to literacy acquisition.

1. Participation of women in the labor force. It is well known that over the past three decades the proportion of women in the paid labor force has increased substantially. Particularly relevant is a dramatic increase in the proportion of married mothers with young children employed outside the home. According to estimates from the U.S. Bureau of the Census, only about 30 percent of married women with young children were working outside the home in 1970, but that number had jumped to 42 percent in 1981, and by 1998, fully 64 percent of married mothers of young children were employed outside the home. Clearly, this major shift in female work patterns reflected, in part, the growing attitude of egalitarianism in American society. More mothers working also meant that there would be greater need for childcare for young children.

Perhaps less obvious and less discussed was the impact of increased work opportunities for women in the teaching profession. As barriers to the advancement for women fell systematically, in recent decades, more talented women have realized their ambitions in medicine, law, business, and universities (Corcoran, Evans, and Schwab 2004; Hoxby and Leigh 2003). In previous decades, these same women, barred from the higher professions, might have chosen teaching. We will return to the implications of this point later in the chapter.

2. *Divorce and family structure.* It is equally clear that over the past two decades the nature of the American family has changed significantly. Divorce is much more common than it used to be. According to some estimates, one-half or more of first marriages will end in divorce, almost twice as many as twenty years ago (Martin 1989; Westoff 1986; Thornton and Young-DeMarco 2001). Further, almost 25 percent of White children and more than 50 percent of Black children are born to unmarried mothers. Consequently, 27 percent of children today live with one parent, and 60 percent of children are estimated to spend at least part of their childhood with only one parent (Hernandez 1993).

3. *Educational attainment and family size.* A lesser-known but no less significant change in the past half century has been the increased educational attainment of women, in particular, mothers. According to recent statistics (Sandberg and Hofferth 2001), only about 5 percent of American mothers with children under age twelve had completed four years of college in 1950. By 1980 that figure had risen to 12 percent and to slightly over 18 percent in 1990. This increase, which presumably has continued in the ensuing years, is significant since more educational attainment is strongly associated with better child rearing. Concurrently, over the last half century the number of children born to the average woman has dropped significantly. The average woman born between 1930 and 1939 had about three children, while women born after 1945 will likely bear no more than two children on average (U.S. Bureau of the Census 1984, 1988, cited in Sandberg and Hofferth 2001).

4. *Shifts in sexual mores.* Sexual behavior and attitudes began to change noticeably during the 1960s. Adolescents and young adults began to question the prohibitions on premarital sex and cohabitation before marriage. Increasing numbers of young unmarried adults became sexually active and experimented with living together. While these behaviors were not unheard of in previous generations, they were

clearly frowned upon and discouraged at a societal level. Beginning in the 1960s attitudes toward premarital sex and cohabitation began to change discernibly. To those with more traditional values, these changes were seen as undermining the sanctity of marriage and family life, with serious negative consequences for the fate of children growing up in such circumstances. To the more progressive minded, these behaviors heralded a new era of honesty and freedom that would liberate Americans from the stultifying moral shackles of earlier eras and ultimately create better relationships, stronger marriages, and healthier children.

5. Patterns of sex-role behaviors. As more women entered the workforce, pressures arose to reexamine and modify the patterns of behavior exhibited by men and women, particularly regarding the household division of labor. Modern couples, in which both partners often worked full-time, were required to sort out the domestic responsibilities that, in former generations, had been carried out exclusively by women at home. Household chores such as cooking, cleaning, dishwashing, laundry, yard work, and bills were now negotiated and renegotiated among couples in an ongoing effort to approximate a 50–50 balance in the relationship. While this was an ideal circumstance for young couples in the 1960s and 1970s, the evidence suggests that in most cases women continued to shoulder the lion's share of domestic responsibilities while still holding a full-time job (Sandberg and Hofferth 2001). Perhaps most important for our discussion, modern couples began to modify their child-rearing behaviors. In contrast to earlier eras where mothers were responsible almost exclusively for childcare, increasing numbers of fathers began to contribute to the care of their children. In truth, the shift in child-rearing responsibilities occurred gradually, but as reviewed below, recent evidence strongly suggests that fathers are now taking a significantly active role in childcare.

6. Declines in religious service attendance. A systematic drop in attendance at religious services occurred over the same period. While several forces were likely operative in shaping this decline, the decrease was seen as part of a more general turning away from the outside influence of arbitrary authority figures. For young adults of the period, there was less need seen to lean on traditional social structures like religious institutions to promote personal happiness. The modern era, with its demonstrated capability of increasing personal health and general well-being, reinforced the view that the individual is the most important entity in society and individual happiness and self-fulfillment are the ultimate goals of human life.

7. *Changing educational philosophy and practice.* Finally, a significant swing in American education took place in the 1960s, away from traditional educational attitudes and practices toward a more progressive stance to teaching and learning (Ravitch 2000). The traditional course of study, in which the teacher created and directed the term's work, was gradually supplanted with more student input and control. In extreme cases, like the progressive school Summerhill (Neil 1960), even attendance, course requirements, and in some cases classes themselves were optional for students. The open education movement reinforced these progressive trends, emphasizing the importance of student freedom in creating more meaning and purpose in learning. This attitude funneled down even to recommendations about the teaching of particular subject matter like reading (Hirsh 1996). The progressive attitudes looked very negatively on the phonics method of teaching early reading from earlier time periods and wholeheartedly endorsed the shift toward the whole language approach, which emphasized student-controlled exposure to meaningful language and literature experiences, which, it was assumed, would naturally produce competent, motivated readers.

Upheavals in the World of Parenting

As the number of divorces has mounted over the last two to three decades, and as the number of children living in single-parent families has jumped over the same period, concerns have been raised about the impact of these demographic and social trends on the nature of family life in America and particularly on the development of children. For it was precisely over the same time period that data began accumulating about the decreasing academic performance of American children from the NAEP studies (reviewed in chapter 1) as well as the low performance of American children compared to their Asian counterparts (Stevenson and Lee 1990). Popular articles then began to appear attributing blame for America's declining educational fortunes to the negative impact of single parenting, to the increases in working women, and to the skyrocketing divorce rate eroding traditional family values. Some even went so far as to claim that the traditional family was dead.

What has really happened over the past two or three decades, and what impact has it had on child development and literacy in America? Did these changes really reflect decreased valuation of the family, parenting, and children? One way to test these claims is to examine the amount of time that parents are spending with their children now versus twenty years ago. To the extent that there has been a systematic erosion in respect for the family or in the importance of parenting, and hence in children's development, we should see that parents are spending correspondingly less time with their children compared to parents of earlier eras. What do the data say? Surprisingly, recent analyses by sociologists and economists have discovered that, contrary to conventional wisdom, the time that parents are spending with their children now has increased substantially from the amounts of time parents were spending with their children in 1981 (Bianchi 2000; Sandberg and Hofferth 2001). For two-parent families in particular, mothers were spending five more hours per week with their children, and fathers were spending over four hours per week more with their children in 1997 than they were in 1981. Somewhat surprisingly, for single-parent families, children in 1997 were not spending less time with either their mothers or fathers than in 1981. Equally revealing is that the increase from 1981 to 1997 has occurred for working as well as at-home mothers, although the increase is slightly greater in at-home mothers. Perhaps most striking is the amount of time children spent with fathers. Overall, in 1997 children spent more time with fathers in two-parent families whether the mother was working or not. However, between 1981 and 1997 the amount of time children spent with fathers jumped sharply in families with working mothers, while the increase for at-home mothers was more modest. As Sandberg and Hofferth concluded, "it appears that fathers may have taken more responsibility for childcare when mothers worked in 1997 than in 1981" (429).

These are important and surprising results that flatly contradict the simple picture that has been portrayed about the negative impact of divorces, single parenting, and working women on the plight of America's families and children. Clearly, these data argue forcefully that we have not seen an erosion in how much we value the family or children's development. In fact, the data imply that, in some ways, exactly the opposite has occurred. For two-parent working families, mothers and fathers are spending more time with their children than they did two decades ago. In particular, fathers are beginning to spend significantly more time with their children, especially when their wives are also working. These trends, at least, suggest that in some ways adults are taking their parenting responsibilities more seriously, at least to the point where they feel that they want to be spending more time with their children than their parents did.

If the demographic trends just described cannot really account for the academic declines over the past twenty years, where can we look for potential answers? There is emerging evidence that the real culprit in the realm of parenting may lie in a series of systematic changes in the attitudes, values, and behavior of parents toward their children over the past two to three decades (Alwin 1984, 1996). Recall that at the beginning of this chapter we emphasized that the generation growing up in the 1960s and 1970s, those becoming parents in the 1980s and 1990s, firmly believed that major qualitative shifts were occurring in the economic, social, and psychological fabric of modern society. An air of idealism, optimism, and positivity pervaded the lives of people growing up in that generation and manifested itself in attitudes toward marriage, relationships, and eventually toward child rearing. In simplest terms, the young parents of that era wanted the whole process of parenting to be more positive. They wanted to raise healthy, happy children who would look upon their parents more positively than many of them had regarded their own parents, whom they viewed as more distant, disciplinary, and formal. The hope of many in this new generation was that parenting did not need to be punitive or negative but could be more joyful and hence create a more harmonious family environment. Parents did not want to rear children who were fearful or slavishly obedient. They vowed that they would never use the phrase "Because I said so." At its foundation, this new generation of parents wanted to create better families—and happier children.

An accumulating body of historical evidence supports these generalizations and can help us to understand the impact of these changes on children's development and, in particular, on the fate of their early literacy development. Evidence gathered by Duane Alwin in a number of studies has demonstrated that over the past half century parental attitudes about the qualities they most want to nurture in their children have shown a systematic and provocative shift. From 1958 until the early 1990s, a series of studies asked parents to rate the importance of a number of child characteristics in preparing for life. Included were characteristics like obedience, popularity, autonomy, hard work, and helping others. Alwin has found that, for the most part, American parents have always valued autonomy in their children, but earlier generations placed obedience a very close second. Over the last three to four decades, parental ratings of the value of autonomy have increased systematically, except for a slight dip in the early 1990s. In sharp contrast, there has been a systematic decrease over the same period in how much parents value obedience in their children (Alwin 1996).

These findings are consistent with the picture of parenting that we have painted—namely, that changes in parenting attitudes, values, and behaviors have been systematically shifting in the latter part of the twentieth century toward less punitive, less discipline-oriented, less negative parenting. Simultaneously, parents have given their children more autonomy, again in the service of creating freer, more independent individuals.

"The Road to Hell . . ."

In contrast to popular notions about the nature and sources of parenting changes, the evidence emerging from social science research reinforces the notion that the real underlying changes in parenting occurred at the level of values and behavior. The generation of parents growing up in the latter half of the twentieth century was attempting to create a different environment in which their children were reared. Gradually, the idealism and optimism of this generation crystallized into a set of child-rearing principles and practices that focused on giving children more freedom, granting them more choices, and simultaneously decreasing the emphasis on arbitrary authority, discipline, and fear induction. In general, these parents have had the best intentions for their children and, consistent with this attitude, they spend more time with their children than did their parents, even when both parents were working.

What is the impact of these changed attitudes and behaviors for our children and especially for their academic lives and success? It is our contention that the evidence emerging from historical, sociological, and economic analyses strongly suggests that in some parents these attitudes led to a series of parenting practices that resulted in lower levels of self-regulation in some children as well as lower levels of literacy. Here again, our emphasis is on variability. What seems to have happened over the past few decades is that an increasing percentage of parents have not exercised sufficient control and discipline over their children to produce independent, responsible, self-regulated learners. This shift in some percentage of parents has served to increase the variability in children's self-regulation skills beginning as early as the preschool years. Hence, in our analysis, increasing numbers of children are coming to school without the learning-related social skills of independence, responsibility, and self-regulation that they need if they are to learn effectively in the classroom. Given the importance of self-regulation in helping a child to pay attention, to concentrate, and to persist in learning efforts, failures to develop self-regulation clearly will have a detrimental effect on the acquisition of important literacy skills, beginning during the preschool period.

In summary, in our analysis, the first major storm affecting literacy in America was brewed in the world of parenting. With the best of intentions, in an effort to sincerely create a happier, healthier generation of children, some parents have unwittingly failed to provide their children with the early self-regulation and literacy skills that they need to be maximally ready for school. As a consequence, contemporary teachers, in contrast to earlier generations, are being presented with increasing percentages of children arriving with lower social, self-regulation, language, and literacy skills. So even under the best of circumstances, teachers would be faced with mounting difficulties in trying to educate all these children. But a separate storm was growing in the world of education. This too, by itself, would have had a great impact on the educational attainment of significant numbers of children growing up in the 1970s and 1980s. The combination of this and the parental changes fomenting during the same period yielded a perfect educational storm whose aftermath laid waste to the educational landscape.

Changes in the World of Teaching

Trends in American instructional philosophy and practice parallel those in the world of parenting and in society as a whole over the latter half of the twentieth century (Ravitch 2000). Battles over school reform have raged throughout the twentieth century (as documented in detail by Diane Ravitch), swinging back and forth pendulum-style between traditional emphases on rigor and discipline to progressive movements emphasizing freedom and openness. In 1955, following a period where the progressive movement dominated American education, Rudolph Flesch wrote an important and influential book, *Why Johnny Can't Read.* In it he lamented the de-emphasis on phonics and traditional reading methods and called for their return. There followed a brief period wherein traditional methods flourished, but this short-lived effort was snuffed out quickly by the cultural and social upheavals of the 1960s. Attitudes toward schooling and instruction veered sharply toward the progressive end of the spectrum, in line with the general emphasis on openness, individuality, and idealism of the emerging generation of the 1960s. As a consequence, Ravitch declares, "the idea of improving performance by intensifying instruction seemed faintly ridiculous and decidedly uncool in the new age of student rebellion" (Ravitch 2000, 384). Alternative schools sprang up throughout the nation. The open education movement flourished, as more and more schools sought to make instruction more child centered and child friendly. As historians have documented, by the mid-1970s the detrimental impact of the sweeping changes began to be seen. First, scores on the influential scholastic aptitude test (SAT) fell sharply from 1963–64 to 1975. During the same period there was a significant decline in enrollment in basic academic courses in favor of more elective offerings. Moreover, absenteeism became more common, and grade inflation and social promotion reached new heights. A gradual erosion in educational standards and rigor seemed to have produced a more poorly prepared generation of students, which, in spiral fashion, served to further erode the level of instruction provided to students.

In the vortex of progressivism that swirled around the educational establishment in the late 1970s and early 1980s, instructional approaches to the teaching of reading were ripe for reform. Specifically, beginning in the 1980s, the whole language movement began to supplant traditional phonics methods as the preferred way to teach reading. With the underlying ideology that written language is a social and cultural phenomenon, educators were told, "Why do people create and learn written language? They need it! How do they learn it? The same way they learn oral language, by using it in authentic literacy events that meet their needs" (Goodman, 1986, 24). Because whole language emphasized the natural connection between early language and early reading, declaring that when children want to read, they will easily do so, it is not hard to see how this approach to reading could take hold in the cultural, political, and social climate of the period. Whole language eschewed the "drill and kill" methods of phonics and focused more on exposing children to real literature in meaningful contexts. Throughout the 1980s, the whole language philosophy and approach swept through large segments of the teaching profession and was adopted in many parts of the country, often to the total exclusion of any phonics instruction. In 1985, noting the potential dangers of exclusive reliance on whole language, a report from the National Academy of Education (called *Becoming a Nation of Readers* [Anderson et al. 1985]) declared that "it is unrealistic to anticipate that one critical feature of instruction will be discovered which, if in place, will assure rapid progress in reading" (4) and that "research evidence tends to favor explicit phonics" (43). Nevertheless, whole language continued to flourish throughout the 1980s, 1990s, and into the new millennium— precisely during the period that reading scores of American children were losing ground.

Shifts in the Teaching Profession

Along with changes in educational philosophy and teaching methods, a shift in the profession itself and in the preparation teachers received could be discerned. As we hinted earlier, one possible consequence of the increase in the number of working women and of the rise of feminism in general starting in the 1960s may have been that significant numbers of women, who in previous years had been limited in their options, could now enter the more lucrative and higher-status professions of medicine, law, and business. Such women may have opted for the teaching profession in earlier epochs. As opportunities for these women opened up, the teaching profession was left to fill the void with students who were, on average, less qualified than their predecessors had been (Corcoran, Evans, and Schwab 2004; Hoxby and Leigh 2003). The impact of this shifting demographic was to increase the variability in the qualifications with which modern teachers entered the profession.

In addition to a shifting pool of applicants, teacher preparation underwent distinct shifts. The emphasis on whole language and more generally on more openness and child-centered approaches meant that teachers received a less uniform curricular preparation for teaching. The heightened variability in the applicant pool coupled with the diversity of preparation received by the fledgling teachers almost of necessity produced significant increases in the variability of instruction children were receiving. Particularly, with regard to basic skills in reading and mathematics, children who required the most explicit instruction in phonics and in other basic skills were now less likely to receive it. While children with strong learning skills and an enriching parenting environment to nourish them continued to flourish, the students at risk for academic failure were now placed at even greater risk.

The Consequences

The impact of these changes in the world of teaching on children's literacy skills and academic development has been nothing short of devastating. Over the past decade or more, we have witnessed a growing disparity between the levels of functioning of more versus less successful students, the so-called Matthew effect (Stanovich 1986). Academically speaking, the rich are getting richer and the poor are getting poorer. On a broader plane, we are witnessing a greater disengagement over time of low-achieving students (Steinberg 1996; Steinberg et al. 1992; Steinberg, Dornbusch, and Brown 1992), exacerbating the differences between more and less successful students. As they fall further behind, these failing and disaffected students become more apathetic and disruptive in the classroom. As a consequence, the teacher's job has become increasingly more difficult, producing rising levels of disaffection among teachers for their jobs and a growing frustration at not being able to help at-risk children. It is no wonder that American teachers suffer from such high burnout rates. The lament, "I can't handle the children" speaks simply but eloquently of the frustration and despair felt by many teachers in many classrooms in American schools today.

Taken together, sufficient evidence has accrued to support our contention that significant patterns of change in parenting as well as in teaching over the last half century contribute significantly, at least in part, to the academic problems we are currently facing. While these two trends were relatively independent on one level, they formed part of the larger societal evolution toward a freer, more just and open society that sought to nurture positive development in our children. In many ways and for a significant percentage of our children these changes were successful. But for a sizable portion of other children there was a downside—they did not develop the skills needed to be ready for school, and they did not receive the kind of instruction needed to bring them to adequate levels of functional literacy. These two "swirling storms," as we have metaphorically called them, collided during the late 1970s and 1980s to produce a massive "educational storm" that devastated the literacy skills of a significant percentage of America's children. In order to improve the literacy skills of these children we will need to directly target these two factors if we are to reverse the damage these storms wrought. We now turn to that effort.

V

Guidelines for Improvement

9

Improving Literacy in America

Go into any inner-city neighborhood and folks will tell you that government alone can't teach kids to learn.

Barack Obama

Improving literacy in America poses a critical but complex challenge. Consequently, it is understandable that researchers, educators, and policy makers have focused on single issues in their efforts to solve the problem. In this book, we have attempted to bring these pieces together, reviewing historical trends as well as current research to better understand the intricate links among parents, teachers, and children and how, in concert, they affect students' success in school. The effort has revealed that these multiple and interconnected sources of influence act to support or undermine children's learning. Therefore, improving literacy in America requires multiple strategies that, ideally, should be pursued simultaneously.

Before we proceed to our recommendations, we need to address one last issue, namely, how do our recommendations relate to the ideas put forth by others for improving literacy in America? National and state policies have tended to focus on strategies such as vouchers, charter schools, and, recently, on reducing class size and on social promotion. While we cannot address all of their suggestions, we would like to focus on one recommendation, reducing class size, and illustrate how our perspective—looking at proximal rather than distal sources of influence—casts that recommendation in a new light, which we feel will ultimately result in more long-lasting positive changes in children's literacy.

Reducing Class Size—Shifting the Focus

Reducing class size to about fifteen children has been shown to significantly improve academic performance for students (Mosteller 1995). Children who spent kindergarten through third grade in smaller classrooms experienced greater school success, even through high school, than did children who spent their early school years in larger classrooms of about twenty-four (Hacsi 2002a). Further, these effects were largest for children at risk for academic failure. Thus for good reason, reducing class size has been viewed as a major strategy in improving achievement in children, and for a significant number of states it has become the education policy of choice. But from our perspective, we have to ask, how does reducing class size work?

We suggest that smaller classrooms succeed, if and when they do, by nurturing proximal sources of influence that promote children's developing literacy. First, smaller classes in principle reduce the chances of disruptive behavior so characteristic of many American classrooms. But, in our analysis, the real cause of the disruptive behavior is the increased number of children coming to school without the self-regulation skills needed to function in the classroom. Second, in smaller classes, teachers might be more likely to attempt to individualize instruction. However, in the absence of an environment that gives priority to individualized instruction, simply reducing class size will have no impact.

This is precisely what happened in California, a state that mandated class-size reductions. Affluent California school districts were quite effective in implementing state-supported class-size reductions because they had a stable and expert teaching force coupled with adequate physical facilities. In contrast, less affluent and urban school districts were forced to hire uncredentialed teachers and make due with inadequate buildings. And it is critical to note that *many teachers did not change the way they taught* even though they now had to instruct and manage fewer students (Hacsi 2002a). Consequently, although both parents and teachers may have preferred the smaller classrooms, the effect on children's achievement was not as great as had been hoped; disparities in teacher quality and facilities between affluent and poorer school districts increased, the intervention was very expensive, and improvements in overall student achievement were uneven. Further, effective teachers, as we have discussed, promote stronger student achievement in larger classes as well as in smaller classes (Taylor et al. 2000), so this expensive intervention would be unnecessary in a world of effective teachers.

A more educationally effective policy would adopt multiple strategies to attract, train, and keep more qualified teachers in the classroom, to promote individualized instruction based on the specific needs of students, and to support parenting efforts before and after children begin school. In our view, focusing on these proximal influences holds greater potential for affecting real long-term change in our children's literacy skills.

We now turn to our recommendations.

Before Children Begin School
1. Start Early!

Whatever steps we take to enhance children's literacy skills, we must remain sensitive to the need to take action as early as possible in the lives of children. This recommendation is obvious at one level, and as a nation we have made great strides in attempting to intervene as early as possible with our most disadvantaged children and families. Witness the heroic efforts of Head Start and other early-intervention projects. Yet, in our view, this admonition needs highlighting and reinforcing for all children at risk for academic problems. Among normally developing children, differences in vocabulary can be seen as early as eighteen months of age (Hart and Risley 1995). Variation in syntactic skills emerges shortly thereafter (Huttenlocher et al. 2002), followed by divergence in phonological, alphabet-naming and emergent-writing skills. Variability across children in critical self-regulation skills has been seen as early as three years of age (McClelland and Morrison 2003). Further, we are beginning to appreciate that these differences are not ephemeral or inconsequential. They can and do persist and stabilize. Consequently, a sizable percentage of children are starting school with two strikes against them. We must take these early individual differences seriously and not focus exclusively on the school years in our efforts to improve literacy. The problems children manifest represent the cumulative impact of many forces acting over long stretches of the child's life. To improve the situation we must also take a cumulative approach, starting with the earliest influences.

2. Promote Effective Parenting

We strongly recommend that, as a nation, we strive to promote the parenting practices that have been demonstrated to enhance children's language, cognitive, literacy, and social skills. Parenting practices represent a crucial source of the individual differences seen in children before they enter school. A clear and specific focus on parents' behavior is vital to improving our children's literacy skills, school readiness, and ultimate school success. To accomplish this goal we need to focus on two issues: the complexity of parenting and the difficulty of changing behavior.

Parenting is complex. This hardly needs emphasizing to the majority of parents. Yet it is something of a shock to new parents when they realize how time-consuming, exhausting, and complicated rearing children can be. These revelations, which are uniquely appreciated by each new generation of parents, should alert us to the fact that knowing how to parent and doing an effective job are not innately provided for human beings. We need to learn to parent effectively, and most of us make plenty of mistakes along the way. From the research we reviewed in these pages, we can see that one of the reasons parenting is difficult is that it involves the orchestration of a number of different dimensions (learning environment, warmth/responsivity, and control/discipline) in conjunction with a particular child's characteristics (language skills, temperament, self-regulation) toward the goal of producing a competent and happy child. Yet recognizing the complexity of parenting should help us appreciate its potential power to shape the skills of our children in profound and sweeping ways. Here we would like to briefly review some of the important dimensions that require parental attention and orchestration.

First is the learning environment, in which effective parenting includes, among other things, talking to your child frequently, reading stories, exposing him or her to letters and numbers, practicing writing, limiting television watching, and taking him or her to plays, movies, museums, and the library. But coupled with those activities, effective parenting also includes large doses of warmth and responsivity. The noted pediatrician Berry Brazelton was fond of claiming that all children should have someone in their life who is crazy about them. The degree to which parents openly express their love for their child and demonstrate it consistently through affection, praise, support, and attention contributes to a child's sense of security, well-being, motivation to learn, and self-control. Finally, somewhat as a counterweight to warmth and affection, parental control/discipline needs to be added to the mix of skills needed to become an effective parent. The unconditional positive regard that comes from love and affection must be tempered by the ability to say "No" at times and to be consistent ("No" means "No"). From the most mundane activities like getting children to brush their teeth at night to the more serious disciplinary issues involving lying, stealing, or aggression, consistent parental efforts to gain compliance in children promote respect for rules, standards, and limits and ultimately contribute to the self-control needed to function effectively in the classroom environment.

It is challenging enough for most parents to try to orchestrate these dimensions competently and consistently. The job is made more difficult because the particular mix of behaviors that will foster children's success depends very much on the child. Some children are more naturally oriented to and interested in books and hence will enjoy bedtime story reading, while for others the activity will be boring or even unpleasant. Some children possess temperaments that make them easier to socialize, and hence the control/discipline needed to deal with them will be very different than with a child who is more active, exuberant, or demanding.

Finally, the job of parenting is complex and difficult because all of these behaviors must be orchestrated during the normal flow of everyday life. Effective parenting can and does require all or most of a parent's resources, literally "24/7." Take the seemingly simple example of reading to our children at night. We are clearly enriching our children's literacy and language skills. But at the very same time, by sitting still for several minutes, our children are also learning to concentrate and are developing an important component of self-control. Simultaneously, sitting together on the bed, with the child snuggled on our laps, we are delivering large doses of love, closeness, and attention, which promote emotional security and motivation.

Can we really change parenting? The second issue that we need to face squarely is the difficulty of changing parents' behavior. We saw in chapter 4 that intervention efforts to date with parents alone have had limited effectiveness. Given the complexity of the behaviors needed for effective parenting for literacy, it is not surprising that simple interventions aimed at one dimension, like the learning environment, would have limited impact. It remains to be seen what a more comprehensive effort combining various facets of effective parenting might accomplish. But there are two more basic issues that must be tackled. First is the pervasive perception that one cannot really change parenting behavior. Second is the fear that we cannot tell parents how to rear their children. Because parenting practices differ so much across families, it is said, agreement on a uniform set of recommendations will never emerge.

Our response to the first concern is that, as difficult as it may be to modify parenting behaviors, we need to try. Parenting remains a relatively untapped resource, in our view, in the effort to improve American children's literacy skills. We know from other initiatives, like antismoking campaigns, that modifying adult behavior is not easy. But we also know that millions of people have stopped smoking and millions of lives have been saved. We recommend a similar national campaign to promote effective parenting. The effort would include intensive interventions for our most at-risk, disadvantaged parents. Educational efforts through the media would also be important. Finally, a focus on prevention of problems in the next generation could be mounted by offering parenting classes (including child development) for students, beginning in middle school.

To the fear that you can't tell parents how to raise their child, we respond that there are a multitude of ways to provide children with the stimulation, love, and guidance they need to grow; each child will need a unique mix of parenting behaviors. There may be a small number of behaviors upon which parents might disagree, like the advisability of corporal punishment. But it is our contention that for the vast majority of parenting behaviors, we will agree on their relative value, albeit with unique cultural adaptations. For example, in families from different ethnic backgrounds, the types of books parents choose to read to their children and their interaction style during a book-reading episode may vary greatly; however, in each circumstance, children can be provided an engaging, language-rich experience in a warm and loving manner. Likewise, what parents talk to their children about will presumably differ across families. However, hopefully we can agree that talking to children in responsive and stimulating ways is important. High-quality and increasingly complex research is helping to identify the facets of parenting that are more or less effective for particular children, thereby illuminating how different children respond to different parenting practices.

3. Provide Uniformly High-Quality Childcare Experiences for Children

In parallel with efforts to improve parenting, we need to appreciate the importance of early care experiences on children's development and strive to maximize the quality of those experiences for everyone. First, for our children and families most in need, we need to guarantee high-quality preschool interventions. The evidence reviewed in chapter 3 clearly documents the psychological and financial benefits (for every dollar spent, seven to nine dollars are returned to society) of intensive interventions for disadvantaged children. We might add that coupled with a comprehensive program designed for parents (along the lines described above), a combined focus on the child and parent can reap enormous benefits for both and substantially boost the language and early literacy skills of at-risk children. Consequently, continuation and expansion of preschool interventions of high quality will contribute measurably to the improvement of the literacy skills of our most vulnerable citizens.

Second, we should extend the same logic and support to all of our children by advocating uniform standards of high quality in childcare environments. Recall that research has demonstrated that the quality of care children receive contributes to variation in children's cognitive and language skills. In particular, childcare environments that provide rich linguistic stimulation coupled with cognitively challenging talk and strong support for parents promote growth of important language and early literacy skills during the preschool years.

4. Foster Children's Self-Regulation as Well as Their Literacy Skills

Repeatedly throughout the book, we emphasized the importance of self-regulation in children's literacy development. The contemporary as well as historical data strongly point to a systematic decrease in the percentage of children who possess the self-regulation skills needed to function effectively and learn in school. Consequently, we recommend that parents and early childhood professionals make self-regulation a priority in their efforts to help children grow. We are not calling for a return to blind obedience to all authority. We are advocating a strategy of socialization by parents and instruction by childcare professionals that takes the development of self-control, concentration ability, independence, and responsibility as seriously as growth of language and literacy skills. It is important to emphasize here that we are not talking about a wholesale change in self-regulation for the majority of American preschoolers. Most are doing just fine. But the number of children who have not learned appropriate self-regulation skills before school entry is high and may have increased over the last several decades, to the detriment of classroom functioning and to individual learning. As parents and teachers we need to give self-regulation a central place in our goals for our children.

Once Children Get to School
5. Strive for Individualized Instruction

The clearest recommendation stemming from recent research on classroom instruction points squarely to the need for a balanced approach to early literacy, combining elements of basic instruction with exposure to rich literature. We want to go a step further and recommend that instruction be tailored as concretely as possible to the level of functioning of each child in the class. We must recognize and act on the insights gained recently that different instructional activities are more or less beneficial for different children. Hence the balance of basic and higher-level literacy-promoting activities will differ depending on the skill levels children bring to class. For too long the prevailing "one size fits all" approach to early literacy instruction has left fully one-third of children without the opportunity to learn in ways that promote their academic success. Top-down policy on curriculum and instruction, scripted basal readers, and the demand that every child in every classroom in the school be on the same page at the same time have bound teachers' hands and proscribed critical flexibility. Good teaching is like dancing; you need to be light on your feet and anticipate where your partner (in this case, your student) will step.

An important corollary of our individualized instruction approach is the need for early and ongoing assessment of children's skill levels in areas of functioning crucial for progress. While teachers have a general idea of how their children are doing, most teachers do not have detailed and concrete information on specific skills like phonological decoding, vocabulary, or comprehension. Only through systematic regular assessments can teachers gain the information they need to construct an accurate profile of each student's strengths and weaknesses and design the instructional package each student needs to advance.

We are not unmindful of the logistical difficulties of implementing classroom practices that will accomplish the goal of providing instruction tailored to each student's level and need. Nevertheless, we attempted to offer some concrete suggestions for ways we could accomplish that goal. Included were using flexible small groups based on assessments, providing enough time for instruction and learning, good classroom management, and promoting effective teaching overall. Our ultimate plea is to *strive* for individualized instruction even in circumstances where it cannot be realized fully for all students. If we keep the focus on students and strive to provide each one with the instruction they need, we will be more likely to avoid the pendulum swings so characteristic of educational practice over the last century (Ravitch 2000).

6. Enhance the Quality and Status of Teachers

While our focus during the school years has been primarily on the act of teaching as the critical proximal factor in need of improvement (chapters 6 and 7), a solid body of evidence points to the critical role of more distal factors directly related to variability in teaching practices: (1) wide discrepancies in the quality of people entering the profession; (2) uneven training they receive to become teachers; and (3) woefully inadequate professional development they are provided once they become teachers. These shortcomings combine with other elements of public perception (Posamentier 2003) to relegate teaching to a surprisingly low status in American society. The low status serves to discourage many highly qualified people from entering the discipline, which reinforces the profession's low status, completing the self-perpetuating vicious circle. We must try to break this cycle, difficult though it may be. Although how to break this cycle is not well studied, there are emerging ideas about how to recast teaching as a respected discipline. Keep in mind, however, that these are largely opinions, and there is no systematic research base for these claims.

First, create viable career paths, reward effective teachers, and stop promoting our best teachers out of the classroom and out of troubled schools. Improve the quality of the education teachers receive with a more rigorous focus on the specialized skills and knowledge teachers need. We also argue that in considering teacher education and credentials, the specialized knowledge of a high school math teacher will differ markedly from that of a first grade teacher. These professional specialties might be better acknowledged and rewarded. With this in mind, we should continue to develop and support high standards for teaching, including accountability for students' academic growth. Also important will be providing more opportunities for professional development. The example provided by New York City's school for principals demonstrates a new approach that might just be successful (*Business Week* 2003). The school district created an intensive summer program for principals, focusing on leadership and other key management skills. Finally, improve teachers' access to research in education so that it can be used to expand the specialized knowledge base teachers need, much the way medicine has over the past forty years.

7. Promote Ongoing Dialogue and Interaction between Researchers and Teachers

Our last recommendation echoes a growing trend in educational circles to bring together the research communities with practicing professional educators in a more systematic way. New research methods are allowing us to examine complex and multifaceted aspects of instruction, including the multilevel influences of children and teachers in classrooms, classrooms in schools, and parents, children, teachers, and schools in communities. Efforts are already under way to make evidenced-based practices the standard for program recommendations and curricular implementation. These initiatives are important in our view and will serve to enhance the quality of instruction provided to children. Parenthetically, related to the above recommendation, we feel that grounding teaching practice in research will help to enhance the status of the teaching profession. But we also strongly urge the research community to become more involved with practicing professionals. Researchers should feel some obligation to explain the meaning and relevance of their work for understanding children's learning as well as to consider research that addresses teachers' most pressing questions in the classroom. The quality of research itself can be enhanced from the knowledge and insights of teachers and other school personnel. Fostering ongoing discussions and collaborations among researchers and educators will enrich both groups and ultimately be most beneficial to our children.

What If . . .

If the above recommendations were implemented, a greater percentage of American children would start school with the language, literacy, and social skills needed to succeed. Teachers would be faced with much less heterogeneity in children's skill levels, which would make teaching more effective in general and would permit more time for individualized instruction. The heightened literacy of a greater percentage of students would serve as a source of continuing gratification for teachers, enhancing their satisfaction and commitment to the profession. Improved teacher training and knowledge, coupled with the ongoing collaboration with scientific researchers, would further enhance the status of the profession as well as its attractiveness. Most important, all elements of American society would have come together to fulfill the potential of each one of our children.

References

Administration for Children and Families. 2003. Details for implementation of the Head Start National Reporting System. *Federal Register* 68 (119).

Alexander, K., and D. Entwisle. 1988. Achievement in the first 2 years of school: Patterns and processes. *Monographs of the Society for Research in Child Development* 53 (2).

Alexander, K., D. Entwisle, and S. Dauber. 1993. First-grade classroom behavior: Its short- and long-term consequences for school performance. *Child Development* 64:801–14.

Alwin, D. 1984. Trends in parental socialization values: Detroit. *American Journal of Sociology* 52:359–82.

———. 1996. Parental socialization in historical perspective. In *The parental experience in midlife,* edited by C. Ryff and M. Seltzer. Chicago: University of Chicago Press.

Anderson, R. C., E. H. Hiebert, J. A. Scott, and I. A. G. Wilkinson. 1985. *Becoming a nation of readers: The report of the Commission on Reading.* Washington DC: National Academy of Education.

Aponte, R. 1993. Hispanic families in poverty: Diversity, context, and interpretation. *Families in Society* 36:527–37.

Applebee, S., J. Langer, and N. Mullis. 1989. *Crossroads in American education.* Princeton, NJ: Educational Testing Service.

Arnold, J., and G. Painter. 2002a. Does the age that children start kindergarten impact their long term success? Poster presented at the twenty-fourth annual Association for Public Policy Analysis and Management (APPAM) research conference, November, Dallas, TX.

———. 2002b. Does the age that children start kindergarten matter? Evidence of long-term educational and social outcomes. Working paper. *http://www-rcf.usc.edu/~gpainter/seasonofbirth2002.pdf.*

Bachman, H. 1999. How did we get here? Examining the sources of white-black differences in academic achievement. In F. Morrison (Chair), Racial differences in academic achievement: When and why? Paper read at biennial meeting of the Society for Research in Child Development, April, Albuquerque, NM.

Bachman, H., and F. Morrison. 2002. Comparing variable-based and person-oriented procedures directly: SEM vs. clustering. Paper read at biennial meeting of the Conference on Human Development, April, Charlotte, NC.

Baker, A., C. Piotrkowski, and J. Brooks-Gunn. 1998. The effects of the Home

Instruction Program for Preschool Youngsters (HIPPY) on children's school performance at the end of the program and one year later. *Early Childhood Research Quarterly* 13:571–88.

———. 1999. The Home Instruction Program for Preschool Youngsters (HIPPY). *Future of Children* 9:116–33.

Barnett, S. 1995. Long-term effects of early childhood programs on cognitive and school outcomes. *Future of Children* 5 (3):25–50.

Barnett, W., E. Frede, F. Mobasher, and P. Mohr. 1987. The efficacy of public preschool programs and the relationship of program quality to efficacy. *Education Evaluation and Policy Analysis* 10 (1):37–49.

Barnett, W. S., J. W. Young, and L. J. Schweinhart. 1998. How preschool education influences long-term cognitive development and school success. In *Early care and education for children in poverty: Promised, programs, and long-term results,* edited by W. S. Barnett and S. S. Boocock. Albany: State University of New York Press.

Baumwell, L., C. Tamis-LeMonda, and M. Bornstein. 1997. Maternal verbal sensitivity and child language comprehension. *Infant Behavior and Development* 20:247–58.

Bayley, N. 1969. *Bayley Scales of infant development.* New York: Psychological Corporation.

———. 1993. *Bayley Scales of infant development.* 2nd ed. New York: Psychological Corporation.

Beals, D. 1997. Sources of support for learning words in conversation: Evidence from mealtimes. *Journal of Child Language* 24:673–94.

Belluck, P. 1999. Reason is sought for lag by blacks in school effort. *New York Times,* July 4, A1, A12.

Belsky, J. 2001. Developmental risk (still) associated with early child care. *Journal of Child Psychology and Psychiatry* 42:845–60.

Berlin, L. J., and J. Brooks-Gunn. 1995. Examining observational measures of emotional support and cognitive stimulation in black and white mothers of preschoolers. *Journal of Family Issues* 16.

Berlin, L. J., C. O'Neil, and J. Brooks-Gunn. 1998. What makes early intervention programs work? The program, its participants, and their interaction. *Zero to Three* 18:4–15.

Bianchi, S. M. 2000. Maternal employment and time with children: Dramatic change or surprising continuity? *Demography* 37 (4):401–14.

Bisanz, J., F. Morrison, and M. Dunn. 1995. Effects of age and schooling on the acquisition of elementary quantitative skills. *Developmental Psychology* 31 (2):221–36.

Blau, F. D., and A. J. Grossberg. 1992. Maternal labor supply and children's cognitive development. *Review of Economics and Statistics* 74:474–81.

Bloom, L. 1998. Language acquisition in its developmental context. In *Handbook of child psychology,* vol. 2, edited by D. Kuhn and R. S. Siegler. New York: Wiley.

Boerst, T. 2003. Deliberative professional development communities as sites for teacher learning. Ph.D. dissertation, School of Education, University of Michigan, Ann Arbor.

Bornstein, M. 1989. Between caretakers and their young: Two modes of interaction and their consequences for cognitive growth. In *Interaction in human development*, edited by M. H. Bornstein and J. S. Bruner. Hillsdale, NJ: Lawrence Erlbaum.

————. 1998. Vocabulary competence in early childhood: Measurement, latent construct, and predictive validity. *Child Development* 69:654–71.

Bornstein, M., and M. Lamb. 1992. *Development in infancy: An introduction.* 3rd ed. New York: McGraw-Hill.

Bourdieu, P. 1985. The social space and the genesis of groups. *Social Science Information* 24:195–220.

Bowey, J. A., and J. Francis. 1991. Phonological analysis as a function of age and exposure to reading instruction. *Applied Psycholinguistics* 12 (1):91–121.

Bradley, L., and P. E. Bryant. 1983. Categorizing sounds and learning to read: A causal connection. *Nature* 301 (3):419–21.

Bradley, R. H., M. R. Burchinal, and P. H. Casey. 2001. Early intervention: The moderating role of the home environment. *Applied Developmental Science* 5:2–8.

Bradley, R. H., and R. F. Corwyn. 2004. Family process investments that matter for child well-being. In *Family investments in children's potential,* edited by A. Kalil and T. DeLeire, 1–32. Mahwah, NJ: Lawrence Erlbaum.

Bradley, R. H., L. Whiteside, B. M. Caldwell, P. H. Casey, K. Kelleheller, S. Pope, M. Swanson, K. Barrett, and D. Cross. 1993. Maternal IQ, the home environment, and child IQ in low birthweight, premature children. *International Journal of Behavioral Development* 16:61–74.

Brandon, P. 2002. The living arrangements of children in immigrant families in the United States. *International Migration Review* 36:416–36.

Bredekemp, S., and C. Copple, eds. 1997. *Developmentally appropriate practice in early childhood programs.* Washington, DC: National Association for the Education of Young Children.

Breznitz, Z., and T. Teltsch. 1989. The effect of school entrance age on academic achievement and social-emotional adjustment of children: Follow-up study of fourth graders. *Psychology in the Schools* 26:62–68.

Brody, G. H., and D. Flor. 1998. Maternal resources, parenting practices, and child competence in rural, single-parent African American families. *Child Development* 69 (3):803–16.

Bronfenbrenner, U. 1986. Ecology of the family as a context for human development: Research perspectives. *Developmental Psychology* 22:723–42.

Brooks-Gunn, J. 2004. What do we know about children's development from theory, intervention, and policy? In *Human development across lives and generations: The potential for change,* edited by P. L. Chase-Lansdale, K. E. Kiernan and R. J. Friedman, pp. 293–340. New York: Cambridge University Press.

Brooks-Gunn, J., L. J. Berlin, and A. S. Fuligni. 2000. Early childhood intervention programs: What about the family? In *Handbook of early childhood intervention,* edited by J. P. Shonkoff and S. J. Meisels. New York: Cambridge University Press.

Brooks-Gunn, J., M. Burchinal, and M. Lopez. 2001. *Enhancing the cognitive and social development of young children via parent education in the Comprehensive Child Development Program.* Manuscript submitted for publication.

Brooks-Gunn, J., G. Duncan, and J. Aber. 1997. *Neighborhood poverty.* Vol. 1: *Context and consequences for children.* New York: Russell Sage Foundation.

Brooks-Gunn, J., W. Han, and J. Waldfogel. 2002. Maternal employment and child cognitive outcomes in the first three years of life: NICHD study of early child care. *Child Development* 73 (4):1052–72.

Brophy, J. 1979. Teacher behavior and its effects. *Journal of Educational Psychology* 71 (6):733–50.

Brophy, J. E., and T. L. Good. 1986. Teacher behavior and student achievement. In *Handbook of research on teaching,* edited by M. C. Wittrock. New York: Macmillan.

Bryant, P., M. Maclean, and L. Bradley. 1990. Rhyme, language, and children's reading. *Applied Psycholinguistics* 11:237–52.

Business Week. 2003. Can Bloomberg fix New York's schools? June 9.

Buzzelli, C. 1996. The moral implications of teacher-child discourse in early childhood classrooms. *Early Childhood Research Quarterly* 11 (4):515–34.

Cabrera, N., C. Tamis-LeMonda, R. Bradley, S. Hofferth, and M. Lamb. 2000. Fatherhood in the twenty-first century. *Child Development* 71:127–36.

Calkins, S., and N. Fox. 2002. Self-regulatory process in early personality development: A multilevel approach to the study of childhood social withdrawal and aggression. *Development and Psychopathology* 14:477–98.

Cameron, C., C. M. Connor, and F. Morrison. 2004. Effects of variation in teacher organization on classroom functioning. Paper read at the Conference on Human Development, April 23–25, Washington, DC.

Campbell, F., and C. Ramey. 1995. Cognitive and school outcomes for high-risk African-American students at middle adolescence: Positive effects of early intervention. *American Educational Research Journal* 32 (4):743–72.

Campbell, J., C. Hombo, and J. Mazzeo. 1999. Trends in academic progress: Three decades of student performance. Washington, DC: NAEP.

Campbell, R., E. P. Pungello, S. Miller-Johnson, M. Burchinal, and C. T. Ramey. 2001. The development of cognitive and academic abilities: Growth curves from an early childhood educational experiment. *Developmental Psychology* 27 (2):231–42.

Caplan, N., M. Choy, and J. Whitmore. 1992. Indochinese refugee families and academic achievement. *Scientific American* (February): 36–42.

Carlisle, J. 2000. Awareness of the structure and meaning of morphologically complex words: Impact on reading. *Reading and Writing* 12 (3–4):169–90.

Catts, H. 1997. The early identification of language-based reading disabilities. *Language, Speech, and Hearing Services in Schools* 28:86–89.

Catts, H., M. Fey, X. Zhang, and B. Tomblin. 1999. Language basis of reading and reading disabilities: Evidence from a longitudinal investigation. *Scientific Studies of Reading* 3 (4):331–61.

———. 2001. Estimating the risk of future reading difficulties in kindergarten children: A research-based model and its clinical implementation. *Language, Speech, and Hearing Services in Schools* 32:38–50.

Cauce, A. M., J. Comer, and B. A. Schwartz. 1987. Long-term effects of a system-oriented school prevention program. *Journal of Orthopsychiatry* 57 (1):127–31.

CBS News. 2002. Pentagon schools. New York: 60 Minutes.

Center for Disease Control and Prevention. 2000. CDC fact book, 2000/2001. Department of Health and Human Services.

Chafouleas, S., L. Lewandowski, C. Smith, and B. Blachman. 1997. Phonological awareness skills in children: Examining performance across tasks and ages. *Journal of Psychoeducational Assessment* 15:334–47.

Chall, J. 1967. *Learning to read: The great debate*. New York: McGraw-Hill.

Chaney, C. 1994. Language development, metalinguistic skills, and emergent literacy skills of three-year-old children in relation to social class. *Applied Psycholinguistics* 15:371–94.

———. 1998. Preschool language and metalinguistic skills are links to reading success. *Applied Cognitive Psychology* 19:433–46.

Chao, R. 2000. Cultural explanations for the role of parenting in the school success of Asian-American children. In *Resilience across contexts: Family, work, culture, and community,* edited by R. Taylor and M. Wang. Mahwah, NJ: Lawrence Erlbaum.

Charity, A. H., H. S. Scarborough, and D. Griffin. 2004. Familiarity with "School English" in African-American children and its relation to early reading achievement. *Child Development* 75(5):1340–56.

Chase-Lansdale, P., R. Gordon, R. Coley, L. Wakschlag, and J. Brooks-Gunn. 1999. Young African-American multigenerational families in poverty: The contexts, exchanges, and processes of their lives. In *Coping with divorce, single parenting, and remarriage: A risk and resiliency perspective,* edited by E. M. Hetherington. Mahwah, NJ: Lawrence Erlbaum.

Chase-Lansdale, P., and L. Pittman. 2002. Welfare reform and parenting: Reasonable expectations. In *Children and welfare reform,* edited by M. K. Shields. Los Altos, CA: David and Lucile Packard Foundation.

Chen, C., and H. Stevenson. 1995. Motivation and mathematics achievement: A comparative study of Asian-American, Caucasian-American, and East Asian high school students. *Child Development* 66:1215–34.

Christian, K., H. J. Bachman, and F. J. Morrison. 2001. Schooling and cognitive development. In *Environmental effects on cognitive abilities,* edited by R. J. Sternberg and R. L. Grigorenko. Mahwah, NJ: Lawrence Erlbaum, pp. 287–335.

Christian, K., F. Morrison, and F. Bryant. 1998. Predicting kindergarten academic skills: Interactions among child care, maternal education, and family literacy environments. *Early Childhood Research Quarterly* 13 (3):501–21.

Christian, K., F. Morrison, J. Frazier, and G. Masseti. 2000. Specificity in the nature and timing of cognitive growth in kindergarten and first grade. *Journal of Cognition and Development* 1 (4), 429–449.

Clark, R. 1983. *Family life and school achievement: Why poor black children succeed or fail.* Chicago: University of Chicago Press.

Clemetson, L. 2003. Hispanics now largest minority, census shows. *NY Times.com,* January 22.

Coates, D., and M. Lewis. 1984. Early mother-infant interaction and infant cognitive status as predictors of school performance and cognitive behavior in six-year-olds. *Child Development* 55:1219–30.

Cohen, D., S. Raudenbush, and D. Ball. 2002. Resources, instruction, and research. In *Evidence matters: Randomized trials in educational research,* edited by F. Moesteller and R. Boruch. Washington, DC: Brookings Institution Press.

———. 2003. Resources, instruction, and research. *Educational Evaluation and Policy Analysis* 25 (2):119–42.

Coleman, J., E. Campbell, C. Hobson, J. McPartland, A. Mood, F. Weinfeld, and R. York. 1966. *Equality of educational opportunity.* Washington, DC: U.S. Government Printing Office.

Coley, R. 2001. (In)visible men: Emerging research on low-income, unmarried, and minority fathers. *American Psychologist* 56:1219–30.

Collins, W. A., E. Maccoby, L. Steinberg, E. M. Hetherington, and M. H. Bornstein. 2000. Contemporary research on parenting: The case for nature and nurture. *American Psychologist* 55:218–32.

Comer, J., and N. Haynes. 1991. Parent involvement in schools: An ecological approach. *Elementary School Journal* 91:271–77.

Conlin, M. 2003. The new gender gap. *Business Week,* May 26.

Connor, C. M. 2000. Reminiscences about her experience at the CIERA Summer Institute for Teachers, July, Ann Arbor, MI.

———. 2002. Preschool children and teachers talking together: The influence of child, family, teacher, and classroom characteristics on children's developing literacy. Ph.D. dissertation, Educational Studies, University of Michigan, Ann Arbor.

Connor, C. M., H. Craig, and J. Washington. 2001. Oral language predictors of reading achievement for African American students. Paper read at the

American Speech, Language, and Hearing Association, November 14–16, New Orleans.

Connor, C. M., F. Morrison, and L. Katch. 2004. Beyond the reading wars: The effect of classroom instruction by child interactions on early reading. *Scientific Studies of Reading* 8(4):305–336.

Connor, C. M., F. Morrison, and J. Petrella. Forthcoming. Effective reading comprehension instruction: Examining child by instruction interactions. *Journal of Educational Psychology* 96(4).

Connor, C. M., S. Son, F. Morrison, and A. Hindman. In review. Teacher qualifications, classroom practices, and family characteristics: Complex effects on first graders' language and early reading.

Cooney, R. 1998. Relations among aspects of parental control, children's work-related skills, and academic achievement. Paper read at the Conference on Human Development, March, Mobile, AL.

Cooper, C., J. Denner, and E. Lopez. 1999. Cultural brokers: Helping Latino children on pathways toward success. *Future of Children* 9:51–57.

Coplan, Robert J., and A. M. Barber. 1999. The role of child temperament as a predictor of early literacy and numeracy skills in preschoolers. *Early Childhood Research Quarterly* 14 (4):537–53.

Corcoran, S. P., W. N. Evans, and R. M. Schwab. 2004. *Women, the labor market, and the declining relative quality of teachers.* http://www.csus.edu/indiv/c/corcorans/research.htm.

Cosden, M., J. Zimmer, C. Reyes, and M. Guttierez. 1995. Kindergarten practices and first-grade achievement for Latino Spanish-speaking, Latino English-speaking, and Anglo students. *Journal of School Psychology* 33:123–41.

Cosden, M., J. Zimmer, and P. Tuss. 1993. The impact of age, sex, and ethnicity on kindergarten entry and retention decisions. *Educational Evaluation and Policy Analysis* 15:209–22.

Cowan, P. A., and C. P. Cowan. 2002. What an intervention design reveals about how parents affect their children's academic achievement and behavior problems. In *Parenting and the child's world: Influences on academic, intellectual, and social-emotional development,* edited by J. G. Borkowski, S. L. Ramey, and M. Bristol-Power. Mahwah, NJ: Lawrence Erlbaum.

Cox, K. E., and J. T. Guthrie. 2001. Motivational and cognitive contributions to students' amount of reading. *Contemporary Educational Psychology* 26:116–31.

Craig, H. K. 1995. Pragmatic impairments. In *The handbook of child language,* edited by P. Fletcher and B. MacWhinney. Oxford: Blackwell.

Crockenberg, S. C. 2003. Rescuing the baby from the bathwater: How conclusions may vary with context. *Child Development* 74 (4):1034–38.

Crockett, L., D. Eggebeen, and A. Hawkins. 1993. Father's presence and young children's behavioral and cognitive adjustment. *Journal of Family Issues* 14:355–77.

Crone, D. A., and G. J. Whitehurst. 1999. Age and schooling effects on emergent literacy and early reading skills. *Journal of Educational Psychology* 91 (4):604–14.

Crosby, B. 2002. *The $100,000 teacher: A teacher's solution to America's declining public school system.* Herndon, VA: Capital Books.

Crosser, S. L. 1991. Summer birth date children: Kindergarten entrance age and academic achievement. *Journal of Educational Research* 54 (3):140–46.

Cunningham, A., and K. Stanovich. 1997. Early reading acquisition and its relation to reading experience and ability 10 years later. *Developmental Psychology* 33 (6):934–45.

Cunningham, A., K. Stanovich, and R. West. 1994. Literacy environment and the development of children's cognitive skills. In *Literacy acquisition and social context,* edited by E. Assink. London: Wheatsheaf/Prentice Hall.

Dahl, K. L., and P. A. Freppon. 1995. A comparison of innercity children's interpretations of reading and writing instruction in the early grades in skills-based and whole language classrooms. *Reading Research Quarterly* 30 (1):50–74.

Darling-Hammond, L. 2000. Teacher quality and student achievement: A review of state policy evidence. *Educational Policy Analysis and Archives* 8 (1).

Darling-Hammond, L., and P. Youngs. 2002. Defining "highly qualified teachers": What does "scientifically-based research" actually tell us? *Educational Researcher* 31 (9):13–25.

Davis, A. R. 1987. A historical perspective. In *Teaching reading,* edited by J. E. Alexander. Glenview IL: Scot Foresman/Little Brown College Division.

Davis, B., C. Glen, S. Trimble, and D. R. Vincent. 1980. Does age of entrance affect school achievement? *Elementary School Journal* 80:133–43.

Debaryshe, B. D. 1993. Joint picture-book reading correlates of early oral language skill. *Journal of Child Language* 20:455–61.

Della Corte, M., H. Benedict, and D. Klein. 1983. The relationship of pragmatic dimensions of mothers' speech to the referential-expressive distinction. *Journal of Child Language* 10:35–43.

Delpit, L. 1995. *Other people's children: Cultural conflict in the classroom.* New York: New Press.

DeMeis, J. L., and E. S. Stearns. 1992. Relationship of school entrance age to academic and social performance. *Journal of Educational Research* 86 (1):20–27.

Diamond, K., A. Reagan, and J. Bandyk. 2000. Parents' conceptions of kindergarten readiness: Relationships with race, ethnicity, and development. *Journal of Educational Research* 94:93–100.

Dickinson, D. K., J. M. De Temple, J. A. Hirschler, and M. W. Smith. 1992.

Book reading with preschoolers: Construction of text at home and at school. *Early Childhood Research Quarterly* 7:323–46.

Dickinson, D. K., and M. W. Smith. 1994. Long-term effects of preschool teachers' book readings on low-income children's vocabulary and story comprehension. *Reading Research Quarterly* 29 (2):105–22.

Dickinson, D. K., and P. O. Tabors. 2001. *Beginning literacy with language.* Baltimore: Paul H. Brookes.

DiPasquale, G.W., A. D. Moule, and R. W. Flewelling. 1980. The birthdate effect. *Journal of Learning Disabilities* 13:234–38.

DiPietro, J. A., S. C. Hilton, M. Hawkins, K. A. Costigan, and E. K. Pressman. 2002. Maternal stress and affect influence fetal neurobehavioral development. *Developmental Psychology* 38 (5):659–68.

Dixon, W., and P. Smith. 2000. Links between early temperament and language acquisition. *Merrill-Palmer Quarterly* 46:417–40.

Dodge, K. A. 2002. Mediation, moderation, and mechanisms in how parenting affects children's aggressive behavior. In *Parenting and the child's world: Influences on academic, intellectual, and social-emotional development,* edited by J. G. Borkowski, S. L. Ramey and M. Bristol-Power. Mahwah, NJ: Lawrence Erlbaum.

DOE. 2002. Meeting the highly qualified teachers challenge. Washington, DC: U.S. Department of Education, Office of Postsecondary Education, Office of Policy Planning and Innovation.

Duncan, G., J. Brooks-Gunn, and P. Klebanov. 1994. Economic deprivation and early-childhood development. *Child Development* 62:296–318.

Duncan, G., W. Yeung, J. Brooks-Gunn, and J. Smith. 1998. How much does childhood poverty affect the life chances of children? *American Psychological Review* 63:406–23.

Durkin, D. 1987. A classroom-observation study of reading instruction in kindergarten. *Early Childhood Research Quarterly* 2:275–300.

Duyme, M., A. Dumaret, and S. Tomkiewicz. 1999. How can we boost IQ's of "dull children"? A late adoption study. *Proceedings of the National Academy of Sciences of the United States of America* 96:8790–94.

Eccles, J. S., and A. Wigfield. 2002. Motivational beliefs, values, and goals. *2002* 53:109–32.

Eccles, J. S., A. Wigfield, and U. Schiefele. 1998. Motivation to succeed. In *Handbook of child psychology:* vol. 3, *Social, emotional, and personality development,* 5th ed., edited by W. Damon and N. Eisenberg, 1017–95. New York, Wiley.

Echols, L., R. West, K. Stanovich, and K. Zehr. 1996. Using children's literacy activities to predict growth in verbal cognitive skills: A longitudinal investigation. *Journal of Educational Psychology* 88 (2):296–304.

Ehrenberg, R. G., and D. J. Brewer. 1995. Did teachers' verbal ability and race matter in the 1960s? Coleman revisited. *Economics of Education Review* 14 (1):1–21.

Ehrle, J., G. Adams, and K. Tout. 2001. Who's caring for our youngest children? Child care patterns of infants and toddlers. Washington, DC: Urban Institute.

Eisenberg, N., R. Fabes, B. Murphy, P. Maszk, M. Smith, and M. Karbon. 1995. The role of emotionality and regulation in children's social functioning: A longitudinal study. *Child Development* 66:1360–84.

Entwisle, D. R., and K. L. Alexander. 1988. Factors affecting achievement test scores and marks of black and white first graders. *Elementary School Journal* 88:449–72.

———. 1993. Entry into school: The beginning school transition and educational stratification in the United States. *Annual Review of Sociology* 19:401–23.

Entwisle, D. R., K. L. Alexander, and L. S. Olson. 1997. *Children, schools, and inequality.* Edited by M. Tienda and D. B. Grusky, Social inequity series. Boulder, CO: Westview.

Entwisle, D. R., and D. Baker. 1983. Gender and young children's expectations for performance in arithmetic. *Developmental Psychology* 19:200–209.

Estrada, P., W. Arsenio, R. Hess, and S. Holloway. 1987. Affective quality of the mother-child relationship: Longitudinal consequences for children's school-relevant cognitive functioning. *Developmental Psychology* 23:210–15.

Evans, M., D. Shaw, and M. Bell. 2000. Home literacy activities and their influences on early literacy skills. *Canadian Journal of Experimental Psychology* 54:65–75.

Ferguson, R. F. 1990. *Racial patterns in how school and teacher quality affect achievement and earnings.* Dallas: Meadows Foundation.

———. 1991. Paying for public education. *Harvard Journal on Legislation* 28 (2):465–98.

———. 2002. *What doesn't meet the eye: Understanding and addressing racial disparities in high-achieving suburban schools.* Naperville, IL: North Central Regional Educational Laboratory (NCREL).

Ferguson, R. F., and H. F. Ladd. 1996. How and why money matters: An analysis of Alabama schools. In *Holding schools accountable: Performance-based reform in education,* edited by H. F. Ladd. Washington, DC: Brookings Institution Press.

Ferrari, M., and R. Sternberg. 1998. The development of mental abilities and styles. In *Handbook of child psychology,* edited by W. Damon. New York: Wiley.

Ferreira, F. and F. Morrison. 1994. Children's metalinguistic knowledge of syntactic constituents: Effects of age and schooling. *Development and Psychology* 30 (5):663–78.

Finn, C. E., and M. Kanstoroom. 2001. Getting better teachers: Time for experimentation. In *Tomorrow's teachers,* edited by M. C. Wang and H. J. Walberg. Richmond, CA: McCutchan.

Flesch, R. 1955. *Why Johnny can't read: And what you can do about it.* New York: Harper and Brothers.

Flores, G., E. Fuentes-Afflick, O. Barbot, O. Carter-Pokras, L. Claudio, and M. Lara. 2002. The health of Latino children: Urgent priorities, unanswered questions, and a research agenda. *JAMA* 288:82–89.

Folk, K. F., and A. H. Beller. 1993. Part-time work and child care choices for mothers of preschool children. *Journal of Marriage and the Family* 55:146–57.

Foorman, B. R., D. J. Francis, J. M. Fletcher, C. Schatschneider, and P. Mehta. 1998. The role of instruction in learning to read: Preventing reading failure in at risk children. *Journal of Educational Psychology* 90:37–55.

Frazier, J. A., F. J. Morrison, and T. R. Trabasso. 1995. Age and schooling influences on growth of narrative coherence. Paper read at the annual conference of the American Educational Research Association, March, San Francisco.

Fritjers, J., R. Barron, and M. Brunello. 2000. Direct and mediated influences of home literacy and literacy interest on prereaders' oral vocabulary and early written language skill. *Journal of Educational Psychology* 92:466–77.

Frymier, J. 1998. Accountability and student learning. *Journal of Personnel Evaluation in Education* 12 (3):233–35.

Fuligni, A. 1997. The academic achievement of adolescents from immigrant families: The roles of family background, attitudes, and behavior. *Child Development* 68:351–63.

Fuller, B., C. Eggers-Piérola, and S. Holloway. 1996. Rich culture, poor markets: Why do Latino parents forgo preschooling? *Teachers College Record* 97:400–418.

Garcia-Coll, C., K. Crnic, G. Lamberty, B. H. Wasik, et al. 1996. An integrative model for the study of developmental competencies in minority children. *Child Development* 67:1891–1914.

Garcia-Coll, C., J. Kagan, and J. Reznick. 1984. Behavioral inhibition in young children. *Child Development* 55:1005–19.

Gardner, H. 1983. *Frames of mind: The theory of multiple intelligences.* New York: Basic Books.

Geary, D. 1996. International differences in math achievement: Their nature, causes, and consequences. *Psychological Science* 5:133–37.

Geary, D., C. Bow-Thomas, L. Fan, and R. Siegler. 1996. Development of arithmetical competencies in Chinese and American children: Influence of age, language, and schooling. *Child Development* 67:2022–44.

Gellman, E., A Guarino, and J. Witte. 2001. Attitudes towards the use of tests and test scores. *Psychological Reports* 86:669–71.

Gleason, J. B. 1997. *The development of language.* Boston: Allyn and Bacon.

Gleitman, L. R., and J.Gillette. 1999. The role of syntax in verb learning. In *Handbook of child language acquisition,* edited by W. C. Ritchie and T. K. Bhatia. San Diego: Academic Press.

Goelman, H., A. A. Oberg, and F. Smith, eds. 1984. *Awakening to literacy.* London: Heinemann Educational Books.

Goldenberg, C., R. Gallimore, L. Reese, and H. Garnier. 2001. Cause or effect? A longitudinal study of immigrant Latino parents' aspirations and expectations, and their children's school performance. *American Educational Research Journal* 38:547–82.

Goldhaber, D. D., and D. J. Brewer. 1999. Teacher licensing and student achievement. In *Better teachers, better schools,* edited by M. Kasteroroon and C. E. Finn. Washington, DC: Thomas B. Fordham Foundation.

———. 2000. Does teacher certification matter? High school teacher certification status and student achievement. *Educational Evaluation and Policy Analysis* 22 (2):129–46.

Goldin-Meadow, S. 2002. From thought to hand: Structured and unstructured communication outside of conventional language. In *Language literacy and cognitive development,* edited by E. Amsl and J. P. Brynes. Mahwah, NJ: Lawrence Erlbaum.

Golova, N., A. Alario, P. Vivier, M. Rodriguez, and P. High. 1999. Literacy promotion for Hispanic families in a primary care setting: A randomized, controlled trial. *Pediatrics* 103:993–97.

Gomby, D. S., P. L. Culross, and R. E. Behrman. 1999. Home visiting: Recent program evaluations—analysis and recommendations. *Future of Children* 9:4–26.

Goodman, K. 1970. Reading: A psycholinguistic guessing game. In *Theoretical models and processes of reading,* edited by H. Singer and R. B. Ruddell. Newark, DE: International Reading Association.

———. 1986. *What's whole in whole language?* Portsmouth, NH: Heinemann.

Goodman, Y. 1984. The development of initial literacy. In *Awakening to literacy,* edited by H. Goelman, A. A. Oberg, and F. Smith. London: Heinemann Educational Books.

Green, J., C. Dixon, L. Lin, A. Floriani, M. Bradley, S. Paxton, C. Mattern, and H. Bergamo. 1992. Santa Barbara Classroom Discourse Group. In *Redefining student learning,* edited by H. H. Marshall. Norwood, NJ: Ablex.

Green, K. D., R. Forehand, S. J. Beck, and B. Vosk. 1980. An assessment of the relationship among measures of children's social competence and children's academic achievement. *Child Development* 51:1149–56.

Greenspan, S. J. 2003. Child care research: A clinical perspective. *Child Development* 74 (4):1064–69.

Greenwald, R., L. V. Hedges, and R. D. Laine. 1996. The effect of school resources on student achievement. *Review of Educational Research* 66 (3): 361–96.

Griffin, E., and F. Morrison. 1997. The unique contribution of home literacy environment to differences in early literacy skills. *Early Child Development and Care* 127–28:233–43.

Grolnick, W. S., and R. M. Ryan. 1989. Parent styles associated with children's self-regulation and competence in school. *Journal of Educational Psychology* 81 (2):143–54.

Guttierrez, J., and A. Sameroff. 1990. Determinants of complexity in Mexican-American and Anglo-American mothers' conceptions of child development. *Child Development* 61:384–94.

Guzman, B., and E. McConnell. 2002. The Hispanic population: 1990–2000 growth and change. *Population Research and Policy Review* 21:109–28.

Hacsi, T. A. 2002a. *Does class size matter?* Cambridge: Harvard University Press.

———. 2002b. *Is bilingual education a good idea?* Cambridge: Harvard University Press.

Haden, C. A., E. Reese, and R. Fivush. 1996. Mothers' extratextural comments during storybook reading: Stylistic differences over time and across text. *Discourse Processes* 21:135–69.

Hansen, E. E. 2001. The unbroken line: Contribution of kindergarten literacy and social skills to sixth grade academic achievement. In *Dissertation abstracts international, section B: The sciences and engineering.*

Hansen, T., S. McLanahan, and E. Thompson. 1997. Economic resources, parental practices, and children's well-being. In *Consequences of growing up poor,* edited by G. Duncan and J. Brooks-Gunn. New York: Russell Sage Foundation.

Harris, J. R. 1995. Where is the child's environment? A group socialization theory of development. *Psychological Review* 102:458–89.

Hart, B., and T. R. Risley. 1995. *Meaningful differences in the everyday experience of young American children.* Baltimore: Paul H. Brookes.

Hartup, W. 1989. Social relationships and their developmental significance. *American Psychologist* 44:120–26.

Hawk, P., C. Coble, and M. Swanson. 1985. Certification: It does matter. *Journal of Teacher Education* 36 (3):13–15.

Haynes, N. M., and J. Comer. 1990. The effects of a school development program on self-concept. *Yale Journal of Biology* 63:275–83.

———. 1996. Integrating schools, families, and communities through successful school reform: The School Development Program. *School Psychology Review* 25 (4):501–6.

Haynes, N. M., J. Comer, and M. Hamilton-Lee. 1988. The School Development Program: A model for school improvement. *Journal of Negro Education* 57 (1):11–21.

————. 1989. School climate enhancement through parental involvement. *Journal of Negro Education* 8 (4):291–99.

Heath, S. B. 1983. *Ways with words.* Cambridge: Cambridge University Press.

Henderson, H. A., and N. A. Fox. 1998. Inhibited and uninhibited children: Challenges in school settings. *School Psychology Review* 27 (4):492–505.

Henke, R. R., P. Knepper, S. Geis, and J. Giambattista. 1996. *Out of the lecture hall and into the classroom: 1992–1993 college graduates and elementary/secondary school teaching.* Washington, DC: U.S. Department of Education.

Hernandez, D. 1993. *America's children: Resources from family, government, and the economy.* New York: Russell Sage Foundation.

Hieshima, J., and B. Schneider. 1994. Intergenerational effects on the cultural and cognitive socialization of third- and fourth-generation Japanese Americans. *Journal of Applied Developmental Psychology* 15:319–27.

Hirsh, E. D. 1996. *The schools we need and why we don't have them.* New York: Doubleday.

Hoff-Ginsberg, E. 1991. Mother-child conversation in different social classes and communicative settings. *Child Development* 62:782–96.

Hoxby, C. M., and A. Leigh. 2003. *Pulled away or pushed out? Explaining the decline of teacher aptitude in the United States 2003.* http://post.economics.harvard.edu/faculty/hoxby/papers.html.

Huttenlocher, J., W. Haight, A. Bryk, M. Seltzer, and T. Lyons. 1991. Early vocabulary growth: Relation to language input and gender. *Developmental Psychology* 27 (2):236–48.

Huttenlocher, J., M. Vasilyeva, E. Cymerman, and S. Levine. 2002. Language input and syntax. *Cognitive Psychology* 45:337–74.

Hyde, J., E. Fennema, and S. Lamon. 1990. Gender differences in mathematics performance: A meta-analysis. *Psychological Bulletin* 107 (2):139–55.

Hyde, J., and M. Linn. 1988. Gender differences in verbal ability: A meta-analysis. *Psychological Bulletin* 104 (1):53–69.

Improving America's Schools Act of 1994. 1994. Public Law 103–382. *http://thomas.loc.gov/cgi-bin/query/F?c103:5:./temp/~c103dy4aOo:e197065.*

Jencks, C., and M. Phillips. 1998a. *The black-white test score gap.* Washington, DC: Brookings Institution Press.

————. 1998b. The black-white test score gap. *Brookings Review* 16:24–27.

Jimerson, S., B. Egeland, L. Sroufe, and B. Carlson. 2000. A prospective longitudinal study of high school dropouts examining multiple predictors across development. *Journal of School Psychology* 38 (6):525–49.

Johnson, D. L., P. Swank, V. M. Howie, C. D. Baldwin, M. Owen, and D. Luttman. 1993. Does HOME add to prediction of child intelligence over and above SES? *Journal of Genetic Psychology* 154:33–40.

Juel, C., and C. Minden-Cupp. 2000. Learning to read words: Linguistic units and instructional strategies. *Reading Research Quarterly* 35 (4):498–92.

Kaestle, C. F. 1993. The awful reputation of education research. *Educational Researcher* 22 (1):23–31.

Kagan, J. 1998. Biology and the child. In *Handbook of child psychology*, edited by W. Damon and R. Lerner. New York: Wiley.

Kamins, M. L., and C. S. Dweck. 1999. Person versus process praise and criticism: Implications for contingent self-worth and coping. *Developmental Psychology* 35 (3):835–47.

Kanstoroom, M., and C. E. Finn, eds. 1999. *Better teachers, better schools.* Washington, DC: Thomas B. Fordham Foundation.

Kantor, R., J. Green, M. Bradley, and L. Lin. 1992. The construction of schooled discourse repertoires: An interactional sociolinguistic perspective on learning to talk in preschool. *Linguistics and Education* 5 (3–4):367–410.

Kaplan, C. 1993. Predicting first-grade achievement from pre-kindergarten WPPSI-R scores. *Journal of Psychoeducational Assessment* (11):133–38.

Kauffman, D., S. M. Johnson, S. M. Kardos, E. Liu, and H. G. Peske. 2002. "Lost at sea": New teachers' experiences with curriculum and assessment. *Teachers College Record* 104 (2):273–300.

Kelly, J., C. Morisset, K. Barnartd, M. Hammond, and C. Booth. 1996. The in fluence of early mother-child interaction on preschool cognitive/linguistic outcomes in a high-social-risk group. *Infant Mental Health Journal* 17:310–21.

Kessenich, M., T. Raviv, and F. Morrison. 2000. Variability and stability in cognitive and language skills of 2- and 3-year-old children in a national sample. Paper read at biennial meeting of the Conference on Human Development, April, Memphis, TN.

Kochanska, G., K. Murray, T. Jaques, A. Koenig, and K. Vandegeest. 1996. Inhibitory control in young children and its role in emerging internalization. *Child Development* 67:490–507.

Korenman, S., and J. Miller. 1997. Effects of long-term poverty on physical health of children in the national longitudinal survey of youth. In *Consequences of growing up poor,* edited by G. Duncan and J. Brooks-Gunn. New York: Russell Sage Foundation.

Kurdek, L. A., and R. J. Sinclair. 2000. Psychological, family, and peer predictors of academic outcomes in first- through fifth-grade children. *Journal of Educational Psychology* 92 (3):449–57.

Ladd, G., and J. Price. 1987. Predicting children's social and school adjustment following the transition from preschool to kindergarten. *Child Development* 58:1168–89.

Lagemann, E. C. 1996. Contested terrain: A history of education research in the United States, 1890–1990. *Educational Researcher* 26 (9):5.

———. 2000. *An elusive science: The troubling history of education research.* Chicago: University of Chicago Press.

Landale, N., and D. Lichter. 1997. Geography and the etiology of poverty among Latino children. *Social Science Quarterly* 78:874–94.

Landale, N., R. Oropesa, and D. Llanes. 1998. Schooling, work, and idleness among Mexican and non-Latino white adolescents. *Social Science Research* 27:457–80.

Landry, S., K. Smith, C. Miller-Loncar, and P. Swank. 1997. Predicting cognitive-language and social growth curves from early maternal behaviors in children at varying degrees of biological risk. *Developmental Psychology* 33:1040–53.

Lane, H., R. Hoffmeister, and B. Bahan. 1996. *A journey into the deaf-world.* San Diego, CA: Dawn Sign.

Langenberg, D. N. 2000. *National reading panel: Teaching children to read: An evidence-based assessment of the scientific research literature on reading and its implications for reading instruction.* Washington, DC: NICHD.

Langer, P., J. Kalk, and D. Searls. 1984. Age of admission and trends in achievement: A comparison of blacks and caucasians. *American Educational Reserach Journal* 21 (1):61–78.

Langlois, J. H., and L. S. Liben. 2003. Child care research: An editorial perspective. *Child Development* 74 (4):969–75.

Lareau, A., and E. Horvat. 1999. Moments of social inclusion and exclusion: Race, class, and cultural capital in family-school relationships. *Sociology of Education* 72:37–53.

Lazar, I., R. Darlington, H. Murray, J. Royce, and A. Snipper. 1982. Lasting effects of early education: A report from the consortium for longitudinal studies. *Monographs of the Society for Research in Child Development* 47 (2–3).

Lengua, L. J. 2002. The contribution of emotionality and self-regulation to the understanding of children's response to multiple risk. *Child Development* 73 (1):144–61.

Lewis, L., B. Parsad, N. Carey, N. Bartfai, E. Farris, B. Smerdon, and B. Greene. 1999. *Teacher quality: A report on the preparation and qualifications of public school teachers.* Washington, DC: U.S. Department of Education, Office of Educational Research and Improvement, NCES.

Leyendecker, B., and M. Lamb. 1999. Latino families. In *Parenting and child development in "nontraditional" families,* edited by M. Lamb. Newark, NJ: Lawrence Erlbaum.

Liang, X., B. Fuller, and J. D. Singer. 2000. Ethnic differences in child care selection: The influence of family structure, parental practices, and home language. *Early Child Research Quarterly* 15 (3):357–84.

Liaw, F., and J. Brooks-Gunn. 1994. Cumulative familial risks and low-birthweight children's cognitive and behavioral development. *Journal of Clinical Child Psychology* 23:360–72.

Liberman, A. M. 1997. How theories of speech affect research in reading and writing. In *Foundations of reading acquisition and dyslexia,* edited by B. A. Blachman. Mahwah, NJ: Lawrence Erlbaum.

Lichter, D., and N. Landale. 1995. Parental work, family structure, and poverty among Latino children. *Journal of Marriage and the Family* 57:346–54.

Li-Grining, C. P., L. D. Pittman, and P. L. Chase-Lansdale. In review. Temperament and early childhood development: Individual differences among young children in low-income urban communities.

Linnenbrink, E. A., and P. R. Pintrich. 2002. Motivation as an enabler for academic success. *School Psychology Review* 31 (3):313–27.

———. 2003. The role of self-efficacy beliefs in student engagement and learning in the classroom. *Reading and Writing Quarterly* 19:119–37.

Linver, M., J. Brooks-Gunn, and D. Kohen. 2002. Family processes as pathways from income to young children's development. *Developmental Psychology* 38:719–34.

Littlewood, E. M. J. 2001. Teaching perspectives of exemplary teachers. In *Tomorrow's teachers,* edited by M. C. Wang and H. J. Walberg. Richmond, CA: McCutchan.

Loban, W. 1976. *Language development: Kindergarten through grade twelve.* Urbana, IL: National Council of Teachers of English.

Locke, J. L. 1993. *The child's path to spoken language.* Cambridge: Harvard University Press.

Lonigan, C., S. Burgess, and J. Anthony. 2000. Development of emergent literacy and early reading skills in preschool: Evidence from a latent-variable longitudinal study. *Developmental Psychology* 36:596–613.

Lonigan, C. J., and G. J. Whitehurst. 1998. Relative efficacy of parent and teacher involvement in a shared book-reading intervention for preschool children from low income backgrounds. *Early Childhood Research Quarterly* 13 (2):263–90.

Loveless, T., ed. 2001. *The great curriculum debate.* Washington, DC: Brookings Institution Press.

Maccoby, E. 2002. Parenting effects: Issues and controversies. In *Parenting and the child's world: Influences on academic, intellectual, and social-emotional development,* edited by J. G. Borkowski, S. L. Ramey, and M. Bristol-Power. Mahwah, NJ: Lawrence Erlbaum.

Maccoby, E., and C. Jacklin. 1972. Sex differences in intellectual functioning. In *Proceedings of the invitational conference on testing problems.* Stanford: Stanford University Press.

———. 1974. *The psychology of sex differences.* Stanford, CA: Stanford University Press.

Maddux, C. 1980. First-grade entry age in a sample of children labeled learning disabled. *Learning Disability Quarterly* 3:79–83.

Magliano, J. P., T. Trabasso, and A. C. Graesser. 1999. Strategic processing during comprehension. *Journal of Educational Psychology* 91 (4):615–29.

Magnuson, K., and G. Duncan. 2004. Parent- vs child-based intervention strategies for promoting children's well-being. In *Family investments in children's potential,* edited by A. Kalil and T. DeLeire, 209–36. Mahwah, NJ: Lawrence Erlbaum.

Magnuson, K. and S. McGroder. 2002. The effect of increasing welfare mothers' education on their young children's academic problems and school readiness. Working paper of the Joint Center for Poverty Research (no. 280). *http://www.jcpr.org/wp/wpprofile.cfm?id=322.*

Malecki, C., and S. Elliott. 2002. Children's social behaviors as predictors of academic achievement: A longitudinal analysis. *School Psychology Quarterly* 17 (1):1–23.

Mann, V. A., D. Shankweiler, and S. T. Smith. 1984. The association between comprehension of spoken sentences and early reading ability: The role of phonetic representation. *Journal of Child Language* 11:627–43.

Mantzicopoulos, P. 1997. The relationship of family variables to Head Start children's preacademic competence. *Early Education and Development* 8 (4):357–75.

Martella, R. C., R. Nelson, and N. E. Marchand-Martella. 1999. *Research methods: Learning to become a critical research consumer.* Boston: Allyn and Bacon.

Martin, R. P. 1989. Activity level, distractibility, and persistence: Critical characteristics in early schooling. In *Temperament in childhood,* edited by G. A. Kohnstamm, J. E. Bates, and M. K. Rothbart. New York: Wiley.

Martin, R. P., and J. Holbrook. 1985. Relationship of temperament characteristics to the academic achievement of first-grade children. *Journal of Psychoeducational Assessment* 3:131–40.

Martin, R. P., S. Olejnik, and L. Gaddis. 1994. Is temperament an important contributor to schooling outcomes in elementary school? Modeling effects of temperament and scholastic ability on academic achievement. In *Prevention and early intervention: Individual differences as risk factors for the mental health of children: A festschrift for Stella Chess and Alexander Thomas,* edited by W. B. Carey and S. C. McDevitt. New York: Brunner/Mazel.

Mason, J., and J. Stewart. 1990. Emergent literacy assessment for instructional use in kindergarten. In *Assessment for instruction in early literacy,* edited by L. M. Morrow and J. K. Smith. Englewood Cliffs, NJ: Prentice-Hall.

Massetti, G. M., and F. J. Morrison. 1997. Cultural and maturational effects on visual-spatial memory development. Poster presented at the annual meeting of the Midwestern Psychological Association, May, Chicago.

May, D., and D. Kundert. 1995. Does delayed school entry reduce later grade retentions and use of special education services? *Remedial and Special Education* 16 (5):288–95.

Mayberry, R. I., E. Lock, and H. Kazmi. 2002. Linguistic ability and early language exposure. *Nature* 417:38.

Mayer, S. 1997. *What money can't buy: Family income and children's life chances.* Cambridge, MA: Harvard University Press.

McCall, R. B., and M. S. Carriger. 1993. A meta-analysis of infant habituation and recognition memory performance as predictors of later IQ. *Child Development* 64:57–79.

McClelland, M., M. Kessenich, and F. Morrison. 2003. Pathways to early literacy: The complex interplay of child, family, and sociocultural factors. In *Advances in child developmental behavior,* edited by R. Kail and H. W. Reese. New York: Academic Press.

McClelland, M., and F. Morrison. 2003. The emergence of learning-related social skills in preschool children. *Early Childhood Research Review Quarterly* 18 (2):206–24.

McClelland, M., F. Morrison, and D. Holmes. 2000. Children at risk for early academic problems: The role of learning-related social skills. *Early Childhood Research Quarterly* 15 (3):307–29.

McCormick, M., J. Brooks-Gunn, K. Workman-Daniels, J. Turner, and G. Peckham. 1992. The health and development status of very low birthweight children at school age. *Journal of the American Medical Association* 267:2204–8.

McCrea, S. M., J. Mueller, and R. K. Parrilla. 1999. Quantitative analyses of schooling effects on executive function in young children. *Child Neuropsychology* 5 (4):242–50.

McLanahan, S., and G. Sandefur. 1994. *Growing up with a single parent: What hurts, what helps.* Cambridge, MA: Harvard University Press.

McLoyd, V. C. 1990. The impact of economic hardship on black families and children: Psychological distress, parenting, and socioemotional development. *Child Development* 61:311–46.

———. 1998. Socioeconomic disadvantage and child development. *American Psychologist* 53 (2):185–204.

Meece, J. L., and S. D. Miller. 1999. Changes in elementary school children's achievement goals for reading and writing: Results of a longitudinal and an intervention study. *Scientific Studies of Reading* 3 (3):207–29.

Meich, R., M. Essex, and H. Goldsmith, and H. Hill. 2001. Socioeconomic status and the adjustment to school: The role of self-regulation during early childhood. *Sociology of Education* 74(2):102–20.

Meisels, S., M. Dichtelmiller, and F. Liaw. 1993. A multidimensional analysis of early childhood intervention programs. In *Handbook of infant mental health,* edited by C. H. J. Zeanah. New York: Guilford.

Mendoza, F. 1994. The health of Latino children in the United States. *Future of Children* 4:43–72.

Meyer, L. A., R. A. Linn, and C. N. Hastings. 1991. Teacher stability from morning to afternoon and from year to year. *American Educational Research Journal* 28 (4):825–47.

Mischel, W., Y. Shoda, and M. L. Rodriguez. 1989. Delay of gratification in children. *Science* 244 (4907):933–38.

Moats, L. C. 1994. The missing foundation in teacher education: Knowledge of the structure of spoken and written language. *Annals of Dyslexia* 44:81–102.

Monk, D. H. 1994. Subject area preparation of secondary mathematics and science teachers and student achievement. *Economics of Education Review* 13 (2):125–45.

Morrison, F., and C. M. Connor. 2002. Understanding schooling effects on early literacy. *Journal of School Psychology* 40 (6):493–500.

Morrison, F., E. Griffith, and D. Alberts. 1997. Nature-nurture in the classroom: Entrance age, school readiness, and learning in children. *Developmental Psychology* 33 (2):254–62.

Morrison, F., E. Griffith, and J. Frazier. 1996. Schooling and the 5–7 shift: A natural experiment. In *Reason and responsibility: The passage through childhood,* edited by A. Sameroff and M. M. Haith, 161–86. Chicago: University of Chicago Press.

Morrison, F., L. Smith, and M. Dow-Ehrensberger. 1995. Education and cognitive development: A natural experiment. *Developmental Psychology* 31 (5):789–99.

Mosteller, F. 1995. The Tennessee study of class size in the early school grades. *Future of Children* 5 (2):113–27.

Murray, A., J. Johnson, and J. Peters. 1990. Fine-tuning of utterance length to preverbal infants: Effects on later language development. *Journal of Child Language* 17:511–25.

Murray, K., and G. Kochanska. 2002. Effortful control: Factor structure and relation to externalizing and internalizing behaviors. *Journal of Abnormal Child Psychology* 30 (5):503–14.

Naito, M., and H. Miura. 2001. Japanese children's numerical competencies: Age- and schooling-related influences on the development of number concepts and addition skills. *Developmental Psychology* 37 (2):217–30.

Nation, K., and C. Hulme. 1997. Phonemic segmentation, not onset-rime segmentation, predicts early reading and spelling skills. *Reading Research Quarterly* 32:154–67.

National Center for Educational Statistics. 1995a. *The condition of education* (NCES statistical report 95–767). Jessup, MD: U.S. Department of Education.

———. 1995b. *The educational progress of Hispanic students: Findings from "The condition of education 1995"* (NCES statistical report 95–767). Washington, DC: U.S. Department of Education.

———. 1999. *NAEP 1999 trends in academic progress: Three decades of student performance* (NCES statistical report 2000–469). Jessup, MD: U.S. Department of Education.

———. 2001a. *The digest of educational statistics.* Jessup, MD: U.S. Department of Education.

———. 2001b. *Educational achievement and black-white inequality* (NCES statistical report 2001–061). Jessup, MD: U.S. Department of Education.

———. 2001c. *The nation's report card: Fourth-grade reading, 2000.* Washington, DC: U.S. Department of Education, Office of Educational Research and Improvement.

———. 2002. *Projection of education statistics to 2012.* Washington, DC: National Center for Education Statistics.

———. 2003a. *The nation's report card: Mathematics highlights, 2003.* Washington, DC: National Center for Education Statistics.

———. 2003b. *The nation's report card: Reading highlights, 2003.* Washington, DC: National Center for Education Statistics.

National Public Radio. 2002. Profile: Focusing on accountability for academic success in public schools, July 31.

National Research Council. 2001. *Science, evidence, and inference in education research.* Washington, DC: National Academy Press.

Neil, A. 1960. *Summerhill: A radical approach to child rearing.* New York: Hart.

Nelson, C. 1973. Structure and strategy in learning to talk. *Monographs of the Society for Research in Child Development* 38 (1–2):1–10.

Nelson, K. 1981. Individual differences in language development: Implications for development and language. *Developmental Psychology* 17:170–87.

Neuman, S. B, and D. K. Dickinson. 2001. *Handbook of early literacy research.* New York: Guilford. NICHD-ECCRN. 1997. The effects of infant child care on infant-mother attachment security: Results of the NICHD study of early child care. *Child Development* 68 (5):860–79.

———. 1998. Relations between family predictors and child outcomes: Are they weaker for children in child care? *Developmental Psychology* 34:1119–28.

———. 1999. Child outcomes when child care center classes meet recommended standards for quality. *American Journal of Public Health,* 89, 1072–77.

———. 2000. Characteristics and quality of child care for toddlers and preschoolers. *Applied Developmental Science* 4 (3):116–35.

———. 2001. Child care and children's peer interaction at 24 and 36 months: The NICHD study of early child care. *Child Development* 72:1478–1500.

———. 2002a. Child-care structure—process—outcome: Direct and indirect effects of child-care quality on young children's development. *Psychological Science* 13 (2):199–206.

———. 2002b. The relation of global first grade classroom environment to structural classroom features and teacher and student behaviors. *Elementary School Journal* 102 (5):367–87.

―――. 2003. Does amount of time spent in child care predict socioemotional adjustment during the transition to kindergarten? *Child Development* 74 (4):969–1226.

―――. 2004. Multiple pathways to early academic achievement. *Harvard Educational Review* 74(1).

O'Brian Caughy, M., J. A. DiPietro, and D. M. Strobini. 1994. Day-care participation as a protective factor in the cognitive development of low income children. *Child Development* 65:457–71.

Ogbu, J. 1988. Black education: A cultural-ecological perspective. In *Black Families,* edited by H. McAdoo, 169–84. Thousand Oaks, CA: Sage.

―――. 1991. Low school performance as an adaptation: The case of blacks in Stockton, California. In *Minority status and schooling: A comparative study of immigrant and involuntary minorities,* edited by J. Gibson and J. Ogbu. New York: Garland.

Olson, Lynn. 1999. Making every test count. *Education Week* 18 (17):11–20.

Olson, S., J. Bates, and B. Kaskie. 1992. Caregiver-infant interaction antecedents of children's school-age cognitive ability. *Merrill-Palmer Quarterly* 38:309–30.

Orellana, M. 2001. The work kids do: Mexican and Central American immigrant children's contributions to households and schools in California. *Harvard Educational Review* 71:366–89.

Owen, M. T., and B. A. Mulvihill. 1994. Benefits of a parent education and support program in the first three years. *Family Relations* 43:206–12.

Padilla, Y., J. Boardman, R. Hummer, and M. Espitia. 2002. Is the Mexican American "epidemiologic paradox" advantage at birth maintained through early childhood? *Social Forces* 80:1101–23.

Palisin, H. 1986. Preschool temperament and performance on achievement tests. *Development and Psychology* 22:766–70.

Palmaffy, T. 1999. Measuring the teacher quality problem. In *Better teachers, better schools,* edited by M. Kanstoroom and C. E. Finn. Washington, DC: Thomas B. Fordham Foundation.

Payne, A. C., G. J. Whitehurst, and A. L. Angell. 1994. The role of home literacy environment in the development of language ability in preschool children from low-income families. *Early Childhood Research Quarterly* 9:427–40.

Peisner-Feinberg, E. S., and M. R. Burchinal. 1997. Relations between preschool children's child-care experiences and concurrent development: The cost quality and outcomes study. *Merrill-Palmer Quarterly* 43 (3):451–77.

Pellegrini, D., A. Masten, N. Garmezy, and M. Ferrarese. 1987. Correlates of social and academic competence in middle childhood. *Journal of Child Psychology and Psychiatry* 28 (5):699–714.

Phillips, M., J. Brooks-Gunn, G. Duncan, P. Klebanov, and J. Crane. 1998. Family background, parenting practices, and the black-white test score gap. In *The black-white test score gap,* edited by C. Jencks and M. Phillips. Washington, DC: Brookings Institution Press.

Phillips, M., J. Crouse, and J. Ralph. 1998. Does the black-white test score gap widen after children enter school? In *The black-white test score gap,* edited by C. Jencks and M. Phillips. Washington, DC: Brookings Institution Press.

Piaget, J. 1960. *The psychology of intelligence.* Paterson, NJ: Littlefield, Adams.

Pinker, S. 1994. *The language instinct.* New York: Harper Collins.

Plomin, R. 1990. *Nature and nurture: An introduction to human behavioral genetics.* Pacific Grove, CA: Brooks/Cole.

Plomin, R., and J. Neiderhiser. 1991. Quantitive genetics, molecular genetics, and intelligence. *Intelligence* 15:369–87.

Porche, M. 2001. Parent involvement as a link between home and school. In *Beginning literacy with language,* edited by D. K. Dickinson and P. O. Tabors. Baltimore: Paul H. Brookes.

Posamentier, A. S. 2003. Grade the teachers. *New York Times,* June 5.

Pressley, M., R. Wharton-McDonald, J. Mistretta-Hapston, and M. Echevarria. 1998. Literacy instruction in 10 fourth and fifth grade classrooms in upstate New York. *Scientific Studies of Reading* 2 (2):159–94.

Ramey, S. L., and R. Campbell. 1984. Preventive education for high-risk children: Cognitive consequences of the Carolina Abecedarian project. *American Journal of Mental Deficiency* 88:515–23.

Ramirez, R., and G. de la Cruz. 2003. The Hispanic population in the United States: March 2002. In *Current Population Reports (P20–545).* Washington, DC: U.S. Census Bureau.

Raver, C. C., and M. Bancroft. 1999. Relations between effective emotional self-regulation, attentional control, and low-income preschoolers' social competence with peers. *Early Education and Development* 10 (3):333–50.

Ravitch, D. 2000. *Left back: A century of battles over school reform.* New York: Touchstone.

———. 2001. It is time to stop the war. In *The great curriculum debate: How should we teach reading and math,* edited by T. Loveless. Washington, DC: Brookings Institution Press.

Raviv, T., M. Kessenich, and F. Morrison. In press. A mediational model of the association between socioeconomic status and preschool language abilities.

Rayner, K., B. R. Foorman, C. A. Perfetti, D. Pesetsky, and M. S. Seidenberg. 2001. How psychological science informs the teaching of reading. *Psychological Science in the Public Interest* 2 (2):31–74.

Reese, E., and A. Cox. 1999. Quality of adult book reading affects children's emergent literacy. *Developmental Psychology* 35:20–28.

Rego, L., and P. Bryant. 1993. The connection between phonological, syntactic, and semantic skills and children's reading and spelling. *European Journal of Psychology of Education* 8 (3):235–46.

Resnick, L. 1992. From protoquantities to operators: Building mathematical competence on a foundation of everyday knowledge. In *Analysis of arithmetic for mathematics teaching,* edited by F. Leinhardt, R. Putnam, and R. Hattrup. Hillsdale, NJ: Lawrence Erlbaum.

Retsinas, G. 2003. The marketing of a superbaby formula. *New York Times,* June 1.

Reynolds, A. J., J. A. Temple, D. L. Robertson, and E. A. Mann. 2003. Age 21 cost-benefit analysis of the Title I Chicago child-parent centers. *Educational Evaluation and Policy Analysis* 24 (4):267–303.

Reznick, J., and M. Goldsmith. 1989. A multiple form word production checklist for assessing early language. *Journal of Child Language* 16:91–100.

Rimer, S. 2002. Critics attack suspension of 33 Philadelphia kindergartners. *New York Times,* December 16.

Rimm-Kaufman, S. E., and R. C. Pianta. 2000. Teacher's judgments of problems in the transition to kindergarten. *Early Childhood Research Quarterly* 15 (2):147–66.

Rivkin, S. G., E. A. Hanushek, and J. F. Kain. 2001. *Teachers, schools, and academic achievement.* Amherst, MA: Amherst College.

Robelen, E. W. 2001. Bush outlines plan to boost pre-k efforts. *Education Week* 21 (30): 1–24.

Rodriguez, J., R. Diaz, D. Duran, and L. Espinosa. 1995. The impact of bilingual preschool education on the language development of Spanish-speaking children. *Childhood Research Quarterly* 10:475–90.

Rothbart, M., and J. Bates. 1998. Temperament. In *Handbook of child psychology,* edited by W. Damon and R. Lerner. New York: Wiley.

Rothstein, R. 2002. Linking infant mortality to schooling and stress. *New York Times,* February 6.

Rowe, D. C. 1994. *The limits of family influence: Genes, experience, and behavior.* New York: Guilford.

Rowe, D. C., A. Vazsonyi, and D. Flannery. 1994. No more than skin deep: Ethnic and racial similarity in developmental process. *Psychological Review* 101:396–413.

———. 1995. Ethnic and racial similarity in developmental process: A study of academic achievement. *Psychological Science* 6:33–38.

Ryan, A. M., P. R. Pintrich, and C. Midgley. 2001. Avoiding seeking help in the classroom: Who and why? *Educational Psychology Review* 13 (2):93–114.

Saigal, S., P. Szatmari, P. Rosenbaum, D. Campbell, and S. King. 1991. Cognitive abilities and school performance of extremely low birth weight children and matched term control children at age 8 years: A regional study. *Journal of Pediatrics* 118:751–60.

Sandberg, J., and S. Hofferth. 2001. Changes in children's time with parents: United States, 1981–1997. *Demography* 38 (3).

Savage, S., and M. Gauvain. 1998. Parental beliefs and children's everyday planning in European-American and Latino families. *Journal of Applied Developmental Psychology* 19:319–40.

Scarborough, H. S. 2001. Connecting early language and literacy to later reading (dis)abilities: Evidence, theory, and practice. In *Handbook of early literacy*, edited by S. B. Neuman and D. Dickinson. New York: Guilford.

Scarborough, H. S., and W. Dobrich. 1994. On the efficacy of reading to preschoolers. *Developmental Review* 14:245–302.

Scarborough, H. S., W. Dobrich, and M. Hager. 1991. Preschool literacy experience and later reading achievement. *Journal of Learning Disabilities* 24 (8):508–11.

Schneider, B., and Y. Lee. 1990. A model of academic success: The school and home environment of East Asian students. *Anthropology and Education Quarterly* 21:358–77.

Schoen, M. J., and R. J. Nagle. 1994. Prediction of school readiness from kindergarten temperament scores. *Journal of School Psychology* 32 (2):135–47.

Schoendorf, K., C. Hogue, J. Kleinman, and D. Rowley. 1992. Mortality among infants of black as compared with white college-educated parents. *New England Journal of Medicine* 326 (23):1522–26.

Schribner, S., and M. Cole. 1978. Literacy without schooling. *Harvard Educational Review* 48 (4):448–61.

Senechal, M. 1997. The differential effect of storybook reading on preschoolers' acquisition of expressive and receptive vocabulary. *Journal of Child Language* 24 (1):123–38.

Senechal, M., and J. LeFevre. 2001. Storybook reading and parent teaching: Links to language and literacy development. In *New directions in child development, no. 92: The role of family literacy environments in promoting young children's emerging literacy*, edited by P. R. Britto and J. Brooks-Gunn. San Francisco: Jossey-Bass.

———. 2002. Parental involvement in the development of children's reading skill: A five-year longitudinal study. *Child Development* 73:445–60.

Senechal, M., J. LeFevre, B. Smith-Chant, and K. Colton. 2001. On refining theoretical models of emergent literacy. *Journal of School Psychology* 39:439–60.

Senechal, M., J. LeFevre, E. Thomas, and K. Daley. 1998. Differential effects of home literacy experiences on the development of oral and written language. *Reading Research Quarterly* 33 (1):96–116.

Share, D., A. Jorm, R. Maclean, and R. Matthews. 1984. Sources of individual differences in reading acquisition. *Journal of Educational Psychology* 76:1309–24.

Shavelson, R. J., and L. Towne, eds. 2002. *Scientific research in education.* Washington, DC: National Academy Press.

Shepard, L., and M. Smith. 1988a. Escalating academic demand in kindergarten: Counterproductive policies. *Elementary School Journal* 89 (2):135–45.

———. 1988b. Synthesis of research on school readiness and kindergarten retention. *Educational Leadership* 44:78–85.

Shilt, David. 2003. The influence of invented spelling on reading development in kindergarten. Paper read at the biennial meeting of the Society for Research in Child Development, April 27, Tampa, FL.

Shoda, Y., W. Mischel, and P. Peake. 1990. Predicting adolescent cognitive and self-regulatory competencies from preschool delay of gratification: Identifying diagnostic conditions. *Developmental Psychology* 26 (6):978–86.

Siegel, L., D. Cooper, P. Fitzhardinge, and A. Ash. 1995. The use of the Mental Development Index of the Bayley Scale to diagnose language delay in 2-year-old high-risk infants. *Infant Behavior and Development* 18:483–86.

Slaughter-Defoe, D. T., K. Nakagawa, R. Takanishi, and D. J. Johnson. 1990. Toward cultural/ecological perspectives on schooling and achievement in African- and Asian-American children. *Child Development* 61:363–83.

Smeeding, T., and L. Rainwater. 1995. Cross-national trends in income poverty and dependence: The evidence for young adults in the eighties. In *Poverty, inequality, and the future of social policy,* edited by K. McFate. New York: Russell Sage Foundation.

Smelsen, N., W. Wilson, and F. Mitchell. 2001. *America becoming: Racial trends and their consequences.* Vol. 1. Washington, DC: National Academy Press.

Smith, J., J. Brooks-Gunn, and P. Klebanov. 1997. Consequences of living in poverty for young children's cognitive and verbal ability and early school achievement. In *Consequences of growing up poor,* edited by G. J. Duncan and J. Brooks-Gunn. New York: Russell Sage Foundation.

Smith, K. 2002. *Who's minding the kids? Child care arrangements: Spring 1997.* Washington, DC: U.S. Census Bureau.

Smith, M. W., and D. K. Dickinson. 1994. Describing oral language opportunities and environments in Head Start and other preschool classrooms. *Early Childhood Research Quarterly* 9 (3–4):345–66.

Smrekar, C., J. Guthrie, D. Owens, and P. Sims. 2001. March toward excellence: School success and minority student achievement in Department of Defense schools. Nashville, TN: Peabody College, Vanderbilt University.

Snow, C. 2001. *Reading for understanding.* Santa Monica, CA: RAND Education and the Science and Technology Policy Institute.

Snow, C., M. Burns, and P. Griffin, eds. 1998. *Preventing reading difficulties in young children.* Edited by N. R. Council. Washington, DC: National Academy Press.

Snow, C., and D. Dickinson. 1990. Social sources of narrative skills at home and at school. *First Language* 10:87–103.

Snow, C., and P. Tabors. 1993. Language skills that relate to literacy development. In *Yearbook in early childhood education,* edited by B. Spodek and O. N. Saracho, 1–14. New York: Teachers College Press.

Stahl, S., and A. Murray. 1994. Defining phonological awareness and its relationship to early reading. *Journal of Educational Psychology* 33:468–79.

Stanovich, K. E. 1986. Matthew effects in reading: Some consequences of individual differences in the acquisition of literacy. *Reading Research Quarterly* 21:360–407.

———. 1994. Constructivism in reading education. *Journal of Special Education* 28 (3):259–74.

State of California Department of Education. 1999. *Language census summary statistics, 1998–1999.* Sacramento, CA: Education Demographics Unit.

Stedman, L. 1997. International achievement differences: An assessment of a new perspective. *Educational Researcher* 26:4–15.

Steele, C. 1998. A threat in the air: How stereotypes shape intellectual identity and performance. In *Confronting racism: The problem and the response,* edited by J. Eberhardt and S. Fiske. Thousand Oaks, CA: Sage.

Steele, C. M., and J. Aronson. 1995. Stereotype threat and the intellectual test performance of African Americans. *Journal of Personality and Social Psychology* 69 (5):797–811.

Steinberg, L. 1996. *Beyond the classroom: Why school reform has failed and what parents need to do.* New York: Simon and Schuster.

Steinberg, L., S. Dornbusch, and B. B. Brown. 1992. Ethnic differences in adolescent achievement. *American Psychologist* 47:723–29.

Steinberg, L., S. Lamborn, S. Dornbusch, and N. Darling. 1992. Impact of parenting practices on adolescent achievement: Authoritative parenting, school involvement, and encouragement to succeed. *Child Development* 63:1266–81.

Stelzl, I., F. Merz, T. Elhlers, and H. Remer. 1995. The effect of schooling on the development of fluid and crystallized intelligence: A quasi-experimental study. *Intelligence* 21:279–96.

Sternberg, R. 1988. *The triarchic mind: A new theory of human intelligence.* New York: Viking.

———. 1997. The concept of intelligence and its role in lifelong learning and success. *American Psychologist* 52:1030–37.

Stevenson, H. W. 1992. *The learning gap.* New York: Summit Books.

Stevenson, H. W., C. Chen, and S. Lee. 1993. Mathematics achievement of Chinese, Japanese, and American children: Ten years later. *Science* 259:53–58.

Stevenson, H. W., C. Chen, and D. Uttal. 1990. Beliefs and achievement: A study of black, white, and Hispanic children. *Child Development* 61:508–23.

Stevenson, H. W., and S. Lee. 1990. Contexts of achievement: A study of American, Chinese, and Japanese children. *Monographs of the Society for Research in Child Development* 55 (221):1–115.

Stevenson, H. W., T. Parker, A Wilkinson, A. Hegion, and E. Fish. 1976. Longitudinal study of individual difference in cognitive development and scholastic achievement. *Journal of Educational Psychology* 68:377–400.

Stigler, J. W., and J. Hiebert. 1999. *The teaching gap.* New York: Free Press.

Stipek, D. 2002. *At what age should children enter kindergarten? A question for policy makers and parents.* Social Policy report, vol. 16, no. 2. Ann Arbor, MI: Society for Research in Child Development.

Stipek, D., and P. Byler. 2001. Academic achievement and social behaviors associated with age of entry into kindergarten. *Applied Developmental Psychology* 22:175–89.

Stipek, D., and R. Ryan. 1997. Economically disadvantaged preschoolers: Ready to learn but further to go. *Developmental Psychology* 33 (4):711–23.

Storch, S. A., and G. Whitehurst. 2002. Oral language and code-related precursors to reading: Evidence from a longitudinal structural model. *Developmental Psychology* 38 (6):934–47.

St. Pierre, R. G., B. Gamse, J. Alamprese, T. Rimdzius, and F. Tao. 1998. *Even Start: Evidence from the past and a look to the future.* Washington, DC: U.S. Department of Education, Planning and Evaluation Service.

St. Pierre, R. G., and J. I. Layzer. 1999. Using home visits for multiple purposes: The Comprehensive Child Development Program. *Future of Children* 9:134–51.

St. Pierre, R. G., J. P. Swartz, B. Gamse, S. Murray, D. Deck, and P. Nickel. 1995. *National evaluation of the Even Start Family Literacy Program: Final report.* Cambridge, MA: Abt Associates.

Stright, A. D., C. Neitzel, K. G. Seras, and L. Hoke-Sinex. 2001. Instruction begins in the home: Relations between parental instruction and children's self-regulation in the classroom. *Journal of Educational Psychology* 93 (3):456–66.

Sugland, B., M. Zaslow, J. Smith, J. Brooks-Gunn, K. Moore, C. Blumenthal, T. Griffin, and R. Bradley. 1995. The early childhood HOME Inventory and HOME-Short Form in differing sociocultural groups: Are there differences in underlying structure, internal consistency of subscales, and patterns of prediction? *Journal of Family Issues* 16:632–63.

Sulzby, E. 1985. Children's emergent reading of favorite storybooks: A developmental study. *Reading Research Quarterly* 20 (4):458–81.

Tabors, P. O. 1997. *One child, two languages.* Baltimore: Paul H. Brookes.

Tabors, P. O., D. Beals, and Z. Weizman. 2001. "You know what oxygen is?" Learning new words at home. In *Beginning literacy with language,* edited by D. K. Dickinson and P. O. Tabors. Baltimore: Paul H. Brookes.

Tamis-LeMonda, C., M. Bornstein, and L. Baumwell. 2001. Maternal responsiveness and children's achievement of language milestones. *Child Development* 72:748–67.

Tamis-LeMonda, C., M. Bornstein, L. Baumwell, and A. Damast. 1996. Responsive parenting in the second year: Specific influences on children's language and play. *Early Development and Parenting* 5:173–83.

Tao, F., B. Gamse, and H. Tarr. 1998. *National evaluation of the Even Start Family Literacy Program, 1994–1997: Final report.* Arlington, VA: Fu Associates.

Taylor, B., D. Pearson, K. Clark, and S. Walpole. 2000. Effective schools and accomplished teachers: Lessons about primary-grade reading instruction in low-income schools. *Elementary School Journal* 101 (2):121–65.

Teale, W. H., and E. Sulzby, eds. 1986. *Emergent literacy: Writing and reading.* Norwood, NJ: Ablex.

Thernstrom, A., and S. Thernstrom. 1998. Black progress. *Brookings Review.*

Thornton, A., and L. Young-DeMarco. 2001. Four decades of trends in attitudes toward family issues in the United States: The 1960s through the 1990s. *Journal of Marriage and the Family* 63 (4):1009–37.

Tomasello, M., and J. Todd. 1983. Joint attention and lexical acquisition style. *First Language* 4:197–212.

Torgesen, J. K., R. K. Wagner, C. A. Rashotte, E. Rose, P. Lindamood, T. Conway, and C. Garvan. 1999. Preventing reading failure in young children with phonological processing disabilities: Group and individual responses to instruction. *Journal of Educational Psychology* 91:579–93.

Treiman, R. 2000. Foundations in literacy. *Current Directions in Psychological Science* 9:89–92.

Tumner, W. E., A. R. Nesdale, and A. D. Wright. 1987. Syntactic awareness and reading acquisition. *British Journal of Developmental Psychology* 5:25–34.

U.S. Census. 2000. *Census 2000 data for the state of California.* Washington, DC: U.S. Census Bureau.

U.S. House of Representatives. 2002. Committee on Education and the Workforce, Subcommittee on Education Reform. *Statement of Grover J. Whitehurst, assistant secretary for research and improvement.* February 28.

Valdez-Menchaca, M., and G. Whitehurst. 1992. Accelerating language development through picture book reading: A systematic extension to Mexican day care. *Developmental Psychology* 28:1106–14.

Varnhagen, C. et al. 1994. Age and schooling effects in story recall and story production. *Developmental Psychology* 30 (6):969–79.

Vellutino, F. R., D. M. Scanlon, E. R. Sipay, S. G. Small, A. Pratt, R. Chen, and M. B. Denckla. 1996. Cognitive profiles of difficult to remediate and readily remediated poor readers: Early intervention as a vehicle for distinguishing between cognitive and experiential deficits as basic causes of specific reading disability. *Journal of Educational Psychology* 88 (4):601–38.

Wachs, T. 1984. Proximal experience and early cognitive-intellectual development: The social environment. In *Home environment and early cognitive development,* edited by A. Gottfried. New York: Academic Press.

Wagner, R., C. Rashotte, S. Hecht, T. Barker, S. Burgess, and J. Donohue. 1997. Changing relations between phonological processing abilities and word level reading as children develop from beginning to skilled readers: A 5-year longitudinal study. *Developmental Psychology* 33:468–79.

Waldfogel, J., W. Han, and J. Brooks-Gunn. 2002. The effects of early maternal employment on child cognitive development. *Demography* 39 (2):369–92.

Wang, M. C., and H. J. Walberg, eds. 2001. *Tomorrow's teachers.* Richmond, CA: McCutchan.

Watson, R. 2001. Literacy and oral language: Implications for early literacy acquisition. In *Handbook of early literacy research,* edited by S. B. Neuman and D. K. Dickinson. New York: Guilford.

Weisskirch, R., and S. Alva. 2002. Language brokering and the acculturation of Latino children. *Hispanic Journal of Behavioral Sciences* 24:369–78.

Welsh, M., R. Parke, K. Widaman, and R. O'Neil. 2001. Linkages between children's social and academic competence: A longitudinal analysis. *Journal of School Psychology* 39 (6):463–81.

Wenglinsky, H. 2000. *How teaching matters: Bringing the classroom back into discussions of teacher quality.* Princeton, NJ: Educational Testing Service.

Wentzel, K. R. 1991a. Relations between social competence and academic achievement in early adolescence. *Child Development* 62:1066–78.

———. 1991b. Social competence at school: Relation between social responsibility and academic achievement. *Review of Educational Research* 61 (1):1–24.

———. 1993. Does being good make the grade? Social behavior and academic competence in middle school. *Journal of Educational Psychology* 85 (2):357–64.

West, J., E. Hausken, and M. Collins. 1995. *Readiness for kindergarten: Parent and teacher beliefs* (NCES statistical report 93–257). Washington, DC: National Center for Education Statistics.

Westat. 2001. *The longitudinal evaluation of school change and performance in Title 1 schools: Final report.* Washington, DC: U.S. Department of Education.

Westoff, C. 1986. Perspective on nupiality and fertility. In *Below-replacement fertility in industrialized societies,* edited by R. Richardo-Campbell. Cambridge: Cambridge University Press.

Wharton-McDonald, R., M. Pressley, and J. M. Hampston. 1998. Literacy instruction in nine first-grade classrooms: Teacher characteristics and student achievement. *Elementary School Journal* 99 (2):101–28.

Whitehurst, G. J., J. N. Epstein, A. L. Angell, A. C. Payne, D. A. Crone, and J.

E. Fischel. 1994. Outcomes of emergent literacy intervention in Head Start. *Journal of Educational Psychology* 86:542–55.

Whitehurst, G. J., F. L. Falco, C. J. Lonigan, J. E. Fischel, B. D. DeBaryshe, M. C. Valdez-Menchaca, and M. Caulfield. 1988. Accelerating language development through picture book reading. *Developmental Psychology* 24 (4):552–59.

Whitehurst, G. J., and C. Lonigan. 1998. Child development and emergent literacy. *Child Development* 69:848–72.

Wigfield, A., and J. T. Guthrie. 1997. Relations of children's motivation for reading to the amount and breadth of their reading. *Journal of Educational Psychology* 89 (3):420–32.

Wilson, W. J. 1987. *The truly disadvantaged: The inner city, the underclass, and public policy.* Chicago: University of Chicago Press.

Wright, P. S., S. P. Horn, and W. L. Sanders. 1997. Teacher and classroom context effects on student achievement: Implications for teacher evaluation. *Journal of Personnel Evaluation in Education* 11:57–67.

Zigler, E., and S. Meunchow. 1992. *Head Start: The inside story of America's most successful educational experiment.* New York: Basic Books.

Index

Abecedarian Project, 49, 52, 57, 59–60, 62, 63, 64, 73

Academic achievement: of Asian and Asian American children, 34–37, 162; and class-size reduction, 174–175; in Department of Defense (DoD) school system, 86; and dimensions of teaching, 123; and entrance age for kindergarten, 90–92; gender differences in, 92–93; high-achieving versus low-achieving Black students, 32–33; of Hispanic children, 37–38; and home learning environments, 81–82; and National Assessment of Educational Progress (NAEP), 10, 13–14, 24–25, 37, 92, 140, 142, 150; and parental warmth and responsivity, 83; predictors of, 29–30, 89, 94–95, 98, 103; and race and ethnicity, 24–38; and social skills, 102–103, 103; and socioeconomic disadvantage, 20–24; and superachievers, 10–11; and teacher qualifications, 141, 142, 145; and test taking anxiety, 27

Accountability, 85, 146, 149–150, 182

Achievement. *See* Academic achievement

Action research, 149. *See also* Educational research

Adolescents, 107, 160–161. *See also* Dropout rates

Adoption, 72, 95

Adult education and adult literacy, 55

Affective climate of home, 45–46, 48, 82–84

Affirmative action in college admissions, 26

African American Vernacular English, 67

African Americans: change agents for, 30; college attendance by, 29; in Department of Defense (DoD) school system, 86; educational aspirations of, 26; educational attainment of parents, 27, 32, 33; and Head Start, 41; high-achieving versus low-achieving Black students, 32–33; high school dropout rates for, 37–38; and infant mortality, 31; and mathematics skills, 38; middle-SES Black students, 29–30; and mothers' employment, 33; parenting in Black families, 26–27, 30, 31–33; population statistics on, 37; poverty of, 19, 26–27, 39; proximal sources of Black-White literacy gaps, 30–34; and reading skills, 29, 31–33; and school environment, 26–28; and Standard American English (SAE), 67; stereotypes of, 28; and television viewing, 32; and test score gap, 6, 24–30, 86; as unmarried mothers, 160; and vocabulary development, 28, 31, 32, 34. *See also* Ethnic and racial differences; Socioeconomic status (SES)

Alcohol use during pregnancy, 76

Alphabet. *See* Letters and letter-sound correspondence

Alternative schools, 167

America Becoming: Racial Trends and Their Consequences (Smelsen et al.), 25–26

Architecture, 156

Arithmetic. *See* Mathematics

Articulation, 65

Asians and Asian Americans, 34–37, 115, 116, 162. *See also* Ethnic and racial differences; Socioeconomic status (SES)

Assessment, 88–89, 132–133, 181

Automobiles, 156–157

Autonomy for children, 158, 164–166

Balanced instruction, 119

Bayley Scale of Infant Development (BSID), 94

Becoming a Nation of Readers, 168

Behavior-genetics studies, 71–72

Behavioral and developmental problems: and childcare, 47–48; of Hispanic children, 42

Bilingual preschool education, 41, 68

Birth outcomes: of African Americans, 31; of Hispanics, 42; infant mortality, 31